EUROPEAN ISLAM
CHALLENGES FOR PUBLIC POLICY AND SOCIETY

SAMIR AMGHAR, AMEL BOUBEKEUR, MICHAEL EMERSON (EDITORS)

CHRIS ALLEN, VALERIE AMIRAUX, TUFYAL CHOUDHURY,

BERNARD GODARD, IMANE KARICH, ISABELLE RIGONI

OLIVIER ROY AND SARA SILVESTRI

CENTRE FOR EUROPEAN POLICY STUDIES
BRUSSELS

The Centre for European Policy Studies (CEPS) is an independent policy research institute based in Brussels. Its mission is to produce sound analytical research leading to constructive solutions to the challenges facing Europe today. The views expressed in this report are those of the authors writing in a personal capacity and do not necessarily reflect those of CEPS or any other institution with which the authors are associated.

This study was carried out in the context of the broader work programme of CEPS on European Neighbourhood Policy, and is generously supported by the Compagnia di San Paolo and the Open Society Institute. The project was initiated at a conference held in Sofia in November 2006, sponsored under International Policy Fellowship programme of the Open Society Institute.

ISBN 13: 978-92-9079-710-4

Centre for European Policy Studies
Place du Congrès 1, B-1000 Brussels
Tel: 32 (0) 2 229.39.11 Fax: 32 (0) 2 219.41.51
e-mail: info@ceps.eu
internet: http://www.ceps.eu

CONTENTS

1. Introduction

Samir Amghar, Amel Boubekeur and Michael Emerson

The 15 million Muslims now living in the European Union, representing 3% of the total population, constitute the largest minority religion in the region and also the biggest Islamic diaspora in the world.[1] Seven countries stand out for the size of their Muslim populations – France, Germany, Belgium, the United Kingdom, the Netherlands, Greece and Bulgaria – where they account for between 3% and 13% of the total populations.[2] In the three Nordic EU member states (Denmark, Finland and Sweden), around 1% of the population is Muslim. To the south, Italy and Spain have been prime destinations for new flows of immigration since the 1990s and have the same proportion of Muslims. And certain countries in the Balkans (Albania, Bosnia, Macedonia...) have long-established if not predominant Muslim populations, which are the legacy of an Islamisation process that began in the 15th century with the expansion of the Ottoman Empire.

In Western Europe, the presence of Islam is mainly the consequence of significant migratory flows in the 1960s from countries of former colonial empires (the Maghreb, sub-Saharan Africa and the Indian sub-continent), but also from Turkey. The arrival of Muslims was the result of organised immigration between the countries of origin and European countries in

---

[1] These figures are a rough estimate, referring to all Muslim cultures; they are not intended to represent religious practice.

[2] In some European capitals, like Brussels, the proportion of Muslims can reach 17%. See C. Torrekens (2006), "La gestion locale de l'Islam dans l'espace public bruxellois", *Les cahiers de la sécurité*, No. 62, 3rd trimester, pp. 139-160 (available at http://www.inhes.interieur.gouv.fr/fichiers/RECH_62CSIinternet.pdf).

order to meet the needs of the latter for manual labour.[3] At the end of the 1960s, this immigration was still widely perceived as temporary. Hanging onto the myth of 'the return', the Turkish, Maghreb or Pakistani immigrant intended to stay in Europe only for the duration of his work contract, and then return home. For this reason, government authorities in the host countries never devised public policies on Islamic issues or their Muslim communities in a structured or nationwide manner.

From the mid-1980s onwards, however, the Muslim populations progressively gave up the idea of returning home and decided to stay in Europe permanently. Gradually, there was a settling on the part of the worker who, having brought his family over from the country of origin, no longer considered himself as a traveller in transit. The signs of this putting down roots became more visible as workers' children were sent to European schools, and places of worship appeared. While practically non-existent in Europe in the 1970s, the number of mosques multiplied rapidly, reaching over 6,000 by the end of the 1990s, and this under the impetus of the first generation of Muslims.[4] Closely linked to their countries of origin, this first generation of immigrants developed a community-minded sense of religion, based on the organisation of worship in their countries of origin. The new mosques of Europe remained tied to these countries (notably Algeria, Morocco and Turkey), which financed them and sent their own imams to manage them.

Despite the fact that the first generations were still linked to their countries of origin, there was nonetheless a profound Europeanisation of Islam already taking place, largely due to the younger generations born and educated in Europe. Although they were practising Muslims and came from a Muslim culture, members of this new generation severed their identification of Islam with their parents' country of origin, and increasingly thought of themselves as French, British, German or Belgian. This re-conceptualisation of Islam coincided with the emergence of claims to equality of treatment with their fellow citizens of European origin.

---

[3] Agreements of this type were signed, for example, by France with Algeria (in 1968), Morocco and Tunisia (in 1963) and by Belgium with Turkey (in 1961), Morocco (in 1963) and Tunisia (in 1965).

[4] Jocelyne Cesari, Sakina Bargach and Damian Moore (2002), «L'islamismation de l'espace public français: vers la fin des conflits», *Les Cahiers du Cemoti*, No. 33.

Struggles against all forms of racial or religious discrimination took shape within the framework of a 'citizenisation' of the Muslim population. For example, as early as 1983, a huge march was organised in Paris by SOS Racism, bringing together nearly 1 million people, mainly from Muslim immigrant communities. They advocated taking part in the political, economic and social life of the host country, by voting and other means. This discourse was also taken up by Islamic religious organisations which, while calling for European Muslims to strengthen their ties with Islam, also invited them to consider themselves as full citizens. Muslim associations encouraged young Muslims to vote and become integrated in the local culture.[5] These demands, based on a European and Islamic citizenship, obliged European policy-makers to no longer consider Islam as a migratory phenomenon, but as an integral and lasting part of the political, social and economic landscape in Europe.

This tendency towards thinking of Islam as fitting into an endogenous integration process, however, began to be undermined and contradicted by the growing tensions linked to what we might call an 'Islam in crisis', highlighted dramatically by the rise in radical Islam, the headscarf controversy and the terrorist acts from 11 September 2001 in New York and Washington to Madrid in 2004 and London in 2005. From the migratory context of the 1970s, policies based on the presence of Muslims have now come to be focused on problems of security and the fight against terrorism. Other conspicuous affairs linked to Islam (e.g. Salman Rushdie's publication of the *Satanic Verses* in 1989 or the Danish caricatures of the Prophet in 2006, not to mention the inflammatory declarations of various imams) have also, since the 1990s, fed a political perception of an 'Islam in crisis', despite its being far-removed from the daily preoccupations of most of the Muslim populations at the grass-roots European level.[6]

---

[5] Samir Amghar (2006), «Les trois âges du discours des frères musulmans en Europe», Samir Amghar (dir.), *Islamismes d'Occident: perspectives et enjeux*, Lignes de Repères.

[6] Amel Boubekeur and Samir Amghar (2007), "The role of Islam in Europe: Multiples Crises?", in Michael Emerson (ed.), *Readings in European Security*, Vol. 4, CEPS, Brussels.

At the outset we highlight two key points of focus, which both concern the search for political solutions to the 'Islam in crisis' in today's Europe.

The first brings an essentialist and culturalist approach to the crises linked to Islam, both as regards the problem and the solution. According to this view, because the tensions have arisen within an Islamic frame of reference, the solution has necessarily to be found within the Islamic religion. Thus, if Islamic terrorists are the cause of attacks in Europe, it is because the religious texts that are supposed to inspire them give explicit incitement to violence. From this viewpoint, one may oppose an external Islam supposedly ill-fitted to European values with a democratic Islam that is European. The solution offered by policy-makers then tends towards European religion-building: whereby a moderate and controllable Islam is promoted in order to combat jihadism. But this solution often proves ineffective. The problem is that this construction of a peaceful Islam is often artificial. It misjudges the attitudes of the local populations, for example in cases that seek to draw upon foreign models of Islam.[7] By placing the supposedly problematic nature of Islam at the heart of the matter, it underestimates the strength of the political and social reasons that are the origin of the riots or jihadist violence, even when these may be undertaken in the name of Islam. In this case the solution should be found within the political sphere, for example by offering means of political participation in their European home countries, and not simply in the religious field via interfaith and intercultural dialogue and the training of peaceful imams.

The second factor regarding European public policy towards Islam is the level of policy-making – at the local, national or European level. When questions of relations between Islam and the West arise, the solution and the framework of analysis tend to favour the national scale and local dimensions, which are undeniably important, but may neglect the European dimension. European values, identities, political and religious means of communication among Muslims living in Europe are a living reality. This was abundantly illustrated by the various responses European

---

[7] For example, the UK requested the assistance of Malaysia in the fight against terrorism. In France, Nicolas Sarkozy, then Minister of the Interior, asked Egyptian theologians for a fatwa forbidding young French Muslim girls from wearing their veils at school.

Muslims gave to the cartoons of the Prophet Mohammad that appeared in a Danish newspaper. Indeed, while some Arab states saw the cartoons affair as a clash of civilisations and a means to put political pressure on the European Union,[8] European Muslims tended to demand respect for their identity and equality as European citizens. In Belgium, France, the UK and many other countries, demonstrations were organised in protest against the publication of the cartoons but very few people attended them. Calls to boycott Danish products pronounced by some preachers and imams were rarely successful among European Muslim communities. The sense of belonging to Europe and having a European identity is therefore highly important to Muslims and should not be underestimated. Furthermore, it is already apparent that the specific features of the national organisational models of Muslim communities in Europe are tending to become blurred. For example both the assimilationist and integrationist models of the French and the multi-cultural models of the British and Dutch are in the process of being re-thought in light of the place these societies wish to give to their Muslim communities. These models are now being re-shaped by the 'Islam in crisis', which is being experienced across the whole of Europe, pushing public authorities to move towards common approaches in search of solutions.

The movement of Muslims, of their ideas and activities from one European country to another, is a considerable phenomenon in itself. The political concerns of Muslims, their media and associations are becoming more and more European. Islamic actors may think of themselves in their respective national contexts, but are increasingly fitting into a European logic. Tariq Ramadan, preacher and intellectual of Swiss nationality and highly regarded by young francophone European Muslims, is the perfect example of this phenomenon. Born in Switzerland, he spent a long time in France and Belgium, and then became a political advisor on terrorism to former British Prime Minister Tony Blair. Another example is the French Muslim Brotherhood, organises a huge demonstration every year in Paris attracting Muslims from all over Europe. The European branch of the Muslim Brotherhood, the Federation of Islamic Organisations in Europe (FOIE), has moved its European headquarters from Markfield in the UK to Brussels, seat of numerous European institutions, and other Muslim

---

[8] It was especially the case of Syria, organising violent demonstrations against EU embassies and trying to negociate EU's demands on Lebanon. See Olivier Roy (8 February 2006), "Geopolitique de l'indignation" in *Le Monde*.

structures are already organised at the European level. Similarly, the European Council of Fatwa and Research, in Dublin, brings together theologians from all over Europe in order to define religious norms in the European context.

It is evident from exchanges between European Islamic actors and policy-makers themselves that Europe is increasingly the forum of choice for devising norms and principles regarding Islam, starting with existing European legislation against discrimination in the labour market, and progressing on from there. European Islam is already a reality for Muslims. How can the EU institutions and its member states catch up with this political reality? Beyond domestic European affairs, there are also questions of how issues relating to Europe's Muslim communities factor into the foreign policies of the European Union, primarily in its relations with the Muslim states of the Mediterranean basin. These merit consideration in positive and participatory terms, rather than simply in the context of the West's latest preoccupation with security, immigration and the fight against terrorism. Europe's new generation of Muslims can also become a valuable human resource in the Union's foreign policy endeavours to come to terms with the challenges of globalised Islam.

*   *   *

These are some of the themes that inform the chapters of this book. More precisely we have structured the contributions in three parts: Ideologies and Movements, Status and Discrimination and Institutionalisation. In what follows we give a succinct guide to their contents.

Part A on Ideologies and Movements contains contributions by Amel Boubekeur, Samir Amghar and Olivier Roy.

Amel Boubekeur surveys the landscape of political Islam in contemporary Europe, defining such movements as those that have recourse to Islam as the first justification of their actions. The plurality and diversity of such movements are stressed first of all, even when focusing on those that seek to work peacefully, to the exclusion of violent jihadism. Political Islam in Europe initially had strong links to activists who came to live in Europe in the 1960s, 1970s and 1980s in exile from repressive regimes at home, and who saw Europe as a safe haven from which to continue to work towards the establishment of Islamic regimes in their home countries. From the 1990s onwards, however, as the immigrant communities became permanent residents and had families that grew up as young Europeans, the focus turned more towards representing European Muslims in the political systems of their new home countries. This was especially true of the groups linked to the Muslim Brotherhood organised under the Union of Islamic Organisation of Europe (UIOE) or the Turkish Milli Görüs, which have become more like political lobbies. By contrast, Sufist movements are still strongly linked to their countries of origin, especially those organised since 2000 around the multinational association known as Participation and Muslim Spirituality (PSM), which attracts Moroccan communities; similarly the Ahbash movement of Lebanese origin also attracts followers from different backgrounds. While Sufism is usually seen as the antithesis of political Islam, in pursuit of a peaceful and non-politicised religiosity, the PSM and Ahbash have adopted an increasingly political role in Europe and act as an alternative to the UIOE, which they view as collaborating too closely with government processes. A third category consists of movements that are driven by a more predicative and missionary logic, notably the Tabligh and Salafist movements, which reject the idea of trying to work within the framework of European political structures.

The Salafist movements are dealt with in more detail by Samir Amghar. Since the beginning of the 1980s Salafist movements have emerged as a main instrument of radicalisation in Muslim communities, mainly among the younger people of immigrant families. Its current success is partly explained by disappointment with the perceived failure of the re-Islamisation efforts of movements such as the Muslim Brotherhood, advocating instead a more literal koranic tradition, driven by the desire to return to the golden age of Islam. Amghar identifies three tendencies within the Salafist family, the first being revolutionary and jihadist, the second pursuing only objectives of predication and conversion, the third advocating political activism to establish the Islamic state and society. Salafists are not numerous, yet their influence is pervasive, dominating the doctrines heard in many mosques.

Olivier Roy goes further into Islamic radicalisation, drawing a portrait of typical West European terrorists, most of whom have adopted some sort of Salafism. The majority of them are second-generation Muslims from immigrant families, but there are also a significant number of converts. They are typically Western educated, often with European citizenship, and the recipient of a 'normal' Western upbringing, but are quite varied in ethnic terms. There is no clear sociological profile. The psychological dimension is more prevalent than a clear-cut social or economic dimension – with an overriding concern for self-image. This radicalisation sees a blending of Islamic discourse with the radicalism of the ultra-leftist movements in the third world of the 1970s. Roy calls them "not the militant vanguard of the Muslim community", but rather "a lost generation, unmoored from traditional societies and cultures, frustrated by a Western society that does not meet their expectations".

Roy goes on to outline what should be done to overcome the current crisis. The objective should be to isolate the Islamic radicals with the aid of the large majority of the Muslim population. The challenge is to make room for Islam as a "mere" religion of Europe among all the others, rather than attempting to sponsor a "good and moderate Islam". Opening up huge themes to discussion, he argues that both the multi-culturalist and integrationist approaches towards the new Muslim communities have failed, and that it would be sounder to encourage the disconnection between religion and culture.

In Part B, Imane Karich and Tufyal Choudhury describe the socio-economic status of Muslims, albeit having to rely on largely inadequate statistical data, in part due to the fact that most countries do not collect data on the basis of religion and the distinction between citizens and non-citizens has become increasingly meaningless. Both authors nonetheless find widespread evidence of disadvantaged economic status, in terms of higher unemployment, lower qualities of employment, low income levels, poorer housing and health. But the picture is not uniformly negative. Karich reminds us of Max Weber's thesis that the link between faith and economic development can be positive, engendering qualities of motivation, ethics and trust. The authors also draw attention to the dynamic development of Muslim niche markets, such as for *halal* meats and for ethnic market entrepreneurship more generally. They also note evidence of upward social mobility and professional achievement of the second and third generations of immigrant families. Educational performance among Muslims is showing significant improvements and UK Muslims now participate in post-compulsory education at a higher percentage level than the national average.

Choudhury discusses the nature of discrimination in the labour market and in other spheres. He notes that the Muslims encounter discrimination of multiple types, including race, ethnicity and gender as well as religion, with imprecise boundaries between these different features in public perceptions. Turning to policies to counter discrimination, Choudhury devotes attention to the significance of European Community law, with two directives adopted in 2000, the 'Race Directive' covering discrimination on grounds of racial or ethnic origin, and the 'Framework Directive' prohibiting discrimination in the labour market on grounds of religion, belief, disability, age or sexual orientation. The weakness of the Framework Directive is its limitation to the labour market, compared to the Race Directive which goes more widely into gender equality, education, housing and the actions of public officials (notably police and immigration staff). In his view, the scope of the Framework Directive could therefore be widened. Further, the EU is deliberating on a new Framework Directive on Racism and Xenophobia, which would make public incitement to violence or hatred for racist or xenophobic purposes a criminal offence.

Isabelle Rigoni examines the treatment of Muslim-related issues by the media. The European significance of this subject has been amply demonstrated by the Danish cartoon affair, which resonated throughout Europe and the Muslim world. The media bear a heavy responsibility in their representation of minority groups, for they profoundly influence the public's perceptions and stereotypes of such groups, and may be a principal agent behind the evident rise of Islamophobia. It is essential for policy measures in the field of integration and the fight against discrimination to include the media as one of the key groups of actors, and in particular the ethnic media. Rigoni favours actions at both the national and European level to promote a better representation of 'visible minorities', citing examples from France, Germany and the UK.

Valerie Amiraux focuses on the headscarf issue, with the increasing trend towards banning the headscarf in public spaces, such as state schools and public sector employment. What do headscarves stand for? Amiraux looks at three elements in the debate: religion, gender and national identity. In other words, she asks: what is religion, and what is politics? The headscarf controversy in Europe tends to mix gender, race and religious issues, triggering a double discrimination on grounds of gender and race/religion. Amiraux identifies two main positions in EU member states towards the headscarf: first an accommodating position, dominant in the 1980s, but declining since the 1990s, and second the positive desire to ban the headscarf in certain public spaces. In her conclusions, she notes that various constitutional court decisions make it seemingly impossible to take a final decision on the basis of abstract reasoning. As a provisional solution she advocates less politicisation and more recourse to the courts of law by individuals to seek redress for specific complaints.

These contributions all flow into the chapter by Chris Allen on Islamophobia, for which he uses the definition coined in the UK Runnymede report: "a shorthand way of referring to dread or hatred of Islam, – and, therefore, to fear or dislike of all or most Muslims". While a more precise and official definition has proved elusive, Allen affirms that this "certain identifiable phenomenon" now impacts on everyday life and has spread as a conceptual and social construct; whereas only five years ago it was an unknown term. He discusses the consequences of "it" for the erosion of multi-culturalism, the hardening of anti-terrorist, security and immigration laws, rising physical abuses and attacks, and looks into the role of political parties and the media in deepening and exploiting the phenomenon. While the phenomenon has grown, so also do we see informed efforts now emerging to counter Islamophobia, mainly at local and non-governmental levels. Although these efforts are so far limited, the issue itself has been transformed in importance and urgency across Europe.

Finally, in Part C, Sara Silvestri and Bernard Godard address issues surrounding the institutionalisation of Europe's Muslims and their representation in political life. Silvestri observes that the increasingly assertive Islam as a transnational presence in the European public sphere is developing in a rather disorganised and fractured way, not least because Islam has no hierarchical structure between the believer and his/her God. European governments are tending to push for an 'artificial' creation of Muslim councils, against a background of competing Muslim bodies – organisations sponsored by governments and diplomatic missions of Muslim states, notably Saudi Arabia, Algeria, Morocco and Turkey, through to Islamist movements of the diasporas, and less formal local groupings. Silvestri argues that the idea of systematising Muslim participation along corporatist lines should be viewed with caution, to say the least. Political participation in Western democracies can take place at the level of the individual and all manner of groups as well as political parties. Muslims should be treated as ordinary individuals, and not be isolated as a special socio-political category.

Bernard Godard, drawing on his extensive experiences in the processes of official relations between government and representatives of Islam, notes that European countries are tending to converge in their approaches to the question of granting official recognition of Islam, whereas initially the national contexts were highly divergent. However, the general pattern becomes one of establishing consultative councils, notwithstanding the difficult issues of designating the representative organisations or individuals, and their often questionable legitimacy at the level of different Islamic factions and movements. Godard also considers the issue at the European level. While the EU has no competence for 'religion', he suggests the creation of a steering group at the European level to study the scope for concerted policies towards the Muslim community.

*   *   *

Works on Islam in Europe often read like a juxtaposition of national case studies covering the history and perhaps the sociology of immigrant groups in the countries considered. Although the sociology of Islam is well-developed in certain European countries such as Germany, France and the UK, it is only in its infancy as a discipline at the European level. The common objective of the chapters in this work has therefore been to supply policy-makers in the member states and EU institutions with an inventory of the main issues concerning the presence of Islam at European level. This is about measuring progress so far registered, but also about revealing the weaknesses and contradictions in initiatives undertaken in Europe in the institutional recognition of Islam. The purpose of this research is to find keys to help unlock what is a complex cultural and political challenge.

Although the manifestations of political Islam in Europe are diverse, it has common features in its sources, structures and practices. The European roots of Islamic political violence are a fact. The perpetrators of recent acts of political violence became radicalised in Europe, and not in Muslim countries as had been the case in the 1990s. Their acts can be viewed as directed towards the polity of Europe as a whole, even if some acts, such as the Madrid and London bombings, have had dramatic impacts on the national scene.

Also, the question of political radicalisation must be differentiated from the question of religious radicalisation. The attempts to build a 'good Islam', aimed at replacing an Islam opposed to European values, are failing and should be abandoned. Policy-makers should not impose their top-down political choices on Muslims concerning the place of Islam in Europe. It will be useless to dictate to them the terms of the debate concerning political Islam and its radicalisation in terms of binary positions (with us or against us), but rather they should be encouraged to express themselves politically with a greater plurality of views, in accordance with the political diversity generally seen in Europe. In order to take the issue of political Islam out of the hands of Islamic political militants, Muslims should be encouraged to engage vigorously in a democratic way with the major debates in society, and at the same time maybe to 'de-Islamise' their political participation.

The visibility of Muslim communities remains problematic in Europe. Since 11 September 2001, in particular, we have witnessed an intensification of the negative portrayal of Muslims in the media. As already mentioned, the media have a major role to play in the construction of a European discourse where Islam and Muslims have a place of legitimacy. Often tainted by Islamophobia, the discourse of mainstream media about Muslims should work towards a better representation of the daily realities of Muslim communities and of Muslims themselves, notably in their link to the question of national and European citizenship. The ethnic and religious-inspired media should also be encouraged by policy-makers to increase their participation in the major debates of society.

This visibility could draw attention to the success stories of Muslim communities, which often go unrecognised. Investment by private Muslim entrepreneurs should be supported, for example, by encouraging self-employment and by promoting access to bank services that conform to the expectations of Muslim populations.

Muslim communities are also mobilising to face the challenges of redefining their European identity. They are emancipating themselves more and more from the question of a purely religious representation, and are investing in the processes of political representation. The initiatives of state-sponsored institutional Islam should therefore take account of this dichotomy between the representation of faith and the question of political representation, which should not be 'Islamised'.

Muslim communities are today subjected to exacerbated forms of discrimination, one of the most widespread being Islamophobia. In light of the multiplication of Islamophobic incidents and tendencies in recent years, a genuine reaction on the part of public bodies in response to Islamophobia is now urgent. The multi-dimensional nature (gender, race, religion…) of the discrimination against Muslims (and in particular against veiled Muslims) today calls for the accumulation of more adequate data on the disadvantages they face in the fields of work, housing and education.

More broadly, the time has come for a new European political and social discourse in relation to its Muslim communities. At the European level this should blend elements of normative doctrine with specific instruments of action, and provide a coherent overall framework for the work of governments and civil society, both at national and local levels.

PART A

IDEOLOGIES AND MOVEMENTS

2. POLITICAL ISLAM IN EUROPE

AMEL BOUBEKEUR

Introduction

Europe is currently home to an extremely diverse landscape of political Islamic[1] movements. This diversity is even greater than in most Muslim countries, where ideological Islamic expression is often limited by the official ideology of the state. In Europe, these movements are often mobilised in defence of European Muslim interests; they work for the recognition of Islam or as its spokesperson in dealing with European states or with the majority of Muslims who are not concerned with political Islam. These movements have been present in Europe for a long while now (between 20 and 40 years for most of them) but their daily realities are still not well known to European policy-makers, neither at the European, national nor local level.

These movements only become really visible when different conflicts[2] emerge in the public sphere. During the various headscarf debates, the

---

[1] Political Islam denotes the recourse to Islam as the first justification of one's political action, notably where demands are made vis-à-vis political authorities or in the methods of mobilisation and engagement proposed to Muslim communities. More specifically, these are descended from the Islamist movements of the Muslim world. They represent only a minority of people within Europe's Muslim minorities. However, their political reach and capacity to focus debates around the place of Islam in Europe often surpass the immediate circles of militants that compose them. In order not to repeat the same term, we will use 'Islamism' in this text synonymously with Political Islam.

[2] Amel Boubekeur and Samir Amghar (2006), "The role of Islam in Europe: Multiple Crises?", in *Islam and Tolerance in Wider Europe*, Open Society Institute, June.

questions concerning individual freedom (such as the crisis over the Salman Rushdie affair, the Danish caricatures of Mohammad, or questions of religious education) and the reaction of European Muslims to international events (such as terrorist attacks in Europe, the war in Iraq or the Israeli-Palestinian conflict), the mobilisation of political Islam has been perceived as fundamentally confrontational both in the media and in institutional discourse. But what about at the grass-roots level? In the context of secular states suspicious of religious engagements in the public sphere, Muslims who are engaged in the defence and the representation of the 'Islamic' issue in Europe are often accused of duplicity in their relationship to democracy and European citizenship. Today the framework and inspiration for the claims of these Islamist movements have much evolved.[3] They now tend to use forms of secular political opposition in the political European tradition. The political Islamic actors mobilised around the interests of political Islam in Europe are very diverse, however, and do not use the same methods to challenge the discourses and public policies that shape the lives of Muslims.

Today this political and publicly militant Islam only represents a minority of Muslims in Europe, but its capacity for mobilisation and the diffusion of discourse in defence of Islam often goes well beyond the circle of its regular militants. It is also this Islam that most attracts European policy-makers' attention the when dealing with questions of radicalisation, institutionalisation of Islam, juridical adaptation of Islamic codes and the defence of citizenship rights for Muslim minorities.

This presentation of the European landscape of political Islam does not aim to be exhaustive. We will concentrate on those movements that are the most active in the political sphere and whose political evolution is the most significant, such as the Islamists in exile from the Muslim world, the UIOE (Union of Islamic Organisations of Europe), the Muslim Brotherhood, the Milli Görüs and political Sufism such as the Participation and Muslim Spirituality movement or the Ahbash. Finally, we will also look at missionary and predicative movements such as the Tabligh and Salafism. We will thus not be looking at jihadist movements or at Shi'ism, nor will we deal with the cultural and ethnic management of certain Turkish, North African, Arab or Indo-Pakistani Islamic movements.

---

[3] See below for the complete definition of Islamism.

2.1   Islamism, a polemical concept

Islamism is not a homogenous phenomenon, its actors are different depending on location and historical era, and the methods of action that they propose also evolve over time. Thus it has moved on from the early 20th century goal of inventing for the Muslim world a modernity autonomous from that of the West, or from wanting to put in place an Islamic state among the militants of the Arab world in the 1970s. More recently it has promoted the leadership of a competitive Islam, especially through the market.[4] However, it is possible to distinguish certain common origins and traits within political Islam.

Historically, Islamism was born in the Arab world towards the end of the 19th century. Above all it aimed to reclaim the 'authentic' Islam of the golden age of the Prophet. Seeking to distinguish themselves clearly from 'classical' Muslims belonging to traditional societies, for whom Islam is lived passively, the promoters of this new current actively defended the precedence of Islamic principles for the whole political and social system. Islamism thus aimed to allow committed Muslims to reposition themselves vis-à-vis the West, in the wake of the abolition of the caliphate and the collapse of the Ottoman Empire in 1924. Islamism sought to present itself as an alternative to new ideologies such as communism and Arab nationalism.[5] For these committed Muslims, it was also a case of halting the intellectual decline of Muslims, seen as incapable of responding to the challenges of 'modernity'.[6] The political identity of Islamism during the 20th century aimed to renew the living environment of Muslims in order to respond to the situation of domination, and even Westernisation of Muslim

---

[4] Amel Boubekeur (2005), "Cool and Competitive: Muslim Culture in the West", *ISIM Review*, No. 16, autumn.

[5] Laurens (1993), *L'Orient arabe: arabisme et islamisme de 1798 à 1945*, A. Colin.

[6] See the works of various Islamist thinkers such as Mawdoudi, Sayyid Qotb, Muhammad Abduh or Rashid Rida. See also Albert Hourani (1962), *Arabic Thought in the Liberal Age*, Oxford: Oxford University Press. Nikki Keddie (1968), *An Islamic Response to Imperialism, Political and Religious Writings of Sayyid Jamal al-Din `Al-Afghani*, University of California Press. Malcolm H. Kerr (1966), *Islamic Reform: The Political and Legal Theories of Muhammad `Abduh and Rashid Rida*, University of California Press. Abdul Ala Mawdudi (1965), *The Political Theory of Islam*, Lahore.

populations.[7] They also sought to reorganise family structures that had been altered by colonisation and to respond to questions of modernisation and progress. The means they used were those of political and social activism, in order to impose new 'Islamic' norms that focused on, among other things, questions of identity, the relationship to Western modernity, the place of women, the relation between religion and the state and the questioning of Western imperialism in its political, economic and intellectual varieties.

Today the concept of Islamism has polemical connotations. It belongs to the language of Western political science, but it is also used in different ways by public opinion, notably in the media. Islamists themselves do not use the term but rather refer to themselves as *islamî* which means 'religious' or 'Islamic'. We use the term here to refer to non-violent activism, both in Muslim and Western states, founded on a particular vision of politics, with a precise political project (not a messianic utopia), organised as a social movement or a political party, with specifically political activities and demands (demonstrations, participation in elections...) and acting within the framework of the state or in dialogue with it.

2.2 The initial role of Islamist militants in Europe

Political Islam in Europe was initially strongly linked to Islamists living in exile on the continent. Certain Islamist militants from the Muslim world "went West",[8] above all those from the network of the Muslim Brotherhood. Under pressure from secular and authoritarian Arab regimes (Syria, Iraq and Egypt, but also Tunisia, Morocco and Algeria), numerous militants and leaders of the Muslim Brotherhood[9] fled to Europe in the 1960s, 1970s and 1980s to escape the political repression they were subject to in their own countries. Saïd Ramadan, one of the leaders of the Muslim

---

[7] John Esposito (1983), *Voices of Resurgent Islam*, Oxford: Oxford University Press.

[8] Olivier Roy (2002), *L'islam mondialisé¸* Paris, Le Seuil.

[9] The Muslim Brotherhood has its origins in an association of the same name created in Egypt in the 1930s and which, opposing the secular state, recommended the establishment of an Islamic state. This association spread rapidly in the rest of the Arab world, then to Europe in the 1970s. On the history of this movement, see Richard Mitchell (1993), *The Society of the Muslim Brothers*, Oxford: Oxford University Press; and Olivier Carré and Gérard Michaud (Michel Seurat) (1983), *Les Frères musulmans*, Paris: Gallimard-Julliard, collection Archives.

Brotherhood (son-in-law of Hassan el Banna, the founder of the Muslim Brotherhood, and father of Tariq Ramadan, a Swiss intellectual and Muslim activist), fled Egypt in the 1960s, moving to Geneva to pursue his political activism. Issam al-Attar, the spiritual guide of the Syrian Muslim Brotherhood, also fled the pressure of President Hafez al-Assad's regime and settled in Aachen in Germany.

Upon their arrival in Europe the exiled leaders of the Muslim Brotherhood met with the engagement of certain Islamic students who were also from Muslim countries and had come to pursue their university studies on the continent. In France, students and Islamic refugees came together within the Islamic Student Association of France (Association des étudiants Islamiques de France – AEIF), which was created in 1963. During this period, numerous people gravitated towards this organisation and were later to occupy important positions in the Islamist movements contesting power within their own countries. Among the future Islamist leaders who were educated in Europe are Rachid Ghannouchi, currently living in the UK, who founded the future Tunisian Islamist party, Islamic Tendency Movement (Mouvement de la Tendance Islamique – MTI) at the end of the 1970s, Hassan al-Tourabi, the great sage of the Islamist military regime in Sudan between 1989 and 1999, and Ali Shari'ati, one of the masterminds of the Iranian Revolution of 1979. The AEIF did not simply operate as a militant Islamic political party, but also as an elite circle of intellectuals, publishing an academic journal and organising conferences and think tanks on the subject of the decline of intellectual Muslims in the world, in the wake of colonisation and the immigration processes that followed. In fact, meeting European Muslim immigrants with low levels of education who had come to Europe to work was quite a shock for these Islamist elites from the Arab world. The Islamist sphere of influence was thus not homogenous but was dominated by the drive to return to 'pure' cultural practices (i.e. in opposition to the more cultural form of Islam practised by the immigrants), as well as by the desire to see Muslims once again active on the global intellectual and political stage.

During the 1970s the Islamist influence in Europe grew and developed in response to the policies of the repressive authoritarian regimes in Muslim countries,[10] and the arrival of contingents of students who had come to Europe to study further and who were sympathetic to the theses of political Islam. These two social groups (political refugees and students) together made up the heart of Islamism in Europe and were behind the creation of European branches of some Islamist parties from the Muslim world.

At the beginning of the 1970s, the decision of the Turkish Constitutional Council to outlaw the Rafah, an Islamist political party directed by Necmettin Erbakan, encouraged a number of its members to create Millî Görüs, meaning 'national vision' in Turkish. This organisation was initially based in Germany and France, but it soon spread to the whole of Europe via the Turkish diaspora. At the end of the 1960s, numerous militants of the Pakistani Islamist organisation founded by Abu lala Mawdudi, Jama'at islami, set up a branch in the UK.

Ten years later, a group of Tunisian students among which Ahmed Jaballah, current director of the European Institute of Human Sciences (in Paris and Chateau Chinon) in charge of training imams, were given the mission of founding a branch of Rachi Ghannouchi's Mouvement de la Tendance Islamique in France.

The overthrow of the electoral process in Algeria in 1991 which prevented the Islamic Salvation Front (Front Islamic du Salut – FIS) directed by Abassi Madani and Ali Belhadj from gaining power, led many of its leaders, militants and sympathisers to leave Algeria for Europe (Switzerland, Belgium, Germany and notably France). Once there, certain members of the FIS created the Algerian Fraternity of France (Fraternité Algérienne de France – FAF) in 1990. Directed by Algerian students, this organisation aimed to represent the FIS in France. At the same time, a certain number of FIS directors decided to organise, from September 1993, a Foreign Executive Committee of the FIS (Conseil Executif du FIS à l'étranger – CEFE). The members of the CEFE aimed to constitute an exiled Islamist opposition and to establish the movement in most European countries.[11]

---

[10] Bassma Kodmani-Darwish and May Chartouni-Dubarry (eds) (1997), *Les Etats arabes face à la contestation islamiste*, Armand Colin.

[11] In its chain of command, the management of the CEFE consists of a political office directed by Rabah Kébir in Germany and vice-directorships in London, the

At the beginning of the 1980s, the use of the European political sphere was purely instrumental. The aim was to use this region of the world as a political tribune to challenge the Turkish and Arab regimes that the Islamists considered to be dictatorships. The different militants thought of their presence in Europe as the means of conceiving 'in safety' a way of reforming the authoritarian regimes of the Arab world – hypothesising that they would eventually return to these countries, once the regimes in question had been overthrown. These movements were thus used as the reserve base of multinational Islamist opposition. Europe seemed to them to be a politically free land, where militants could be trained, in anticipation of the liberalisation of the political situation in their countries so that Islamic states could be constructed there. To their opposition of the authoritarian regimes in the Arab world was added a critique of Europe denouncing the political, cultural and ethical imperialism of the West that Muslim societies were supposed to submit to. On one hand, the reading of Islam by these exiled movements was founded on the re-Islamisation of the social practices of immigrants who were seen to be perverted by Western societies (with regards to the loss of the Arabic language, religious practices and the difficult transmission of this identity to children born in Europe). On the other hand, it was founded on the politicisation of religion, presented as an all-encompassing system capable of resolving the political, social and economic problems of Muslims.

Nevertheless, the influence of Islamist discourse on immigrant populations remained marginal and only reached certain segments of the Muslim community (overseas students and Islamist refugees). This general indifference is explained by the fact that the immigrants were still closely linked to the consulates of their country of origin, which were concerned with religious matters[12] (construction of mosques, organisation of classes in religion or in the Arabic language). Moreover, these immigrants considered their presence in Europe as temporary, only just tolerated by the authorities

---

US and Switzerland, held by Abdallah Anas, Anouar Haddam and Mourad Dhina, respectively.

[12] The Kingdom of Morocco has a network of Mosques in France, Belgium, the Netherlands, Italy and Spain. The Turkish Minister of Foreign Affairs also controls a number of places of worship in France, Belgium, the Netherlands, Austria and Denmark.

who were not favourable towards political actions that might disturb the public order. In addition, the aspirations of the Islamists regarding the politicisation of religion found no favour with immigrants whose daily cultural practices were much more pragmatic. The instances of political protest regarding Islam among immigrants were therefore sporadic, limited for example to the demands of Muslim workers in certain European factories for the provision of a place of prayer in their workplace.

Confronted with this lack of success, many of those who defended the establishment of Islamic states in the Muslim world changed their argument at the beginning of the 1990s. From this point on, these organisations no longer considered Europe as the reserve base for the Islamism of Muslim countries, preparing their return to the Arab, Pakistani or Turkish political stage. They now saw themselves as structures that represented the interests of Muslim immigrants and their children in Europe, having themselves definitively renounced the objective of returning to their home countries.

2.3   Movements linked to the Muslim Brotherhood

From the 1990s onwards Islamic militants abandoned the theme of the establishment of an Islamic state that resembled the Islamism of the early days and founded their claims on the representation of European Muslims. This second current of militant Islam accentuated the importance of political and social activism in their host countries, as a way of defending and representing European Muslims. In this perspective, former Islamist actors joined in the general phenomenon of re-islamisation with the emerging generations of young Muslims born in Europe, particularly students who were in a position to reach the middle classes.[13] In order to claim rights for European Muslims, the privileged vectors were to be the associative system and the political party. Within these associations new

---

[13] In Europe, re-Islamisation is not Islamism in itself but rather the process of re-appropriation of an Islamic heritage. It uses the tools of Islamism to provide Muslim youth born in Europe with a feeling of religious commitment. Re-Islamisation should not be confused with the transmission of religious sentiment by parents who come from Muslim countries to their children. See Amel Boubekeur (2006), «L'islamisme comme tradition. Fatigue militante et désengagement islamiste en Occident», in Samir Amghar (ed.), *Islamismes d'Occident. État des lieux et perspectives*, Lignes de repères.

Islamic militants would create specific groups for youth, students, women, theological training and humanitarian work.

Although these structures were heavily inspired by the experiences of opposition and protest in the Arab world, the discourses had to be adapted to the very different political sensitivities of European-born Muslims. This movement militates for an integration of Muslims into the social and political landscape, for example by calling on Muslims to enrol and to vote. In this way, the organisations that belong to this tendency try to set up an 'Islamic citizenship', proposing themselves as privileged interlocutors to the public authorities, at local and national levels, on issues as diverse as religion, racism and problems of delinquency in difficult suburbs.[14] In wanting to define the contours of European Islam, these organisations also offer young Muslims a model of integration inspired by the British multicultural model: to be both European and Muslim at the same time – without that implying assimilation to the dominant secular ideology.

The Union of Islamic Organisations of Europe (UIOE) is a militant supranational structure founded in 1997 by a group of political refugees and Islamist students from North Africa and the Middle East. It is directed by Chakib ben Makhlouf, an activist of Moroccan origin who recently succeeded Ahmed al-Rawi, a British citizen of Iraqi origin. Linked to the international organisation of the Muslim Brotherhood, the UIOE regroups close to 500 associations throughout Europe. It is active in the UK via the Muslim Association of Britain (MAB), in Switzerland via the Ligue des musulmans de Suisse (LMS), in Germany via the Islamische Gemeinschaft in Deutschland (IGD), and finally in Belgium via the Ligue interculturelle islamique de Belgique (LIIB). Of the 500 European associations federated with the UIOE, nearly 250 of them are present on French territory and are controlled by the Union of Islamic Organisations of France (UIOF), the French branch of the UIOE. The UIOF was created in 1983 by the Iraqi Mahmoud Zuhaïr and the Tunisian Abdallah Benmansour, and became the welcoming organisation of Islamist militants from the Arab world. The UIOF was initially strongly characterised by its Islamist parentage and was not very interested in political action in its host country. Towards the end

---

[14] Swiss intellectual Tariq Ramadan was one of the promoters of this 'Islamic citizenship'. This discourse principally had an effect on francophone Europe: France, Switzerland and Belgium.

of the 1980s, the organisation changed its orientation and became persuaded of the relevance and the necessity of basing its action in France. In fact, in a context of rising Islamism (especially in Algeria with the FIS), the UIOF aimed to negotiate its entry onto the French political scene as an important protest movement, weighing in heavily with regards to the place of Islamism on the international political chessboard. The Union thus sided with the high school students expelled from school in 1989 for refusing to remove their headscarves, organising demonstrations and monopolising media attention on this issue. Along the same lines, it also tried to have the French publication of Salman Rushdie's *Satanic Verses* banned. Every year the UIOF organises a huge assembly at Le Bourget in Paris, offering a four-day conference on the place of Islam in Europe, focused on the compatibility of religious practices with European social and political reality. This assembly is the largest reunion of Islamic associations at European level, with over 80,000 Muslims participating in past years. They attend conferences and request fatwas (religious decrees) from a number of sages, as well buy Islamic books and clothing.

The UIOE also possesses one of the first European university institutes with the responsibility of training imams and religious leaders: the European Institute of Human Sciences (EIHS), based in Paris. This institute regroups 300 Muslim students from all over Europe. The UIOE has also founded the European Council for Fatwa and Research (ECFR), based in Dublin. The Council brings together Muslim theologians living in Europe[15] and aims to define an Islamic practice that takes into account the reality of Europe in responding with fatwas to questions posed to them by Muslims.[16]

As the heirs of Islamism, this part of the Muslim Brotherhood movement has nonetheless evolved, especially with the emergence of young Europe-born Muslims in its ranks. The different national federations that are members of the UIOE have engaged to differing extents, and with varying degrees of success, in the representative councils for Muslims in

---

[15] The list of European members of this Council includes four British citizens, four French, three Germans, one Irish, one Bulgarian, one Dane, one Norwegian, one Belgian and one Swiss.

[16] These fatwas may deal with issues as varied as: relationships, use of bank loans, Islamic banking, the consumption of certain foods, political participation, voting and politics...

European countries. Thus the French federation (UIOF) participated in the process of the institutionalisation of Islam in France and won a large number of seats in the elections of the French Council of the Muslim Religion (Conseil Français du culte musulman – CFCM)[17] in 2003 and 2005. Via the CFCM the current leadership of the UIOF has developed a negotiating strategy with the French political authorities in order to defend the interests of French Muslims, thus breaking with the political culture of the previous leadership, which preferred confrontation to cooperation.

Today the UIOE generally, and the UIOF in France and the LIIB in Belgium in particular, are no longer the confrontational actors they were in the 1990s. Their methods of intervention on the question of Islam have become more consensual, and more routine, which has enabled them to present themselves as socially acceptable interlocutors to the political authorities.

However, even though the UIOE remains a dominant actor in the landscape of political Islam, it is currently suffering from an increasing lack of legitimacy among young Muslims because it downplays conflictual questions, which is a consequence of its 'clientelist' relationship with governments. Thus the position of the UIOF on the French law concerning religious symbols in 2003 was very reticent, although a part of the UIOF criticised this position. The fatwa against urban violence that was issued by the UIOF, at the request of the Minister of the Interior during the November 2005 riots, thus castigating the rioters on the basis of their supposed affiliation with Islam, contributed still more to the deepening of the rupture between the Muslim Brotherhood and their base.

The second major international organisation to structure the landscape of associations that militate for the defence and integration of Muslims in Europe is the Turkish Milli Görüs (MG), founded in Germany in 1973 with its headquarters in Cologne. Whereas the UIOE regroups Arab and converted Muslim populations from around Europe, the MG is

---

[17] The CFCM was designed as a representative body for French Muslims in dealing with the political authorities and as the body that organises and manages the Muslim religion (pilgrimages, Ramadan, burials, mosques…) in France. It was created in 2003 by Nicolas Sarkozy, the then Minister of the Interior.

essentially frequented by European members of the Turkish diaspora and their children.[18]

The MG was first founded in Turkey in 1969 by Necmettin Erbakan, who would later found and lead the Turkish Islamist party. In the same mould as the associations founded by exiled Islamists and inspired by the Muslim Brotherhood, the MG was implanted into Europe by militants of the Erbakan party who had fled Turkey for Switzerland and Germany in 1972, following the decision of the Constitutional Council to prohibit the Islamist group in 1971.[19] The MG has many branches throughout Europe, particularly where there are large Turkish communities (Belgium, France, the Netherlands, Germany, Denmark, Switzerland, Austria...). Bringing together nearly 30 associations in as many European countries, the organisation has a large network of mosques with nearly 511 places of worship, 2,137 youth, women's and student groups, 17,841 directors and over 252,000 members – which makes it without a doubt the biggest Muslim organisation in Europe.

Following the example of the UIOE, the MG provides a framework for the Turkish population of Europe via the organisation of religious and social activities. Contrary to the UIOE, however, its objective is not to gain religious leadership over all European Muslims, but rather to offer political and religious representation for the European Turkish community of nearly 4 million people. The MG is thus in competition with the Dyanet, which is the representative of the official Islam of the Turkish Minister for Religious Affairs and is responsible for dealing with the religious affairs of the Turkish community in Europe (appointing imams, setting up koranic schools...). However, the MG maintains a good relationship with the Muslim Brotherhood (UIOE), which sometimes leads them to organise common events, such as the shared electoral lists UIOF/MG during the elections of the CFCM in France.

---

[18] For a wider view of the history of Turkish Islamism in Europe, see Ural Manço, "Les organisations islamiques dans l'immigration turque en Europe et en Belgique", in Felice Dassetto (ed.) (1997), *Facettes de l'islam belge*, Bruylant-Academia.

[19] For the description of the evolution of Islamist movements in Turkey, see Jean Marcou (2004), "Islamisme et post-islamisme en Turquie", *Revue Internationale de Politique comparée*, Vol. 11, No. 4.

Originally the MG was very influenced by its Islamist and nationalist heritage and it emphasised objectives based on political and social issues specific to Turkey and its community in Europe. However, in the middle of the 1990s the organisation was obliged to reposition itself in order to appeal to the European-born younger generations of Turkish origin. Taking its inspiration from the UIOE, the MG developed a discourse on the necessity for the Muslim populations of integrating into European society. Their means of action for enlarging their influence in Europe, previously only oriented towards political militancy, were also modernised. In fact, the MG now possesses Islamic banks, clothing brands, radio stations and magazines throughout Europe. In order to demonstrate their openness, the head of the Dutch branch of the MG even went so far as to the lengths of organise a football game between young militants and members of the gay community, which provoked strong opposition within the traditionalist Turkish community.

It should also be noted that in 2000 a schism occurred between the French branch of the 'young MG' and their parent organisation, as the former decided to place emphasis on the 'Europeanisation' of their political identity. The new organisation has a network that covers all of Europe, is called the Cojep League of Popular Education (Ligue cojépienne d'éducation populaire – LICEP).[20] It is behind the creation of a network of young Turkish businessmen in Europe and is also active in public debates and lobbying concerning Turkey's accession to the EU.

2.4 Political Sufism

Sufism in Europe is usually seen as the antithesis of political Islam and linked to a peaceful, tolerant, non-politicised and almost folkloric type of religiosity. Sufism has always played an important role in politics, however, especially during the colonisation processes in the Middle East and Africa. Indeed, its political activities, networks and demands have always been implemented through the powerful structures of Sufi brotherhoods.

---

[20] Samim Akgonul (2006), "Millî Görüs: institution religieuse minoritaire et mouvement politique transnational (France et Allemagne", in Samir Amghar (ed.), *Islamismes d'Occident. État des lieux et perspectives*, Lignes de repères.

For around 15 years now, and since the decline of the traditional hegemony of the major Islamist movements (like the Muslim Brotherhood), the political role of Sufism has become more and more important in the landscape of political Islam in Europe. These movements could also be called neo-Sufism.[21]

In their relations to European public actors, these neo-Sufis movements have the advantage of being less stigmatised and their visibility or commitment to public life appears to be less problematic. However, as with the other movements and tendencies linked to political Islam, Sufi actors are claiming specific rights, and have their well-identified 'project' of society as well as their enemies.

The association Participation and Muslim Spirituality (Participation et Spiritualité Musulmane – PSM), established in 2000, is characterised by the originality of its doctrinal heritage. Although its methods of mobilisation are inspired by political Islam, it claims Sufism as an orientation. The PSM is the European emanation of an unofficial Moroccan movement of both Sufi and Islamist tendency: the Al'Adl wa-Ihsan party, founded by Abdessalam Yassine in 1987. The PSM was initiated by Moroccan students who were pursuing further study in Europe at the beginning of the 1990s, and experienced a certain development during the years 2000; it is today one of the most active European associations of political Islam. It is active in countries with a large Moroccan immigrant population (France, Belgium, Spain, Italy, the Netherlands, but also in North America). Much more discreet in its activities than the associations previously mentioned, the PSM principally recruits among the emerging re-Islamised middle class, who are disappointed by the overly bureaucratic discourses of the older associations like the UIOE. It is an attractive movement because its method of militancy is quite unique in Europe. It functions like a refuge for its members. It does not ask them to commit to an exclusive militant membership, but encourages them to take on political roles at the local level and to invest themselves in associations that defend citizens' rights. Nor does it require its members to make specific reference to the movement in the public sphere. In France, the PSM was actively involved in protesting against the law pertaining to religious symbols at

---

[21] Sean O'Fahey and Bernd Radtke (1993), "Neo-Sufism Reconsidered", *Der Islam*, IXX.

school, through the 'One School for All' action, which became a protest movement that united both Muslim and secular associations.

The spiritual side of the movement is another reason for its success, through the organisation of evening prayer meetings for members, and the transmission of religious experiences shared exclusively among group members such as the religious explanation of dreams and the recital of incantations for the well-being of the group. The question of religious sentiment having been somewhat attenuated by the political strategy of the UIOE and its obsession with the relationship with the political authorities, the PSM seems to offer an Islamic structure that allows for the combination of spiritual life with political aspirations, and this remains quite revolutionary. The key to the success of the PSM lies internally in the very important relationship of trust with the figure of the Sheikh (the guide), especially for the Sufi methods, and externally in the freedom of manoeuvrability within the secular state. Although they do not control many mosques in Europe, the influence of this movement is continuing to increase, thanks to preaching that is effective but not polemical (conferences, camping, courses, music festivals...).

One of the political axes of the PSM comes from the transposition of the Moroccan political situation to Europe (the Al'Adl wa-l'hsan party, from which comes the PSM, is not recognised in Morocco and regularly undergoes waves of violent repression). In addition, Nadia Yassine, the daughter of Sheik Yassine, who is currently the figurehead of the movement, comes to France regularly to give conferences on the compatibility of Islam and the dynamics of political modernisation, almost exclusively emphasising questions relating to democracy and human rights. It is also responsible for an association for the defence of human rights that has no reference to Islam, the Alliance for Freedom and Dignity (AFD), which is responsible for organising some of Nadia Yassine's European conferences. Finally, during the periods of repression against the central organisation in Morocco, the European members of PSM worked actively to spread information, once again without reference to religion but under the banner of the 'defence of human rights'.[22]

---

[22] Amel Boubekeur and Samir Amghar (2006), "Islamist Parties in the Maghreb and their Connections with Europe: Growing Influences and the Dynamics of Democratization", *Euromesco report*, November.

At the beginning of the 1960s in Lebanon, a theologian of Ethiopian origin, Sheik Abdallah al-Habachi, founded the Association of Islamic Charitable Projects (AICP) which is more commonly known as the Ahbash.[23] This movement has existed since the 1980s in Europe and has its headquarters in Paris. The movement spread throughout Europe thanks to the religious activism of Lebanese students studying in Europe, and political refugees here to escape the civil war in Lebanon. The Ahbash claims to be a Sufi movement and defends a political reading of Islam. Today they are active in more than 15 European countries (France, Germany, Switzerland, Denmark...), and even in Australia where the son of the movement's founder, Abderrahman Al Habachi, supervises the activities. They have several centres in the US, notably in Philadelphia, as well as in Ukraine where they have a large mosque in Kiev.

In France, where the association emerged in 1991, several public figures belong, or have belonged, to the movement, such as the rapper Kéry James (whose last two albums sold over 150,000 copies) or Abd Samad Moussaoui (the brother of Zacarias, one of the presumed authors of the September 11 attacks in 2001). In Switzerland the movement is older; its establishment dates from the end of the 1970s. Here, under the auspices of Lebanese students studying at the University of Lausanne, an association was created called the Centre Islamique de Lausanne (CIL). In just a few years the movement became the official representative body for Muslims of that region. It is the principal interlocutor of the Swiss authorities and is solicited to appoint chaplains in prisons and hospitals.

In Lebanon the movement has been used by the Syrian regime to contain the growing influence of Islamists in that country.[24] In Europe, anti-Islamist rhetoric is also one of the ways public opinion is mobilised by the Ahbash, especially after the September 11 attacks. In reality, this group fights for the ideological monopoly of European Islam, as much among young Muslims as with the public authorities. In presenting itself as the incarnation of Sufi and moderate Islam, the Ahbash attempt to play the 'defence against Islamism' card. Each year, the French branch of the AICP

---

[23] A. Nizar Hamzeh and R. Hrair Dekmejian (1996), "A Sufi response to political Islamism: Al-ahbash of Lebanon", *International Journal of Middle East Studies*, No. 28.

[24] Mustafa Kabha and Erlich Haggai (2006), "Al-Ahbash and Wahhabiyya interpretations of Islam", *International Journal of Middle East Studies*, 38(4).

organises an evening meal during Ramadan in the Salons of UNESCO in Paris, where they affirm before an array of international Muslim officials and European political personalities their moderate reading of Islam and their condemnation of Islamism. This initiative proves, among other things, that they are not exempt from political motivations, even if it is more discreet. They also often collaborate with European authorities that appreciate their opposition to the other tendencies of political Islam in Europe. On several occasions Abd Samad Moussaoui has condemned the religious jihadist experience of his brother on television, whilst simultaneously ensuring the promotion of his own more moderate movement.[25] Finally, it must be added that the movement organises regular demonstrations in support of the Syrian presence in Lebanon.

2.5 Missionary and predicative movements: The Tabligh and the Salafis

Whereas Turkish and Arab Islamic militants extol the defence and recognition of social and cultural rights for Muslims in Europe, and political Sufis fight for the conquest of power in their countries of origin (Morocco and Lebanon), the third feature of the European militant Islamic landscape, represented by the Tabligh and Salafists, has a more predicative and missionary logic. This third group of movements is characterised by a strong missionary activity that seeks to bring back to Islamic practices those who have turned away from them. Taking the Prophet as their example, these movements seek to enliven religious life, encouraging knowledge of the Koran and of the *hadiths* (sayings of the Prophet). They offer their members a pious vision of the world, which is founded on a concept of society in which the islamisation of the whole of humanity is an inescapable element. Thus, their concern is neither the establishment of the Islamic state, as was the case for the exiled Islamists, nor the defence of European Muslim interests, as is the case for the UIOE and the Milli Görüs, but rather a messianic vision that consists of bringing straying believers back to Islam. They seek to breathe a 'pure' Islamic conscience back into Muslims, through a return to the religious practice of the Prophet, a practice purified of any addition since the koranic revelation and the

---

[25]Abd Samad Moussaoui and Florence Bouquillat (2002), *Zacarias Moussaoui, Mon frère*, Denoël – Impacts.

prophetic apostolate. Their framework of political protest is historically fixed by the Prophet's example and thus, by consequence, maladjusted to the profane reality of contemporary Europe. Thus, the hope for social justice is postponed until the day of the Last Judgement in a millenarian fashion, this day being when the true Muslims return en masse to the pure practice of Islam. For them, protest should be passive and founded on the quiet strength of numbers that they are currently acquiring. They believe that through predication a social movement can be created that will overthrow the hierarchical organisation of the world and give Islam the predominant place that it deserves. These movements are thus not directly concerned with politics, but are rather concerned about correcting belief and religious practices through Islamic education, with a global reform in sight. This means a literal application of the koranic message that insists on the unity of God, a principle that is not respected, according to them, by Muslims and which is behind the political and social decadence of the umma (the community of believers).

Moreover, these movements are opposed to all 'westernised' forms of political participation by Muslim populations within European societies, because such participation would be contrary to Islam. Democracy is assimilated to the replacement of God, because European deputies legislate in the name of values that are not those of the sharia (Islamic law). Thus, in Europe these movements promote an attitude of withdrawal from the official political stage even though it directly concerns European Muslims. For these movements and contrary to the opinions of the Islamic militants who defend European Muslims, the future of Islam on the continent cannot be reduced to a process of negotiation with the state. The primacy of Islam over all other systems, especially secular ones, prevents them from considering themselves as participants in a non-Muslim political system. Thus they offer an interpretation of the world that explains Islam as the solution to all evil. Although they are apolitical, they maintain an element of symbolic protest through this attitude of withdrawal, due to the disappointing living conditions of Muslim Europeans (religious and social discrimination, economic exclusion, the everyday immorality of the public space...). Advocating a religiosity based on the rejection of the dominant values of society and the necessity of living one's faith in private, they do not demonstrate any violence. This religiosity often allows young Muslims with family, school or personal problems (particularly those from difficult suburbs), to develop a sense of atonement for their previous lack of religiosity. It also allows them an alternative to violence produced by the frustration at daily experiences of discrimination and exclusion in Europe.

Islam will ultimately compensate the oppressed, explain the followers. This feeling of oppression is reinforced by the stigmatisation that is associated with their participation in the movement, either in the public space because of their physical appearance (long beard, total veil and clothing from the Middle East), for which the media labels them a nest of 'suicide bombers', or even by the incomprehension of their friends and family.

The Tabligh, which means to bring the message, was created in 1880 at Merwat, not far from Dehli. Its founder, Muhammad Ilyas, responding to the desire for re-Islamisation among the local population which he esteemed to be only superficially Islamised, sought to preserve Indian Islamic identity through religious predication, in opposition to the English colonial presence and the Hindu majority. Before its arrival in Europe, this movement had a significant influence on the Indian sub-continent, such that many people were Islamised or re-Islamised through contact with the proselytism of the Tabligh. In 1944, upon the death of the founder, Ilyas' son decided to internationalise the organisation by taking it out of India and setting up permanent missions in the rest of the world. At the beginning of the 1950s it set up branches along the main pilgrimage routes in the Middle East and in East Africa. In the 1960s it spread to West Africa and South East Asia. In just a few years the Tabligh had, following in the footsteps of the Muslim Brotherhood, become a multinational religious organisation. Wherever it operated it practised a systematic policy of regulating Islamic activity by controlling the construction of mosques and other predicative activities.

The internationalisation of the movement, which led to its presence in almost 100 countries, was a result of the leaders' desire to spread their message in a universal fashion. It was also a result of the fact that in the 1940s the movement had reached its peak in India and in order to continue its development it was necessary to recruit a new clientele in other parts of the world. In the 1960s the movement turned towards Europe as a new land of predication, through the intermediary of the Indo-Pakistani community in the UK. The first Tabligh missions were set up in the UK at the same time as the first immigrants arrived from the Indian sub-continent, as some of them were members of the Tabligh. They set up their headquarters at Dewsbury in Yorkshire and from there, with the help of missionary activists from India, the movement expanded across Europe –

above all in those countries with Muslim immigrant populations at the time (Belgium, the Netherlands, Germany and France).[26] Other European countries such as Spain, Switzerland and Italy would only experience the predication of the Tabligh from the 1980s, with the arrival of Muslim immigrants. In France, although the movement was present as early as 1968 it was only officially organised in 1972 with the creation of a Muslim association called Faith and Practice (Foi et Pratique). Imbued with communitarian logic, the members of this movement did not recognise the dominant values of French society, such as pluralism or secularism. This lack of recognition brought indifference rather than any attempt to challenge or reject these values. In Belgium, the Tabligh progressively became an important Islamic actor from its foundation in 1974.

Religious predication is at the heart of the activity of the Tabligh: in groups of four or five they travel Europe, and the world, calling on people to come to Islam (khuruj fi sabillilah – preaching on the path of God). As a religious obligation, each disciple must spend between three days and four months proselytising on predicative missions in Europe or in the rest of the world. Their protest is symbolic, as in the rejection of the dominant aesthetic norms: a militant Tabligh characteristically wears a long robe (qamiss), a skullcap and has a beard. Each militant conforms to a great moral rigour. The Tabligh does not concern itself with the daily problems of young Muslims beyond their spiritual needs. Membership is conceived as a passage, more or less long, to the eventual goal of the militant re-Islamisation of the self. This passage may however, lead unsatisfied individuals to question the quietist nature of the Tabligh and to engage in violent political action once out of the movement. This was notably the case of Khaled Khelkal, former member of the French Tabligh who was responsible for the 1995 bombings in the Paris metro, as was also the case for the attacks in Casablanca in 2003, which were organised by former members of the European Tabligh.

Salafism makes reference to the salaf, the pious ancestors incarnated by the three generations of Muslims that succeeded the Prophet and who

---

[26] Felice Dassetto (1988), "L'organisation du Tabligh en Belgique", in T. Gersholm and Y.G. Lithman (eds), *The New Islamic Presence in Western Europe*, London, New York: Felice Dasseto (1988), *Le Tabligh en Belgique. Diffuser l'islam sur les traces du prophète*, Academia Sybidi Papers, 2. Moustapha A. Diop (1994), "Structuration d'un réseau: la Jamaat Tabligh (Société pour la Propagation de la Foi)", *Revue européenne des migrations internationales*, Vol. 10, No. 1.

represent the golden age of Islam. It is strongly inspired by the national Saudi religious doctrine: Wahhabism, named after its founder: Muhammad Ibn Abd al-Wahhab.[27] The adepts of this movement seek to base their daily life on the example of these three generations. Salafism came to Europe at the beginning of the 1990s thanks to the predication of graduates of Saudi Islamic Universities, as well as the proselytism of former militants and sympathisers of the Salafi wing of the Islamic Salvation Front (FIS), the Algerian Islamist party that settled on the continent in the 1990s, notably in the UK, France and Belgium.

Having no desire to engage in society and having no political project other than the messianic expectation of divine justice, Salafism controls numerous mosques (in Madrid, Copenhagen, Geneva, Brussels, the suburbs around Paris...), and like the Tabligh, they defend an apolitical non-violent vision of Islam, based on the will to mechanically align life with the fatwas of Saudi religious authorities. The current success of Salafism among young Muslims in Europe can be partly explained by a feeling of disappointment at the failure of re-Islamisation movements such as the UIOE.[28] Salafis criticise these movements for wanting to defend European Muslims using Western political categories and wanting to reform Islam in line with Western modernity. Thus they consider the majority of the political concessions and evolutions on questions of identity that have been obtained by these movements as unacceptable alterations of the koranic reference and the tradition of the Prophet. Salafis also reproach these currents of the Muslim Brotherhood for having accepted to negotiate with the state, especially on the different projects regarding the institutionalisation of Islam. The emergence of Salafism in Europe must be interpreted as the refusal of an excessive politicisation of Islam according to European standards, and a critique of the integration of values seen to be foreign to Islam, such as democracy and citizenship, into Islamic heritage. Negotiations between public authorities and militant Muslims have thus supposedly led to a banalisation of Islamic discourse, diluting its potential

---

[27] On the historical path and current dynamics of Wahhabism, see Madawi Al-Rasheed (2007), *Contesting the Saudi State: Islamic Voices from a New Generation*, Cambridge: Cambridge University Press.

[28] Samir Amghar (2006), "Le salafisme en Europe: la mouvance polymorphe d'une radicalisation", *Politique étrangère*, 1.

for protest and leaving room for Salafism, whose potential for effective protest and opposition has however yet to be tested. For many followers it has become the means of regenerating a mythology for an ageing Islamism. We are describing here the 'pious' tendency of Salafism. We return in the next chapter to a more detailed treatment of Salafism and its own different tendencies.

Conclusions

European political Islam is a varied movement composed of multiple strains. Overplaying the religious variable without taking into account the complex relationships that these different militant groups have with their political environments, national and international, would mean considering political Islam as a homogenous group, which is not the case. The different militant groups can be distinguished by the political methods they mobilise in the defence of Islam.

Thus the Sufi movements remain closely linked to and are controlled by the structures in their countries of origin (notably Morocco and Lebanon), whereas for those militant groups close to the Muslim Brotherhood and Milli Görüs, the rupture with their home countries has led them to refocus on Europe and adapt to its political culture. These latter groups act like political lobbies, seeking to influence European states by resorting to methods of engagement sanctioned by European legislation such as demonstrations, petitions or calls for economic boycotts. These actors work within a dialectical political framework where dynamics of negotiation and mutual influence interact with civil society and European political authorities. Finally, movements that are more withdrawn from the secular dimension of political Islam, such as Salafism or the Tabligh, voluntarily place themselves outside the framework of the state when it comes to negotiations about the rights of European Muslims. Their protest is manifested by their symbolic estrangement from the dominant values of society such as voting or the citizenship of a country they consider to be merely a host country, thus constantly affirming the primacy of an idealised religious micro-community over any other form of social organisation.

Overall, one can discern a form of political participation that is relatively serene emerging from among a large number of militant Muslims, notably in comparison with the minority of violent jihadists. Those who developed an interest in politics during the major crises concerning Islam, such as the headscarf affair in France or the Danish cartoons of Mohammad, have mostly done so not in exclusive reference to religion but to European law, in soliciting the national jurisdiction of the European Court of Human Rights. The cultural and religious 'otherness' emphasised by Islamism is no longer the privileged means of expressing contestation. During these crises the overwhelming majority of militant political Islamists asserted the European values of freedom of religion as the basis for their political demands, rather than the idea of a Western-based hatred of Islam. For committed Muslims, change would no longer come via the contestations of outsiders who only react to their own marginalisation. Establishing a relationship of opposition with the majority would no longer be, in the same way, the only means of obtaining visibility. Today their prime concern is the need to renew and update their political discourses, which have only scarcely been efficient up until now, and which are emblematic of the supposedly intrinsically oppositional nature of Islam. The issue for these militant Muslims henceforth is to find new ways of expressing their religiosity in the public sphere, without that being interpreted as an opposition to European values. These new discourses will also test, for committed Muslims and public authorities alike, their capacity to adapt to the political evolution of European society. A renewal of the spirit of committed Islam, where the reference to Islam in the context of political claims is not a disqualification, seems thus to be a major development of European political Islam.

Recourse to radical forms of political Islam, particularly by young people, is often the expression of a lack of political representation and participation by those who are excluded and socially and culturally discriminated against. On the other hand the mainstreaming of the political participation of these militants (through voting, participation in local political life, membership of political parties) will allow for a greater identification with national and European interests, with their citizenship leading them de facto to look beyond those questions only relevant to political Islam. In other words, these militants should be induced to participate in the construction of European society via the methods used by all European citizens. An increasing focus by militant Muslims on the general concerns of the society in which they live will disqualify the logic of opposition that leads to violence and the rejection of state institutions.

Moreover, greater political coordination between member states on the question of political Islam now seems to be called for, in light of the often trans-European nature of these movements, although it is true that the national contexts are of great importance. In order to understand what is at stake in the question of political Islam in Europe, the roots of present tensions and emerging conflicts must also be seen as European roots corresponding to particular national realities. The responses to these conflicts should therefore be considered by European institutions not as a matter of intercultural dialogue as was the case during the episode of the cartoons of Mohammad, but as a European political responsibility to European citizens. The place of European Islam and immigrant communities needs to be made visible in the cultural, political and historical heritage of Europe.

3. SALAFISM AND RADICALISATION OF YOUNG EUROPEAN MUSLIMS

SAMIR AMGHAR

Introduction

European Islam is more than half a century old. Since the end of the 1980s, a new form of religiosity has emerged among young people of North African, Turkish or Indo-Pakistani origin, some of whom were born in Europe. This new variation of Islam was first of all largely the result of 're-islamisation' movements such as the Muslim Brotherhood. However, the 1990s also saw the emergence of another movement in the 're-islamisation' dynamics in Europe: Salafism. It is possible to distinguish three streams of Salafism here. The first is revolutionary; it places 'jihad' at the heart of religious beliefs. The second is predicative Salafism, which bases its actions on preaching and religious teachings. The last is political Salafism, which organises its activities around a political logic. Each one of these currents entertains a specific relationship with European societies, with Muslim societies and with the means – including jihad – of hastening the eventuality of the Islamic state.

The new relationship towards Islamic teachers that is prevalent among these young people is not simply the reproduction of the communitarian religiosity of their parents. If the religious affiliation of the previous generation was founded on an ethno-national logic, as well as on the dominance of traditional attitudes towards religion, these young people refuse to reproduce the inclinations of their parents.[1] Until the beginning of

---

[1] F. Khosrokavar (1997), *L'Islam des jeunes*, Paris: Flammarion.

the 1990s, both the Muslim Brotherhood and the Tabligh,[2] played a central role in re-islamisation, effectively enjoying a monopoly in the supply of Islam to Europe. Since then, we have witnessed the diversification of this supply with the arrival of new actors. Among them, Salafism, a once marginal group in Europe,[3] has become a pillar of re-islamisation at the beginning of the 21st century, competing with the more traditional structures. While both the Muslim Brotherhood and the Tabligh present a doctrinal and organisational homogeneity, Salafism appears to be a movement that is both pluralist and contradictory,[4] of which it is necessary to identify its multiple European components.[5]

3.1   The origins of Salafism

Salafism was born with the beginning of Muhammad's apostolate in the 7th century. His teachings brought together men and women, the most famous among whom were the four first Caliphs of Islam – Aboubakr, Omar, Othman and Ali, who were later to become, among others, what Muslim theologians would call the Companions of the Prophet; the *sahâba*. To these companions were added the successors (*tâbi'ine*), and then the successors of the successors (*tâbi'i at tâbi'ine*).[6] These three groups formed what the theologians were to call "Salaf", the pious predecessors: three generations that represented the golden age of Islam. The Salaf were distinguished by their exemplary piety, and by their military conquests, which were the foundations of a great empire stretching from Spain to India. Theologians and clerics thus established a causal relationship between the faith of the Salaf and their military and political success. Since then, each time a Muslim society is confronted with an economic, political or social crisis,

---

[2] The Muslim Brotherhood Association was founded in Egypt in 1928.

[3] See S. Amghar (2005), «Le paysage Islamique français: acteurs et enjeu» in JF Dortier and L Testot, *La religion. Unité et Diversité*, Paris, Sciences humaines, pp. 195-201.

[4] Expression taken from F. Frégosi (2005), «Les musulmans laïques en France: une mouvance plurielle et contradictoire», *Maghreb-Machrek*, No. 185, printemps.

[5] For a typology of different tendencies within Salafism in France, see S. Amghar (2005), "Les salafistes français: une nouvelle aristocratie religieuse?», *Maghreb-Machrek*, No. 185.

[6] S. Mervin (2000), *Histoire de l'Islam, Doctrines et fondements*, Paris: Flammarion, pp. 25-29.

certain theologians will recommend a return to the Islam of the Salaf. The first to have formalised this idea at a religious level was Ibn Hanbal (780-855), at a time when the Muslim empire was prone to fighting amongst politico-religious factions. Ibn Taymiyya (1263-1328) reiterated the idea when his Damas region was subjected to the Mongol invasions.

This idea of a return to the pious ancestors as a response to the decline of Muslim society was later taken up by Muhammad Ibn Abdel Wahhab (1720-1792), who was inspired by the writings of Ibn Hanbal and Ibn Taymiyya, and who hoped to define the causes of the Ottoman Empire's waning strength in terms of its opposition to European hegemony. The origin of the crisis of the Ottoman Empire would thus not be imputable to political or economic considerations but to the betrayal by Muslims of the original koranic message, organised around the concept of *tawhid* (the unity of God), such as the Salafs had understood and applied it.

3.2 Three forms of Salafism in Europe

Three antagonistic tendencies in Europe associated with this heritage today claim an explicit link with Salafism.[7]

The first is the so-called 'revolutionary' or jihadist Salafism.[8] This movement was initially associated with the political doctrine of the Muslim Brotherhood. It conserved only one element of that ideology: political and social action must necessarily fit within an Islamic perspective – a perspective linked to a literalist reading of the politically-oriented koranic texts that deal with the management of power, authority and the caliphate, all aiming towards revolutionary action. This discourse is radical and is opposed to any idea of engagement or collaboration with Muslim[9] or Western societies. Even in the West, this discourse defends opposition to the state and the fight for the establishment of the Islamic state and, eventually, the caliphate. Partly inspired by the religious opinions of the 13th century Damascene theologian Ibn Taymiyya, who justified the resort

---

[7] The majority of Islamist and neo-fundamentalist movements claim a link with Salafism, (see O. Roy (2002), *L'Islam mondialisé*, Paris, Le Seuil.

[8] G. Kepel (2003), *Jihad, Expansion et déclin de l'islamisme*, Paris, Gallimard/Folio, pp. 341-342 (Original Edition: Paris, Gallimard, 2000).

[9] This contrasts with the majority of Muslims, who are mostly integrated (they vote, take part in the social and economic life of Western societies).

to jihad against the Mongols (whom he doubted belonged to the umma), this movement defends direct action to implement the reign of God on earth. Hostile to religious action that restricts itself to conversion, (*da'wa*), the revolutionary Salafis place the jihad at the heart of Islamic faith.[10]

The forms of violence associated with the jihad are of two orders: vertical when they contest the state, either European or Arab, horizontal when they affect individuals accused of contravening a religious norm that the jihadists expect to have respected by all means.[11] In the West, this violence is only aimed at contesting the legitimacy and the actions of Western regimes, with the support of European countries to Arab regimes seen as an obstacle to revolution and the eventuality of the Islamic state in Muslim countries. The terrorist attacks in Madrid on 11 March 2004 did not aim to punish the victims for their non-respect of Islamic norms, but to pressure Western states, Spain in this case, into withdrawing their troops from Iraq. Another earlier example, the attacks by the GIA (the Armed Islamic Group) on a regional train in Paris in 1995, was an attempt to push France into withdrawing its support for the Algerian regime. This vertical violence is thus different from the Islamic terrorism that rages in the Arab-Muslim world. In addition to the pressure on the states, action in Arab states aims to get individuals to respect religious obligations. When the GIA massacre civilians in Algeria, they also intend to sanction those populations who, according to them, are acting in contravention of the religious norm.

The idea of the vertical jihad is developed in the text "Knights under the banner of the Prophet" by Ayman Al-Zawahiri, who is a theorist of Egyptian origin associated with al Qaeda. In this text he affirms that it is necessary to obtain the support of the Muslim masses in order to overthrow Arab regimes. Al-Zawahiri suggests a strategy of exporting the jihad to the West, and particularly to the US, in order to, on the one hand, obtain the support of the undecided Muslim masses, and on the other hand, to weaken the Western support for those Muslim countries considered impious. Strikes against the Western enemy would, by ricochet-

---

[10] B. Rougier (2004), "L'Islam face au retour de l'islam", *Vingtième siècle*, No. 82, April-June, p. 111.

[11] F. Burgat (2002), *L'Islamisme en face*, Paris: La découverte, p. 113. See also F. Khosrokhavar (2003), *Les Nouveaux Martyrs d'Allah*, Paris: Flammarion.

effect, weaken the Arab states, which would facilitate the ultimate objective of seizing power and establishing of the Islamic state.[12]

It must be stressed that the jihad, as it is conceptualised in Europe, stems from two strategies, depending on whether it operates in the West or in the Arab-Muslim world – although they may overlap. Jihad undertaken in Europe must be qualified as *offensive*: it expresses the desire to destabilise or at least unnerve Western governments so that they cease supporting the Arab-Muslim regimes that the Salafis are fighting against. In the case of the jihad launched by young Muslims from Europe in Muslim countries, it must be considered *defensive*. For European jihadists, military action (in Iraq, Bosnia-Herzegovina or Chechnya) demonstrates their desire to support those Muslim populations that are victims of aggression often perpetrated by Western powers.

Many organisations situate their actions within a Salafist logic of the revolutionary type. This is the case for the group Kaplan, the result of a schism within the Turkish Islamic party, the Refah (Party of Prosperity). Active in France, Germany and Belgium, this group defends the installation of the caliphate by all means. This discourse is also found within the Hizb ut-Tahrir (Liberation Party), the product of a split within the Muslim Brotherhood. Founded by Taqieddin Nabhani in 1958, it is active in the UK and Denmark.

The second tendency pursues the objective of conversion and predication. In Europe, this tendency represents the great majority within Salafism.[13] In opposition to revolutionary Salafism, which it sees as violent and heretical, this movement believes that it is neither the jihad[14] nor armed

---

[12] G. Kepel (2004), *Fitna. Guerre au cœur de l'Islam,* Paris: Le seuil; see also under his direction: *Al-Qaïda dans le texte,* Paris, PUF, (2005). See also the text by Ayman Al-Zawahiri (2002), «Al wala'wa al-baraa», September.

[13] For example, this stream has nearly 500 militants in France, 5000 sympathisers and controls nearly 20 mosques out of some 1800. Despite being in the majority within the Salafist movement in Europe, it is part of the minority streams compared to those which are more firmly implanted, such as the Muslim Brotherhood or the Tabligh.

[14] For example, a collection of fatwas condemn the attacks in Algeria, *Fatâwas al 'ulamâ alkabir fîma* ouhdira *mi dima' fi-il jaza'ir* (Fatwas of the great religious scholars on the blood spilt in Algeria), (Editions Maktaba al furqa).

action that will allow the establishment of an Islamic society and state. Many of those who today claim to belong to predicative Salafism are thus opposed to the entry of Muslim militants into political or revolutionary activism. A famous comment by the Albano-Syrian Salafist Sheikh Nasir ud-Din Al-Albani explains: "Part of [good] politics today is the abandonment of politics". This theologian, who was the most remarkable figure of Salafism along with the Grand Mufti of Saudi Arabia, Abdelaziz Ibn Baz, from the 1960s until their deaths in 1999, participated extensively in the diffusion of predicative Salafism throughout the world. Both these men were convinced that the only solution to the problems encountered by Muslims was what they called *At-Tasfiyatu wa-Tarbiyya*: purification and education. This meant purification of the religion from 'innovations' that sullied its dogma and its precepts, in order to return to the religion as it was taught by the Prophet and the education of Muslims, so that believers may conform to this religion and abandon their bad habits. Any other solution (political or revolutionary) would be to lead them astray. Critical of revolutionary Salafism, seen as incapable of bringing the kingdom of Allah to earth, these theologians offer an opposing vision based on piety, which has its foundations in a faith that is both eschatological and apodictic, and in which the purification of belief and of Islamic education are written into human destiny. This means bringing an Islamic conscience back to Muslims, by returning to a religious practice purified of all additions subsequent to the last koranic revelation and to the apostolate of the Prophet. Through preaching, a new social movement would be created to lead to a world order in which Islam is accorded a pre-eminent place. Pious Salafis are thus not primarily concerned with politics but rather with the correction of belief and religious practices.[15]

In Europe, this current is for the most part found in Wahhabi-inspired Salafism. Linked to the official religious institution in Saudi Arabia (*Dar el Ifta*) and to the different Islamic universities in that country, this movement has counted among its chief theologians Ibn Baz, the former Mufti of the kingdom, Al-Albani,[16] and Ibn Uthaymin[17] (who died in 2001).

---

[15] Roy, op. cit., note [7].

[16] Al-Albani, a specialist of the science of the hadith, emigrated from Albania to Syria in the 1940s with his father, a Hanafi Mufti. He was called on to teach the science of the hadith at the University of Medina, when it was built in 1962. This university educated foreign students, many of them beneficiaries of scholarships from the Saudi government. Two years after he began this post, his contract was

Fawzan,[18] Al-Madkhali[19] and the Great Mufti of the Saudi Kingdom, Al-Cheikh, and the Yemenite Muqbil[20] (who also died in 2001) have been the contemporary representatives of this movement.

Predicative Salafis oppose all forms of political participation for Muslim populations within European society, with the motive that such participation would be contrary to Islam. Democracy is assimilated to a form of associationism (*chirk*) that leads to heresy, because Western parliamentarians legislate in the name of values that aren't those of the sharia. Salafis in the west advocate an attitude of withdrawal, even though this concerns European Muslims. During the protests organised by Muslim associations against the proposed law banning religious symbols at school[21] in France in December 2003 and January 2004, among the few thousand participants there were few who belonged to this current of Salafism (according to our observations). This absence may be interpreted as a demonstration of indifference towards these political questions. These

---

terminated. He then lived for some time in Lebanon, and in the United Arab Emirates, before moving to Amman where he lived until his death in 1999. His disciples, mostly of Jordanians and Palestinian origin, then founded the centre Al-Albani in the Jordanian capital.

[17] Former member of the Saudi Committee of the Wise, he is the author of a famous fatwa: the perpetrator of a suicide attack will be in hell forever.

[18] Salih Al-Fawzan is a member of the Saudi Committee of the Wise.

[19] The Saudi Rabi Ibn Had Al (Madkhali) is without a doubt the official spokesman for this tendency in Saudi Arabia. Former head of the department of the Sunni sciences at the University of Median, he was a student of Al-Albani at this same university. Extremely vehement towards revolutionary Salafis, and the Muslim Brotherhood, he is the doctrinal reference for many Muslims in Europe who claim links to Wahhabi-inspired Salafism. He currently occupies a chair at the University of Medina.

[20] Muqbil Ibn Hadi was trained in Saudi Arabia before being expelled. Extremely critical of the Saudi government up until his death, he reformed his position when Saudi authorities welcomed him and transferred him to the US, and then to Saudi Arabia, for treatment. See F. Burgat (2005), *L'Islamisme à l'heure d'Al-Qaida*, Paris: La Découverte, pp. 32-39.

[21] This law, of 15 March 2004, pertained to the application of the principle of laicity, the wearing of religious symbols or clothing demonstrating a religious affiliation in public school and high schools.

Salafists do not engage in negotiations with the state: Islam would never be content with such negotiation. Their interpretation, based on the belief of the primacy of Islam above any other system – *a forteriori* secular – forbids them to consider themselves as active participants in a non-Muslim political system. To participate in this way would mean implicitly recognising an identical status between Islam and the problems of society: withdrawal is thus preferable to all forms of participation. This attitude vis-à-vis European societies is confirmed by the fatwas of the Saudi theologians, who make emigration (*hijra*) to a Muslim country a religious obligation for any practising Muslim living in the West.

Although they refuse all forms of integration, these Salafists develop a non-confrontational relationship to the dominant power structure, refusing all violent action. Whilst predicative Salafism is active in the Netherlands and in Belgium as a result of Moroccan immigration, in France it is partly based on the proselytism of individuals of Algerian origin. The movement was consolidated in France in the 1990s by the intervention of Abdelkader Bouziane in Lyon and Abdelhadi Doudi in Marseille.

The third tendency emphasises political activism as the means of convincing the Muslim masses of the necessity of the Islamic state and society. This tendency is in the extreme minority within the Salafist movement. Although it draws on the Muslim Brotherhood's repertoire of political action (participation, creation of associations, demonstrations etc.), so-called political Salafism criticises them on a number of points. It accuses them of excessively modernising Islam. This current is partly the product of the combination of the political reading of Islam of the Muslim Brotherhood, with the religious literalism of the predicative Salafists, particularly the Saudi-Arabians.

This Saudi Arabian dimension traces back to the refuge given there to the Syrian and Egyptian Muslim Brotherhoods, when they had been disgraced by Nassar and the Alaouite regimes respectively. These Brotherhoods thus constituted the bureaucratic framework for the major Islamic institutions of Saudi Arabia, such as the WML (World Muslim League) or the World Assembly of Muslim Youth (WAMY).[22] In Europe, this current of Salafism is above all implanted through the intermediary of the LIM, active in many countries thanks to the large network of mosques

---

[22] Kepel, op. cit., note [12], pp. 208-210.

that it finances.[23] In Switzerland, this movement is incarnated by Youssouf Ibram, Imam of the Cultural Islamic Foundation of Geneva, linked to the LIM. Originally of Moroccan origin, in the 1980s he obtained a Masters in Shari'a Law at the Islamic University of Riyad. At the beginning of the 1990s the LIM name him Imam of the Zurich mosque, before moving him to Geneva in 2000. As a member of the European Council of the Fatwa and Research, an organisation linked to the European Muslim Brotherhood, he participates in the implementation of a European-style Islam. Youssouf Ibram defends the idea of Muslim integration in Europe. He is close to the vision of the Muslim Brotherhood but nevertheless remains opposed to it by virtue of his literalism and his religious rigour.

In addition to this Salafism, which is close to the Brotherhood ideology, there is another tendency, represented for example by Farid Benyettou, who as a 23 year-old delivered sermons in the mosques of the Paris region encouraging young French people to fight the American army in Iraq. If the actions of this man lie within a jihadist logic, they also have a political dimension, in terms of negotiations with the French authorities. Of Algerian origin, Benyettou frequented militants of the Islamic Salvation Front (FIS) for a time in France, through the intervention of his brother-in-law, who initiated him in literalist and rigorous religious readings. Claiming links with Ali Behadj, Saïd Qotb and Safar Al-Hawali, he argues that European Muslims must have recourse to democratic instruments and liberty of expression in order to influence national policy. Opposing all forms of violence on French territory and in the West in general, in the name of Islam, he was active in all the meetings and demonstrations against the proposed law on secularism, including those organised both by Muslim associations or secular structures, and even those organised by the extreme left.

3.3   Common Islamic heritage and political myth

Although deprived of all organisational synergy and distanced from each other by mutual ex-communication, the three streams of the Salafist movement have common ideological foundations and myths that structure

---

[23] The mosques in Brussels, Geneva and even Mantes-la-Jolie were constructed and financed by the WML.

their political imagination – all things that it shares with Islamists.[24] The first element that can be identified with the Salafists, and which is also a central theme for the Islamists, is the idea that Islam cannot be reduced to its religious dimension; cannot be summarised by ritual practices. On the contrary, Islam is a global system that reigns over all domains of life, both sacred and profane. Like the Muslim Brotherhood, the Salafists, whatever their tendency, refuse an exclusively cultural understanding of confessional belonging.[25]

The second element shared with Islamism is the systematic effort to define the contribution of Islamic civilisation to Western society. Salafists, like Islamists, see European society as being confronted with a political and economic impasse that only Islam can overcome – an Islam that, seen as a global system, has the necessary resources to confront the difficulties and crises of European and Muslim societies.

Many myths also contribute to the foundation of the political 'imaginaire' of the Salafist movement, revolutionary, political or predicative. One of the first resorts of the political mythology of Salafism is the myth of decadence. Islam is, according to this myth, in decomposition and Muslim identity is becoming lost in the haze of Western hegemony. For Salafists, as for Islamists, the decay of irreligious youth hastens the end of time. Muslim society and Muslim minorities in the West have entered a state of generalised anomie (disregard for divine law and values),[26] in particular the product of divisions between Muslims that only Islam can combat. Salafist political mythology also emphasises an apocalyptic millenarian dimension: the end of the world is near, numerous signs of the

---

[24] Salfism has many points in common with political Islam. But in contrast to Salafism, political Islam is based on the activism of groups that have a precise political vision and a political project (and not a messianic utopia), which are organised as social movements or political parties, with recourse to strictly political activities and initiatives (demonstrations, petitions, participation in elections, etc.), acting in a real political and institutional framework (of the state), and are non-violent in their methods of action.

[25] The Muslim Brotherhood call this principle *chûmuliyya al islam*. See S. Amghar, "Les Frères musulmans francophone: vers un islamisme de la minorité", in S. Amghar (dir.).

[26] These comments are inspired by the work of R. Girardet (1990), *Mythes et Mythologies Politiques*, Paris: Le Seuil, and the writings of M. Winock (2004), *Nationalisme, antisémitisme, et fascisme en France*, Paris: Le Seuil.

prophetic tradition announce its imminence, and it will be preceded by a holy war, between Muslims and non-Muslims, where Islam will triumph over evil as incarnated by the West.

For the Salafists, the decline of Muslim society is certainly the result of the betrayal of the original koranic message, but it is also the product of a conspiracy. Along with the idea of the alteration of Islamic practice, this conspiracy theory is one of the elements that fundamentally explain the weakness of Muslims around the world. Behind this plot are the West and the Jews who have concocted a plan to keep Muslims dominated and prevent Islam from developing.[27] In this ideological representation, Islam is the only power able to overthrow Western imperialism and dominance that is manipulated by an occult power for which the Jews are responsible. "Conspiracy theory" wrote Karl Popper, is a vision according to which "whatever happens in society – especially happenings such as war, unemployment, poverty, shortages, which people as a rule dislike – is the result of direct design by some powerful individuals and groups".[28]

3.4 Salafism: A response to the failure of political Islam?

The current success of Salafism within certain segments of Europe's Muslim population is partly explained by the disappointment resulting from the failure of Islamist-inspired re-islamisation movements, such as the Muslim Brotherhood. The development of Salafism in Europe in the 1990s must therefore be analysed in light of the aporiae of political Islam.[29] Salafists reproach Islamist movements originating with the Muslim Brotherhood for wanting to establish an Islamic state 'top-down' (for the predicatives), for using Western political categories (for the jihadists) or for wanting to regenerate Islam in keeping with Western modernity (for the political stream). Thus the Salafists, be they political, jihadist or quietist, still share the essential belief that the concessions of the Muslim

---

[27] This expression comes from L. Poliakov (1980), *La causalité diabolique, essai sur l'origine des persecutions*, Paris: Calmann-Lévy. See also, P-A Taguieff (2005), *La Foire aux Illuminés: ésotérisme, théorie du complot et extrémisme*, Paris: Mille et une nuits.

[28] K.R. Popper (1985), *Conjecture et réfutations. La croissance du savoir scientifique*, Pris, Payot (original edition: London 1963).

[29] O. Roy (1992), *L'échec de l'Islam politique*, Paris: Le Seuil.

Brotherhood are unacceptable alterations of the koranic references and the tradition of the Prophet.[30] In France, a number of predicative Salafists (Wahhabi-inspired) reproach the representatives of the Muslim Brotherhood (in the *UOIF*) for having accepted to negotiate with the public authorities, notably during the process of the institutionalisation of Islam in France, which led in the end to the betrayal of the koranic message.

The emergence of these different forms of Salafism must thus be analysed as a refusal of the excessive politicisation of Islam by means borrowed from Western political culture. This is why Salafists criticise the Muslim Brotherhood for having integrated into Islamic heritage values such as democracy, which are foreign to the Muslim religion. This position must be understood less as the total negation of Western political culture than as a rejection of the methods of appropriation of Western modernity proposed by the Muslim Brotherhood.

Negotiations with the public authorities and civil society in the West make the discourse of the Muslim Brotherhood routine to a certain extent, thus diluting its confrontational impact and leaving room for a Salafist movement of which the potential for contestation has not yet been tested. This movement now appears to be an 'Islamist variant', seductive for those groups that are marginalised and excluded from all political participation. The mobilisation power of Salafist discourse is thus the consequence of the rejection of the strategies of social and political participation associated with the Muslim Brotherhood – particularly by those people initially convinced by the radical rhetoric of this organisation in the 1980s and 1990s. In entering the negotiation process, the Muslim Brotherhood stopped representing a utopia capable of mobilising people. In light of this, Salafism would now be a way of regenerating Islamic mythology, as well as a new way of engaging the domain of political participation. For the jihadists this happens through political violence and for the predicatives

---

[30] F. Burgat (2005), *L'Islamisme à l'heure d'Al-Qaida*, Paris, La Découverte, p. 117. The current Great Mufti of Saudi Arabia, Cheikh Al-Cheikh, said of the Muslim Brotherhood: "Among the principal aspects of their attraction we count: secrecy, dissimulation, versatility, closeness with those who are potentially useful for them […]. On the other hand, the ultimate goal of the Muslim Brotherhood is to obtain power […] The fact that people are saved from the wrath of Allah and go to Paradise is of little importance to them." Speech recorded on a cassette entitled *Fatâwa Al 'Ulamâ'i fil-jamâ'ati wa atharuhâ 'alâ bilâd il-h' aramayn* (Editions Minuit, 2002).

through indifference. It is a matter of moving beyond the limits of traditional Islam and overcoming the security barriers of both Western and Arab regimes. A non-negligible number of French Salafists initially frequented the Muslim Brotherhood before joining Salafism and were seduced by the discourse of Tariq Ramadan, who is close to the Muslim Brothers and the Tabligh.

Finally, Salafism criticises the Muslim Brotherhood less for their political openness than for their partisan instrumentalisation of Islam (*hizbiyya*). This latter point, for the Salafists, leads to the fragmentation of the *umma*, which is unacceptable to the extent that it results in the weakening of Islam and *fitna* (division of the *umma*) – a cause of war for Muslims.

Conclusions

As we have seen, European Salafists divide into three distinct poles, the revolutionary, the predicative and the political. Derived from the same desire to return to the golden age of Islam, the three poles are opposed to each other on the question of which methods should be used to create the Islamic state. Their different operating methods represent three different relationships to the Western 'other'.

These three tendencies have always maintained multiple links to each other. Since the Algerian civil war, and above all since the September 11 attacks, the demarcations between the three movements have solidified. In the wake of these events, there is an increasing autonomy amongst and between these movements. Predicative Salafists present themselves as the best defence against revolutionary Salafism, which they refer to as *takfiri* (he who pronounces the anathema); as for the revolutionary Salafists, they continue to accuse the predicative Salafists of being in the pay of monarchies and Arab regimes.

However they share a common understanding of Salafism's political functions, which are also three: that of protest, of a tribune and as an elective function.

The first consists in the expression of *opposition* to the social and political system, to the dominant political and religious choices on offer, rather than in proposition: hence the absence of a precise political project, which is more often than not reduced to the establishment of the Islamic state, without further precision. Salafists mistrust Islamists, most of all those of the middle and upper classes which, according to them, maintain

Muslims in a subordinate position. Rejected by the well-off, true Islam attracts those who have a quarrel with the dominant order and the social hierarchy.

It is from this conflictual dimension that the *tribune* function develops: Salafism becomes the tribune for a mass of malcontents that neither the political parties nor the other religious currents can accommodate.[31] Thus the emergence of Salafism appears to be the consequence of the crisis of political representation in Europe, manifested by a defiance vis-à-vis political structures incapable of incorporating the aspirations of a part of the resident Muslim population. Salafism expresses a rebellion in which religion symbolises an affirmation of the self in opposition to the dominant values of society.

The third function is *elective*. For the Salafists, belonging to Salafism means being part of an elite, avant-garde movement responsible for the realisation of God's design on earth. As actors in a story defined by God, Salafists take care of those Muslims not yet touched by divine grace.

---

[31] G. Lavau (1981), *A quoi sert le Parti communiste?*, Paris: Fayard.

4. ISLAMIC TERRORIST RADICALISATION IN EUROPE

OLIVIER ROY

4.1 The West European terrorist

Since 9/11, a great deal of data has been accumulated on the terrorists linked to al Qaeda.[1] The picture that emerges shows the growing role played by Western Muslims. They constitute the bulk of the terrorists involved in actions perpetrated here in Europe. But they are also involved in terrorist actions abroad and participate in the different international military jihad (from Faluja to Kashmir). These Western Muslims have varied personal histories and include different categories: the majority are second-generation Muslims who were either born in Europe or came as children; we also find people who came as students or as political refugees; thirdly, there has been a significant number of converts.

They all share common patterns. They speak European languages, are Western educated, and many have citizenship of a European country. They have had a 'normal' Western teenager's upbringing, with no conspicuous religious practices, often going to night clubs, 'womanising' and drinking alcohol. None have previous religious training. Most of them are born-again (or converts): they became religious-minded Muslims in Europe, even if a few of them, in the aftermath of (re)discovering Islam, went to Middle Eastern *madrasa* (school or college) to improve their

---

[1] Marc Sageman (2004), "Understanding Terrorist Networks", Pennsylvania University Press; Robert Leiken (2006), "The Quantitative Analysis of Terrorism and Immigration: An Initial Exploration", *Terrorism and Political Violence,* December, Nixon Institute.

religious knowledge (this is mainly true of British Pakistanis and of converts). When they went to university, their curricula were modern and secular (computer science, engineering, etc.). In many ways they are modern.

They do not represent an Islamic tradition; on the contrary they break with the religion of their parents. When they convert or become born-again, they always adopt some sort of Salafism, which is a scripturalist version of Islam that discards traditional Muslim culture. They do not revert to traditions: for instance when they marry, it is with the sisters of their friends or with converts, and not with a bride from the country of origin chosen by their parents. There is also a growing number of female converts among the terrorists. The case of Muriel Degauque (a Belgian woman who killed herself in Iraq in 2005) is probably the harbinger of a new generation of al Qaeda activists recruiting far beyond the usual pool of second-generation Muslims and numbering people who, 40 years ago, would have joined ultra-leftist groups, like the Red Army Faction.

The groups are rarely homogeneous in ethnic terms: the Hofstad group of Holland includes second-generation Moroccans (Bouyeri himself), 'white' (the former policewoman Martine van der Oeven) and 'black' Dutch citizens (the brothers Jason and Jermaine Walters): the deeds of this group may have destroyed the concept of 'multiculturalism' in Holland, but it is typically 'post-culturalist'.

The radicalisation of Western Muslim youth is often considered a spill-over of the crisis in the Middle East (Palestine, Afghanistan, Iraq). But in fact the chronology of events, the geographical origin of the radicals and their own claims most often contradict this assumption. No Palestinian, Afghan or Iraqi has been involved in terrorist actions in Europe. There are very few Arabs from the Middle East (some Egyptians and Syrians). People of Pakistani (in the UK) or Moroccan origin are overrepresented. We also find East African activists living in the UK. The perpetrators of the failed terrorist attack in London on 21 July 2005, were Ethiopian (Osman Hussain), Somalian, Eritrean and Ghanaian; another Ethiopian, Binyam Mohammed, had been arrested in connection with the José Padilla case. Converts make up 10% (according to the Nixon Institute) to 25% (the Beghal group) of the militants in Europe.[2] Many converts are Black

---

[2] Leiken, ibid.

Caribbeans (Richard Reid, the Bonte brothers, Grandvisir, Willie Brigitte, Jermaine Lindsay), or 'white' people (Jérôme Courtailler, Lionel Dumont, Christian Ganczarski); an interesting case is that of Eisa al-Hindi (alias Dhiran Barot) a former Hindu, born in Kenya, a British citizen who went to Afghanistan and then Malaysia where he married, before being arrested in London for planning attacks in New York: all of al Qaeda is embodied in this trajectory.

In a word, there is no relation between the geographical map of the radicalisation and the map of existing conflicts. This geographical discrepancy can be pushed further: almost none of the 'born again' who became terrorists returned to the country of origin of his/her family to fight jihad: none of the French of Algerian descent went back to Algeria during the 1990s, despite the fact that there was some sort of a jihad there. The few exceptions are related to British Pakistanis, but they went back to Pakistan not to fight against the regime of President Musharraf, but to join the global terrorist hub which is nowadays centred in that country. Instead all the European radicals preferred to go to peripheral jihads (Afghanistan, Bosnia and Chechnya); none went to Palestine (with the exception of two Britons). They did not target specific Jewish or Israeli objectives in Europe (contrary to their secular leftist Palestinian predecessors in the 1970s), but 'global' targets (namely transport systems).

Moreover, the terrorist actions perpetrated in Europe have rarely been expressed in direct connection with the events in the Middle East, (with the possible exception of the Madrid attack in 2004). 9/11 was expressed in terms of a global war between Islam and the West. When Mohamed Bouyeri killed Theo Van Gogh in Amsterdam, he did not mention in his letter the presence of Dutch troops in Iraq and Afghanistan; he referred instead to the desecration of Islam in Holland.

It is also interesting to note that none of the Islamic terrorists killed or captured so far in the West had been active in any legitimate anti-war movements or even in organised political support for the people they claim to be fighting for. They don't distribute leaflets or collect money for hospitals and schools. They do not have a rational strategy to push for the interests of the Iraqi or Palestinian people. On the contrary, the few of them who have joined a militant group before turning radical, did so in joining global and supranational Islamic movements like Jama'at ut Tabligh or Hizb ut-Tahrir.

There is no clear-cut sociological profile of the radicals or anything that could link them to a given socio-economic situation. More precisely, the reasons that may push them towards violence are not specific enough, but are shared by a larger population that deals with such a situation in a very different way. Explanations based on poverty, exclusion, racism, acculturation, etc., are simply not specific enough. There is clearly a generational dimension: Islamic radicalism is a youth movement. Frustration is obviously a key element in their radicalisation, but has more to do with a psychological than a social or economic dimension. They tend to become radical within the framework of a small local group of friends, who either met on a destitute estate (as the Farid Benyettou group in France in 2006), a university campus, a gang of petty delinquents and drug addicts or … in jail. Jail is a favoured place for recruitment, especially as far as converts are concerned.

A common factor among known radicals is a concern for self-image and the endeavour to reconstruct the self through action. In this sense they are more in search of spectacular action where they will be personally and directly involved, than with the long-term and painstaking building of an anonymous and underground political organisation which could extend the social and political basis of their networks. They are more activists than constructivists. They are very different from the *komintern* agents of the 1920s and 1930s. This narcissistic dimension explains both the commitment to suicide actions and the difficulty of working underground without the perspective of action. Without terrorism, they cease to exist. This commitment to immediate or mid-term action as opposed to long-term political action is probably their greatest weakness.

Another significant element of radicalisation is the blending of 'Islamic' wording and phraseology with a typically Western anti-imperialism and third-world radicalism: their target is the same as the Western ultra-leftist movements of the 1970s, even if they proceed to mass terrorism (except that they do not target political or business personalities, as the European ultra-left used to do). But the paradigm of ultra-leftist terrorism from the 1970s might provide a bridge with non-Islamic radicals.

The Western-based Islamic terrorists are not the militant vanguard of the Muslim community; they are a lost generation, unmoored from traditional societies and cultures, frustrated by a Western society that does not meet their expectations. And their vision of a global umma is both a mirror of and a form of revenge against the globalisation that has made them what they are. Al Qaeda and consorts offer a narrative of revolt and violence that appeals to an unmoored youth and gives a religious and political dimension to youth revolt that could have been expressed in other forms of violence (gangs, Columbine-style school-shootings, drugs, delinquency). It is not by chance that jails in the West seem to be as much recruiting grounds as mosques.

4.2   What can be done?

The picture is quite variable in Europe. There are countries where Muslims are mainly first-generation immigrants (Spain, Italy), while in France, Germany, the UK, Belgium and the Netherlands, they are mainly made up of second and even third generations. Polls also show that there is an impact of the host country's political culture on the Muslims: the bulk of the French Muslims claim individual integration as full citizens and complain about discrimination on the job-market, while a majority of the British Muslims seem to be more in favour of living as a community with its own rules (see the polls carried out the Pew Institute).[3] But nowhere is there a real Muslim 'community' with legitimate leaders and institutions.

In Europe it is common to oppose two approaches: the British 'multi-culturalism' (where Muslims are defined by a distinct ethno-cultural identity) and the French *assimilationnisme* (where Muslims may become full citizens only by shedding their pristine identity). But paradoxically both approaches share the same premises: religion is embedded in a culture, so if one is a Muslim one belongs to a different culture. Interestingly enough, the level of radicalism has nothing to do with state policy: there have been as many terrorist threats in the UK, France, Spain, Belgium and Holland, although the policy toward Islam is very different in each country. Radicals do not answer to a specific national policy, but to a global perception of the state of the umma. In any event, both policies – multiculturalism and assimilation – have failed for the same reason: Muslims in the West, with the exception of many British Muslims, do not push for an ethno-cultural identity, but want to be recognised as a mere faith community. Religion is dissociated from culture: as we have seen

---

[3] Pew Institute (2006), "The Great Divide: How Westerners and Muslims View Each Other" (report available at
http://pewglobal.org/reports/display.php?ReportID=253).

radicals don't express a traditional Islam, but try to recast Islam as a militant ideology. In the UK, the born-again Muslims don't care for traditional culture and thus do not answer to traditional community leaders. But secularist France was very surprised to see that the erosion of traditional Muslim culture has gone hand in hand with a strong religious assertiveness: the 'headscarf affair' in French schools is not the result of an imported culture but a consequence of the construction of a purely religious identity among educated and integrated school-girls. The idea was that cultural assimilation would take place alongside secularisation. The concept of a 'non-cultural' religious revival was seen as unthinkable, but it did happen. By creating a French Council of Muslim Faith, the government reluctantly acknowledged the existence of Islam as a 'mere' religion.

So what are the solutions to the current crisis? European countries should pursue a clear objective: isolating the Islamic radicals with the support of the Muslim population, or at least the neutrality of the non-violent conservative fundamentalists. The issue is not to solve the crisis in the Middle East (which nevertheless would be a good thing *per se*), but to accompany the process of de-culturation and the assertion of Islam as a 'mere' religion. It means making room for Islam in the West as a western religion among others, not as the expression of an ethno-cultural community. This is the real process of 'secularisation', which has nothing to do with theological reformation (are the two last Popes 'liberal', not to say Protestants?), but could of course entail a theological debate, as an almost forced secularisation did for the Catholic Church in continental Western Europe (the emergence of the Christian Democracy, that is the full acceptance by the Church of democracy, is a consequence and not a pre-requisite of the process of secularisation).

Calling on Muslims to adapt the basic tenets of their religion to the West is a mistake for several reasons. To sponsor officially 'good and liberal' Muslims would be a sort of kiss of death and would deprive them of any legitimacy. The main motivation for youth radicalisation is not theological: political radicalisation is the main driving force. Youth is not interested in a theological debate. In modern secular states, theology should not and could not be a matter of policy. Pluralism is the best way to avoid being confronted by a tight-knit Muslim community. Conservative and even fundamentalist views of religion are manageable, as shown by the Protestant, Catholic and Jewish cases.

Political authorities should not look for traditional 'moderate' religious thinkers from the Middle East to appease Western Muslims, nor should they expend state subsidies to promote 'civil' or 'liberal' Islam. They should not negotiate the management of Western Islam with conservative and authoritarian Arab regimes: these regimes are not interested in reforms, democracy or tolerance; they are using the Muslims in Europe as leverage for their own interests. And by the way most Muslims in Europe feel no sense of loyalty to the existing regimes. European authorities should simply make room for Islam without changing laws or principles. Genuine pluralism is the best way to avoid confrontation with a Muslim population, itself very diverse, but that could feel coerced into a ghettoised community. Conservative and even fundamentalist views of religion can be manageable in a plural environment, and a pluralistic approach allows civil society to reach the cadres of youth that could be prime targets for radicals and neo-fundamentalist groups. State policy should be based on integration and even 'empowerment'[4] of Muslims and community leaders on a pluralistic basis. The priority should be to weaken the links with foreign elements by pushing for the 'Europeanisation' of Islam and preventing the deepening of the ghetto syndrome. Transparency and democracy should be the aim.

The problem is that some governments (i.e. in France) and the bulk of public opinion equate European Islam with 'liberal' Islam. What can be done about this? Waging a 'global war on terrorism' is playing al Qaeda's game. The growing isolation of the radicals should allow the Europeans to continue with their 'soft' approach: police and intelligence services are efficient and sufficient tools of counter-terrorism.

But such a policy will never totally eradicate terrorism. The European tradition of terrorism and political violence may have forged the experience of the counter-terrorist institutions, but it also makes the entry into violence of young activists easier. It is impossible to prevent some young guys from becoming radical and looking for some sort of spectacular action. Concentrating on sociology and the motivations of the radicals is important in understanding their mode of recruitment, but will be of little use in drying up the ground on which they prosper. The aim is not total eradication, but to make terrorism a residual factor.

---

[4] See the example of Lord Ahmed (Britain's first Muslim peer) in the Upper House of the UK Parliament.

Such a 'soft' approach is sustainable on one condition: that Islamic radicalism is kept as a fringe movement. The real danger would be to see Islamic radicalism enlarging its social basis or connecting with other potentially radical movements. The issue is not going to the roots of terrorism to eradicate it, but to prevent the radical fringe from finding a political basis among the Muslim population.

But this political and social analysis, while allowing us to take some distance from the usual clichés such as the roots of Muslim wrath and Islam's views on violence, jihad and suicide bombers? – not to mention the 'clash of civilisations' – does not answer the key question: What is going on with Islam?

4.3   Pushing for a Western Islam

The key issue is thus the attitude of the Muslim population in Europe. It has a far greater political stake and plays a far greater role than its counterpart in the US for three reasons: it is the main source of immigration, and has thus a demographic weight that bears no relation to the percentage of Muslims in the US. It originates from the closely neighbouring southern countries, bringing a risk of connection between radicalisation in the countries of origin and Europe. It is made up largely of the under-class and jobless youth; hence the social tensions tend to aggravate the feeling of discrimination and alienation. Social, geographic, political and strategic implications are thus intertwined.

We have seen that both the multi-culturalist and the integrationist approaches have failed. A more sound approach would be to acknowledge and encourage the disconnection between religion and culture. The second and third generations are no more the bearers of a traditional culture, even if they may reconstruct a tradition (by wearing the veil for instance). Such a disconnection is clearly demonstrated by the fact that a significant percentage (between 10- 20%) of al Qaeda recruits in Europe are converts.

But it should be clear that building a Western Islam does not mean interfering in theology. It will not work and will brand any reformer as a tool for manipulation. It will also unduly interfere in a debate that is taking place among Muslims. Another problem is that many 'Muslims' advocating reform in Islam are in fact avowed non-believers (Ayan Hirsi Ali for instance), which could accredit the idea that for the West a good Muslim is a non-Muslim. In fact the issue is to promote Western Muslims – not Western Islam.

A 'Western' Islam is not necessarily a 'liberal' Islam (for the same reason that a Western Christianity or Judaism is not necessarily liberal), but is an Islam that considers itself as a faith community, based on a voluntary adhesion. To stress the voluntary dimension of such a faith community, we should avoid considering as 'Muslim' anybody with a Muslim background. It also means that people could change their religion: apostasy will certainly become a more and more important issue, as well as intermarriages and endeavours to define a non-religious 'alien' identity (on racial or ethnic criteria). Defining Islam as a 'mere' religion also means encouraging the training of imams in Europe, in institutions that are linked with other European teaching institutions. It means also that Islam should be treated and recognised by the same laws and principles that deal with the other religions (Christianity in particular).

A consequence is that the issue of Islam should not be managed through the help of foreign governments or institutions, which have no interest in delinking Muslims in the West with their countries.

My argument translates into a number of concrete proposals:

- Establish a tighter control on fund-raising and subsidising from abroad, which means also a better access to open domestic fund-raising and subsidies (for building mosques).
- Build bridges and links between Islamic religious teaching institutions and the universities and academies.
- Let instances of religious representations emerge without monopoly.
- Enlist Muslim professionals in the mainstream political parties, not as 'community leaders' but as citizens.
- Avoid cornering Muslims by imposing a black-and-white choice (either you are with us or against us), and let them express a diversity of opinions in line with the spectrum of political diversity in the West.
- Stress above all the issue of citizenship above any communal affiliation.

Such a set of policies would meet the aspirations of mainstream Muslims in Europe: the recognition of Islam as a Western religion and Muslims as full citizens, while discouraging the creation of closed communities, ghettos and minority status. This would also isolate the terrorists and prevent them from building a political constituency.

PART B

STATUS AND DISCRIMINATION

5. ECONOMIC DEVELOPMENT OF MUSLIM COMMUNITIES

IMANE KARICH

Introduction

This chapter gives an overview of the current economic development of European Muslim communities and suggests initiatives that could be taken to improve the situation. The exercise was quite challenging since there is an absence of reliable statistics and figures on Muslim communities in Europe.[1]

Since 9/11, several subjects have monopolised the main discourses on Muslim communities: the debate around the radicalisation of Muslims, their integration and so-called 'identity', their visibility and their necessary adaptation into the host society. In a contemporary Europe characterised by the secularisation and privatisation of religious identity, the presence of Muslim communities claiming their faith is perceived by some as disturbing.

On the other hand, socio-economic issues such as unemployment, discrimination and exclusion, while given less attention in the current debate,[2] are at the same time considered to be causes of extremism and

---

[1] In the UK, however, an ethnic and religious census has been conducted and a map of minorities drawn up, based on the research of the Statistics Office. See M. Selignan (2006), "L'example britannique'", *Le Figaro*, 24 November.

[2] F. Buijs and J. Rath (2002), "Muslims in Europe, the State of Research", Russell Sage Foundation, New York, NY, October.

terrorism,[3] and by the Muslims themselves as their most important worry for their future.[4] As advocated by some sociologists,[5] it is imperative to get away from the essentialism that dominates reflections on Islam and the Muslim communities in Europe.[6] Pointing to Islam, its practices and its visibility as the main reason for the problems of integration risks widening the existing gap between this religious minority and the secularised host society.

The objective of this study is to investigate what the Muslim community can contribute to the development of society, to look at how religious discourse can help the younger generations identify with success, and how the faith factor can be a success factor for economic integration.

5.1 Economic development and faith

Since Max Weber, there has been an active debate on the impact of religion on people's economic attitudes. He was the first to identify the significant role that religion plays in social change.[7] Surveys have shown that religious belief is generally positively linked to behaviour that fosters free markets and better institutions, emphasising the potentially transformative power

---

[3] Discussion in the Assembly on 29 January 2004 (6th session) (Report of the Commission on political questions, rapporteur: M. Mercan, Committee of Experts on Terrorism (CODEXTER), Council of Europe, Strasbourg). Text adopted by the Assembly on 29 January 2004 (6th session).

[4] Pew Center (2006), "Muslims in Europe: Economic Worries Top Concerns About Religious and Cultural Identity Few Signs of Backlash from Western Europeans", Pew Global Attitutes Project, Washington, June.

[5] H. Boussetta (2003), «L'Islam et les musulmans en Belgique, enjeux locaux et cadres de réflexion globaux», Synthesis note, Fondation Roi Baudouin, Brussels, septembre.

[6] Ibid.

[7] M. Weber (1964), "L'éthique protestante et l'esprit du capitalisme", Paris: Plon, originally published in 1904-1905 as "Die Protestantische Ethik und der 'Geist' des Kapitalismus".

of religion as a capacity to develop new motivation and activities. Trust in others, in politics and in legal systems is characteristic of religious people.[8]

The Islamic ethos emphasises the importance of education, trust and hard work as the main components of economic development. The importance of trade, free-market economics and profit as material reward are supported by many koranic and Prophetic quotes. One might then ask why such principles have not turned out to be effective for the main Muslim nations. The fact that Muslim nations are among the poorest and least educated have brought many scholars to link religious faith with their economic and educational fate.[9] However, our opinion is that this situation is more due to corrupt autocratic leaders manipulating people's fears to keep them in ignorance and under control than to Islamic values as such. The example of Malaysia illustrates how Islam, when associated with democracy, modernity, pluralism and freedom, can foster and sustain economic growth.[10] Another study comparing different religious cultures and the work ethic also supports this idea and shows how Muslim cultures display the strongest of work ethics.[11]

While it could be an exaggeration to assert that entrepreneurship and economic development are mainly fostered by culture and religion, culture may be a creative resource that immigrants can use to transform their environment. This characteristic is significant in Chinese immigrant entrepreneurship. The dynamism and proliferation of Chinese entrepreneurship is influenced by the Confucian ethos, considered as a real code of business ethics based on practical and rational values. Beyond common values such as a belief in thrift, honesty, trust and loyalty, the Confucian ethos also covers more specific values. Risk-taking and profit-seeking are assumed to be imperatives to generate wealth, and

---

[8] L. Guiso, P. Sapienza and L. Zingales (2002), *People's Opium? Religion and Economic Activities*, NBER Working Paper 9237, National Bureau of Economic Research, Cambridge, MA.

[9] T. Kuran (2005), *Islam and Mammon: The Economic Predicaments of Islamism*, Princeton, NJ, Princeton University Press.

[10] M. Bin Ahmad (2003), "Islam and Economic Growth in Malaysia", Naval Postgraduate School, Malaysia, December.

[11] P. Norris and R. Inglehart (2004),"Sacred and Secular, Religion and politics worldwide", Harvard University, Cambridge, MA.

organisational skills are a key feature of a successful business, as is protecting and using family and community trust.[12]

As far as the Muslim community is concerned, cultural and religious principles are already seen to have positive aspects for economic behaviour. Migrant groups come with a business culture, working harder, saving their money and being more disposed to dedicate their lives to their businesses. This would explain why they go into business in such large numbers.[13] Culture also plays an important role in networking abilities, especially in the necessary financial and human resources. Community and family links are factors that help the entrepreneur launch companies, by finding cheap or free financial loans, and using family members as their main employees.[14]

5.2 Economic situation of the Muslim community

Notwithstanding these positive features, several studies on the economic level of immigrant communities in Europe show unfavourable results. In France, the national institute of statistics concludes that around 15% of families of foreign origin and 20% of people of Moroccan and Turkish origin live in poverty, against a national average of 6.2%.[15] In the UK, 75% of Bangladeshi and Pakistani children live in households below the poverty level (60% of average income). This compares with under a third (31%) of children in all households.[16] In the Netherlands, a study confirms the high level of poverty among persons from immigrant communities, at least two or three times higher than the national level.

However these rather alarming figures should be handled with care.

---

[12] K.B. Chan and S.N.C. Chiang (1994), "Cultural Values and Immigrant Entrepreneurship: The Chinese in Singapore", *Revue Européenne des Migrations Internationales*, Vol. 10, No. 2, p. 87.

[13] A. Pecoud (2005), "The cultural dimension of entrepreneurship in Berlin's Turkish economy", *Revue Européenne des Migrations Internationales*, Vol. 17, No. 2.

[14] Ibid.

[15] N. Perrin and B. Van Robaeys (2006), "La Pauvreté chez les personnes d'origine étrangère chiffrée", in *Pauvreté chez les personnes d'origine étrangère*, Fondation Roi Baudouin and GERME, ULB, Bruxelles.

[16] UK Department for Work and Pensions, "Households Below Average Income 1994/5 - 2000/01", London.

As mentioned, it is very difficult to find statistical data on Muslims themselves as the data are mainly based on nationality. For several years, many European countries have eased the acquisition of the host nationality.[17] Consequently, naturalised migrants and their descendants born in Europe are not included in these statistics. For example in Belgium, in 2000, the number of naturalisations increased mainly because of the acquisition of the Belgian nationality by Turks and Moroccans.[18] Besides the sole naturalisation effect, there are other reasons why these statistics cannot be applied to the whole Muslim community. The acquisition of the nationality eases access to the employment market and consequently to a better standard of living. Moreover these statistics do not take into account Muslim converts.

Nonetheless, even if not fully reliable, these figures at least give a rough indication of the current economic situation of the Muslim population in Europe: the Muslim communities in Europe have a relatively low standard of living and encounter socio-economic barriers that impede their integration into society.

Social mobility, namely the improvement of work status of the same individual during his/her career, while relatively limited as far as immigrants are concerned, is real and increases with time.[19] In France, around 30% of young people of the second generation born before 1968 had the status of junior executive in 1986.[20] Thus young people coming from

---

[17] For instance, in Belgium, the 1984 law grants Belgian nationality to the children born from a mixed union and the 1991 law allows children from the third generation to automatically obtain Belgian nationality.

[18] "Immigration en Belgique, Effectifs, Mouvement & Marché du travail", Rapport 2001, Direction Générale Emploi et Marché du travail some 70% of Turks living in Belgium enjoy Belgian nationality, against 66% of Moroccans, 35% of French and 22% of Dutch.

[19] J-L Richard and A. Moysan-Louazel (2002), "De l'immigration étrangère parentale à la mobilité sociale des jeunes adultes: Lignée familiale et dynamiques professionnelles individuelles au début des années 1990", *Journées d'Etudes CEREQ*, Rennes, May.

[20] J-L Dayan, A. Echardour and M. Glaude (1996), "Le Parcours professionnel des immigrés en France: Une analyse longitudinale", *Revue Economie et Statistique*, No. 299.

immigrant families have more chance of accessing better employment than their parents and possess better social prospects. However, the passage of one generation at least is necessary to see the full effect of this social mobility.[21]

Self-employment and entrepreneurship has become an important attribute of the Muslim population on the labour market. Until the end of the 1970s, self-employment among immigrants was considered a secondary aspect as the immigration flows were first and foremost a response to the request for labour in Western countries.[22] But since the 1980s, ethnic entrepreneurship has become significant. The self-employment level of the Turkish population in Europe grew from 3% in 1985 to 5.2% in 1996 and several Turkish entrepreneurial organisations have been founded since the 1990s.[23] In France, in 1999, the number of second-generation entrepreneurs has grown by 18% in 10 years, compared to a decrease in the total number of entrepreneurs by 9% for the same period.[24] In the UK, immigrants and their descendants are proportionally over-represented among self-employed workers compared to their native counterparts:[25] the rate of self-employment is high amongst all Asian ethnic minority groups, among which are Pakistanis and Bangladeshis.[26] In Germany, the number of independent foreigners is growing compared to the indigenous level and in Belgium, the number of self-employed persons of Moroccan and Turkish

---

[21] Ibid.

[22] S. Palidda (1992), "Le développement des activités indépendantes des immigrés en Europe et en France", *Revue Européenne des Migrations Internationales*, Vol. 8, No. 1.

[23] U. Manço (2003), Journées Bruxelloises de la Méditerrannée, Journée Histoire, Octobre, originally published in U. Manço (2000), "Turcs d'Europe: de l'image tronquée à la complexité d'une réalité sociale immigrée" dans Hommes et Migrations, No. 1226, juillet-août 2000, Paris, pp. 76-87.

[24] Body-Gendrot S., E. Ma Mung and C. Hodeir (1992), "Entrepreneurs entre deux mondes. Les créations d'entreprises par les étrangers: France, Europe, Amérique du Nord", *Revue Européenne des Migrations Internationales*, Vol. 8, No. 1.

[25] Ibid.

[26] Open Society Institute (2005), "Muslims in the UK: Policies for engaged citizens", Open Society Institute and EU Monitoring and Advocacy Programme.

origin has also been growing fast, especially among the Turks.[27] What was first perceived as a marginal consequence of immigration has become a major trend.[28] Difficulties of professional integration encourage some immigrants and their descendants to launch their own businesses. Ethnic entrepreneurship sometimes also offers social mobility opportunities that cannot be found in the general employment market.

Europe-wide, 75% of Turkish businesses are concentrated in the retail business (general food, itinerant sales, hotel and catering).[29] In the UK, Germany, Belgium and the Netherlands, immigrants' self-employment is concentrated in the service sector, except in the latter, where Turkish immigrants are seen in relatively large numbers in the clothing industry.[30] These businesses often occupy niche markets abandoned by the indigenous population.[31] Examples are seen in food production and distribution, tourism and transportation companies towards countries of origin, communication services, translation, administration and mediation services to ease socio-cultural adaptation.[32] Businesses launched by the next generation are characterised by the larger diversification of sectors and qualifications within the immigrant population.[33]

The development of self-employment among immigrants also goes with the creation of national and international networks that can positively stimulate international exchanges[34] and business opportunities. Ethnic solidarity can help overcome class disadvantages, with internal organisations that provide members access to capital or credit.[35] Financing

---

[27] A. Manco (2005), "L'Entreprenariat immigré en Belgique: Contextes, exemples et perspectives", IRFAM, Brussels.

[28] A. Pecoud (2005), "The cultural dimension of entrepreneurship in Berlin's Turkish economy", *Revue Européenne des Migrations Internationales*, Vol. 17, No. 2, pp. 153-168.

[29] Ibid.

[30] Palidda, op. cit.

[31] Pecoud op. cit.

[32] Manco (2005), op. cit.

[33] Ibid.

[34] Palidda op. cit.

[35] Pecoud op. cit.

may come from friends and relatives, where there are no possibilities of a bank loan, or where there is reluctance to use interest-bearing money forbidden by Islamic law.[36] The shaping of this business class in Europe has allowed a certain dynamism among the immigrant communities, helping ease socio-economic marginalisation.[37]

Muslim women and the labour market. As regards their situation has improved compared to that of the first generation of immigrants.[38] It is still far from reaching average European levels, however. Muslim women are still mainly economically inactive despite increasing levels of education. When they work, their profile is generally low and they occupy posts requiring low qualifications in the most precarious sectors. Again, however, these observations should be tempered by the fact that most figures are based on nationality: naturalised women are almost invisible in the statistics. For instance, in France, the activity rate is greater for naturalised women, as 52% of women originally from Morocco are active, compared to 29% of women with Moroccan nationality. In the Netherlands, the employment rate of Moroccan women increases from 16% in the early 1990s to 23% in 1998.[39] Moreover, the second generation has a better level of education. Young women currently hold better jobs in the structured service sectors such as trading, banking and the liberal professions.[40] Discrimination may be a factor in explaining the low levels of economic activity among Muslim women. Cultural reasons also have an influence, although these are decreasing in importance.

The specific emphasis on women and Muslim girls' performance is also interesting as they present certain characteristics that cannot be applied to their male fellows, as shown for example by the 'veil debate' that began in France in 2003 and that led to the French law forbidding religious

---

[36] Islamic law forbids the receiving and the giving of interest because this money is not considered as having been earned directly by the beneficiary.

[37] L. Muller and S. Tapia (2005), "Un dynamisme venu d'ailleurs: La création d'entreprises par les immigrés", Paris: L'Harmattan.

[38] C. Catarino and M. Morokvasic (2005), "Femmes, Genre, Migration et Mobilités", *Revue Européenne des Migrations Internationales*, Vol. 21, No. 5.

[39] M. Khachani "La Femme Maghrébine Immigrée dans l'Espace Economique des pays d'accueil: Quelques repères", Rabbat, Morocco.

[40] Ibid.

signs in public schools in March 2004 and the exclusion of hundreds of girls from public education. Some of these students turned to correspondence education, while others excluded themselves wholly from education.[41] Besides its direct consequences, this legislation and the associated debate had repercussions far beyond the school environment, extending to workplaces and universities. A negative image of veiled Muslim women is undeniable in the minds of many opinion leaders, and this has helped to worsen the current exclusion of a large part of the Muslim community from the labour market.

The Halal[42] business. In a context where Islam is a minority religion, Muslim immigrant populations try to adapt their environment to their religious values. Many consider Islamic prescriptions to be absolutely mandatory as a condition of their integration into the host society. It is not surprising then that the halal market has seen rapid growth.

The first market influenced by Islamic rules is the food sector, especially the meat industry. In most European countries, the primary Muslim businesses have been the numerous halal butcher shops. Even if some religious opinions allow the consumption of meat from Christian and Jewish sources, a majority of European Muslims still require their meat to be slaughtered according to Islamic methods. Over the last few years, the consumption of halal food has increased tremendously in France. This need has seen second-generation Muslims taking to the Burger King Muslim (BKM) as the first Muslim fast-food chain in the Paris region. The Zaphir company also offers all varieties of cooked meats similar to the non-halal varieties. The growth of this market is further illustrated by the growing interest of big distribution names such as Carrefour supermarkets, which have begun selling halal foods.

Initially limited to the meat industry, the halal market is in fact much bigger: alternative sodas, clothes, music, etc. The halal concept transcends

---

[41] P. Tevanian (2005), "La loi sur le voile, un an après, un bilan désastreux" (www.mrap.fr). Other figures presented by the Comité du 15 mars et libertés (March 15 and Freedom Committee) assess the number of 'victims' of this law as 250, among which 70% currently follow correspondence education, 10% are totally excluded from education and 20% have left for other countries such as Belgium, Turkey or the UK. (see www.saphirnews.com).

[42] Halal is the Arabic translation of 'Islamic compliance'.

the sole fact of knowing if the product is proper to Islamic consumption: it also concerns the conscience and the moral sense of the Muslim, beyond the simple consumption of food. An ethical dimension has been added to the simple halal seal, directly inspired by Islamic sources. Islamic clothing brands are numerous in main European cities, such as Capsters in the Netherlands and HNA in Belgium. The Islamic music industry recognises the pull of Islamic singers' concerts: tickets for Sami Yusuf and Yusuf Islam concerts are always sold out. Although there are no official figures, it is estimated that 10% of the food in France is halal, while the Europe-wide business is valued at around €5 billion.[43] The halal market is reckoned to be worth $150 billion worldwide and is expected to grow at a rate of 15% per year.

This growing market illustrates two important facts: the first is that the Muslim population is increasingly considered as an important potential market with specific needs. The second is that the building of a European identity of the Muslim community is reconciling capitalist consumption norms and Islamic values.

Migrant remittances. Another indicator of the economic development of the European Muslim community is linked to their immigrant origins, rather than to their religion. Like the majority of immigrant-origin populations, Muslims, especially of the first-generation, maintain strong links to their countries of origin and regularly send home money. According to the World Bank, $100 billion are transferred every year by immigrants. To this official figure, $300 billion should be added, representing the money not transferred by official channels. For example Germany and Belgium are the sources of remittances totalling $8.2 billion and $8.1 billion respectively each year. According to the European Investment Bank, these amounts represent 1% of the GDP of European countries with significant immigrant communities, exceeding the total direct investments and development aid of these countries.[44]

This little known phenomenon might be expected to slow down, with the increasing integration of Muslim communities in Europe. But the

---

[43] "More and more young people are attracted by halal consumption", *Le Monde*, 13 June 2005.

[44] Banque Européenne d'Investissement (2006), "Etude sur les transferts de fonds des migrants méditerranéens d'Europe", (see www.bei.org).

figures show an increasing trend. It is difficult to identify the reasons for this paradox. One explanation is simply the continuing attachment of many immigrant descendants to their families and to the development of their countries of origin. Another reason could be the absence of Islamic-compliant investment products in Europe and the need on the part of some new middle-class Muslims to invest their excess liquidity.

5.3 Policy issues

No specific policy has been defined towards the economic development of the Muslim communities in Europe. Yet in all European countries, traditional policies are now showing their limits. Discrimination in housing, employment and education still exists and is even on the increase for new generations, despite having being born in Europe. However, the current debate at European Union level in terms of integration and the fight against discrimination illustrates the political importance that the member states attach to the successful integration of their immigrants and their descendants. In its spring 2003 report, the European Commission referred to the need for instruments to better integrate immigrant workers that can substantially contribute to self-employment.[45] Also, the need to find a solution to integration and employment issues by harmonising rules between member states is increasing.[46] Challenges for the future mainly concern the discrepancies in comparative employment rates between European, non-European immigrants and their second-generation off-spring, the support for the full participation and employment of the second-generation, the necessity to adequately respond to female immigrants' needs, the fight against discrimination and the transformation of undeclared work into declared work.[47]

We could say that economic issues have been underestimated in the current debate around the Muslim community's situation and the threat of

---

[45] European Commission (2003), Le Rapport au Conseil européen de printemps du 21 mars 2003 sur la stratégie de Lisbonne pour le renouveau économique, social et environnemental (COM(2003) 5 of 14th January 2003).

[46] V. Spidla (2006), "Relever le défi de l'immigration et de l'intégration", European Commission speech, February.

[47] "Successful Integration on the Labour Market" (2002), European Commission Conference, Report, Copenhagen 4-5 July.

fundamentalism and terrorism, although poverty and exclusion are the main factors behind identity fallbacks and the vulnerability of young people to extremist discourses. While there is no hesitation in considering religious identity as part of the problem, we often paradoxically have qualms about seeing it as part of the solution.[48] Although this approach is justified in order to avoid the Islamisation of integration issues, the faith and community factor should not be excluded from the solutions considered. Individual integration and the preservation of community life are not contradictory phenomena.[49]

The first barriers to integration are the different forms of discrimination that Muslim minorities still face. The current climate of mistrust around Islam and Muslims in the Western world has worsened the already existing segregation of these communities in the areas of housing, employment and education. While different actions, policies, laws and other instruments are available to combat all kinds of discrimination, discrimination towards minorities has increased in recent decades. The consequences of this discrimination are also often understated. Stress, loss of self-confidence, discouragement, frustration, insecurity and the absence of prospects or the ability to plan projects are all perfect ingredients for marginalisation. Discrimination on the labour market for highly educated minorities dispels the idea that education can help break the class barriers and ease upward mobility and sends a paradoxical message to younger generations. Recognised and unpunished discrimination towards young, highly educated, veiled Muslim women on the labour market is actually hindering their autonomy and emancipation from traditional constraints.

Given the failure of existing policies, more radical preventative and curative policies should also be considered, such as temporary positive discrimination in some areas in order to ensure better prospects and foster social diversity. Also, Muslim communities need to be made aware of the different instruments available to them to denounce all signs of discrimination. They should be informed of existing legislation forbidding religious and ethnic discrimination in order for them to know what protection they have.

---

[48] J. Rath and F. Buijs (2002), "Muslims in Europe: The State of Research", Essay prepared for the Russel Sage Foundation, New York, N.Y., October.

[49] U. Manço (1997), op. cit.

As mentioned earlier, the quality of education is one of the most critical determinants in successful integration. There are still areas for improvement in the current education systems in different European countries. Effective measures should be taken to tackle unacceptable voluntary and involuntary educational segregation and to encourage social diversity within schools. The refusal to admit Muslim children to elite schools and the direction of Muslim students towards low-level education areas should be identified and effectively managed. Training of educators and teachers should be improved to instil in them an understanding of cultural diversity issues in the classroom. School inspectors should be trained to recognise discrimination based on religion.

Given the current low level of employment among the European Muslim communities compared to average levels among other groups, proactive policies should be defined in order to minimise the gap. The first step is to ensure that Muslims are not disadvantaged by their religion when trying to enter and progress within the labour market. One way to ensure diversity on the labour market is by defining targets[50] for the minimum level of ethnic and religious diversity, starting with the public services.

Often, entrepreneurship is seen as the solution to an inaccessible labour market. Entrance into the business world requires certain skills that help integration: knowledge of the national language and of administrative procedures, ability to connect with people outside the group for potential partners, employees, providers and clients. Government policies can play an important role in the evolution of ethnic economies by determining their legal framework, but also through the elaboration of instruments that meet the specific needs of potential Muslim businessmen and women.[51]

One of these specificities is the reluctance to use interest-based financing and the preference for venture capital financing. However, while this kind of instrument already exists, lack of knowledge on the part of Muslim minorities impedes their access. Specific coaching and financing should be offered to young Muslims who express the desire to become self-employed, helping them to choose the right sector, deal with

---

[50] Target levels differ from quotas in the non-compulsory characteristic. See Open Society Institute (2005), op. cit.

[51] Pecoud, op. cit.

administration, including marketing and management concepts.[52] In France, the Besson report presented to the National Assembly underlined the inadequacy of the help given to minority entrepreneurs under the French system, compared to the American system, which reserves a large part of public subsides for certain groups.[53]

The establishment of cultural and community business and elite organisations can have certain advantages for younger generations. Among these advantages are role models, the emphasis on success stories, the transfer of knowledge, networking skills and suitable coaching. These organisations help fill the gap between existing practices and the specificities of Muslim communities. Educated and well integrated Muslims can transmit to their fellows the importance of education, work and progress as core Islamic values.[54] The advantage of such organisations is for instance illustrated by the case of a German-Turkish business organisation. The entity initiated an impressive sector diversification allowing their members to be present in almost all sectors of the German economy, including highly successful and competitive sectors like software and new technologies.[55]

Ghettoisation is a main factor in exclusion and marginalisation. The recent riots in France showed the consequences of the anger that housing isolation may engender. Social diversity can be achieved by offering easier access to housing possibilities outside the ghettos. A good illustration is the example of the city of Frankfurt: the municipality practises social diversity policies by limiting the proportion of immigrants in social housing to 30%.[56]

---

[52] Ibid.

[53] E. Besson (1998), "For an emergency plan to support the creation of small entreprises", Information report No. 1804, Observatory of European SMEs, European Commission, DG Enterprise, Brussels.

[54] An important Islamic principle is the fact that the situation of people will not change if they do not reform themselves first, rejecting all victimisation behaviours whatever the hostility of the environment (Koran, S. 8, V. 53).

[55] Pecoud, op. cit.

[56] C. Calla (2005), "L'intégration réussie des immigrés à Francfort", Le Figaro, December.

Home ownership is also considered as a facilitator in successful economic integration. Several reasons explain the difficulty for Muslims in accessing the property market. One of the factors rarely emphasised is the importance for an increasing proportion of the Muslim communities of having access to Islamic-compliant means of finance. As Islam rejects all forms of interest defined as the price of money, Muslim populations limit their access to banking services to the minimum, in the absence of services in compliance with their beliefs.[57] Besides offering more adequate solutions to their banking needs, Islamic banking can be seen as a positive sign of genuine efforts to understand the Muslim community.

Conclusions

Taking into account Muslim specificities should not be seen as threatening the neutrality of the policy environment, but as recognising the legitimacy of a religious minority within the host society. Denying these characteristics or confusing the respect of Islamic values by Muslims with signs of fundamentalism increases the gulf between the Muslim community and the rest of society. For a large majority, practising Muslims are moderate people who want to live as European citizens in peace and in respect of their faith. Diversity should also include the religious characteristics of Muslims. In fact, in most diversity policies, race or ethnicity is largely taken into account, but this tends not to be so for Muslim characteristics. The economic development of Muslim communities, linking integration, identity and insertion issues, requires more attention from local, national and European communities. Proposals for action have been listed above, focusing on the importance of including Muslim specificities in the proactive policies to be promoted by authorities.

---

[57] CEREI (2003), "Quantification of the Muslim Financial Needs", December (www.cerei.net).

6. MUSLIMS AND DISCRIMINATION

TUFYAL CHOUDHURY

Introduction

The urgent need to tackle the discrimination faced by Muslims in Europe has emerged as a key concern of European policy-makers.[1] Discrimination is considered a significant contributor to alienation and disaffection among Muslims, a barrier to integration and a risk factor for radicalisation. Developing effective and coherent policy interventions requires a clear understanding of the nature of the discrimination faced by Muslims as well as an assessment of the strength and limitations of existing policies.

The first part of this paper examines the nature of the discrimination faced by Muslims in Europe. It sets out some of the research and statistical data that are available on performance by minority groups in relation to key socio-economic indicators. While this provides important information about the disadvantages experienced by minority groups that are predominately Muslim, the paucity of information on Muslims, as a group, limits our understanding of both the disadvantages and the discrimination Muslims encounter. In examining the data, the difficulty of identifying the role of 'discrimination' from data is explored. Furthermore, even when there is sufficiently robust data to allow statistical regression that can identify an 'ethnic', 'religion' or 'migrant' penalty, the nature of discrimination that Muslims are confronted with remains complex and varied.

It is suggested that the main grounds for discrimination that Muslims face vary between different Muslim groups. For some, the first order of

---

[1] A. Al Hussani (2005), *Islamophobia in Europe*, ENAR Shadow Report, European Network against Racism, Brussels.

discrimination may be on the basis of nationality, refugee or immigration status. For others, colour and racial discrimination may be prevalent and for others it may be religious discrimination. Most importantly, attempting to identify a particular area of discrimination overlooks the potential for discrimination on intersectional and multiple grounds. Finally, even when it is possible to identify religious discrimination, the experience and impact of it can vary among Muslims.

A second part of this paper explores the possibilities, potential and limitations within the current EU policies aimed at tackling discrimination. It begins therefore, by setting out the developments in EU anti-discrimination legislation and policy – with a focus on the EC Directive for tackling discrimination on the grounds of religion and belief in employment (the Framework Directive) – considering the relationship between equality and discrimination. It is argued that a fundamental constraint on the use of tools provided by the legal framework is the absence of any consensus on a vision of what equality for Muslims looks like. The paper then explores some of the limitations of the Framework Directive; these include the limited scope of the application of the directive, the potential for addressing multiple or intersectional discrimination and the continuation of an approach that relies on individuals making complaints.

6.1 Disadvantage and discrimination

Socio-economic disadvantage

Disadvantage is measured through data. Patterns of disadvantage revealed by data are, in part, a product of prior decisions about how to categorise people. These decisions, in turn, reflect political decisions about which patterns are likely to be important and which groups deserve protection. The UK is one of the few EU member states where the national census includes a question on religion and thus allows the data to be disaggregated and analysed by religion. In many European countries, there are legal prohibitions on the collection of data on the basis of personal characteristics such as religion. In others, while there is no legal prohibition on the collection of such data, the official practice has been to collect data on the basis of ethnicity, national origin or country of birth. In the absence of data on Muslims, as a group, some ethnic or national categories can provide a proxy for data on Muslims.

Within the research literature, the most significant Muslim proxy ethnic groups are Bangladeshi, Maghrebi, Pakistani and Turkish groups. The use of data for these groups in understanding the position of Muslims is problematic. Firstly, not all members of the proxy group are Muslims. Secondly, such data tell us nothing of the situation of Muslims beyond that group. Furthermore, where the data are based on country of birth they provide limited information on the situation of second- and third-generation, European-born Muslims from such ethnic or national groups.

It is only possible, within the confines of this paper, to provide a snapshot of some statistics and data relating to Muslims, or to proxy groups for Muslims, which indicate disadvantage in respect of some key socio-economic indicators within the EU.[2] Disadvantage in the labour market can be measured in several ways, for example, higher unemployment rates; lower employment rates or concentration in unskilled or semi-skilled sectors of the economy. Unemployment rates running at twice the national average can be found for children of Moroccan and Algerian immigrants in France[3] and for Turkish nationals in Germany.[4] In the Netherlands, the unemployment rate amongst Moroccans and Turks is

---

[2] See http://www.eumap.org/topics/minority/reports/eumuslims for reports reviewing the existing research literature on Muslims in relation to key socio-economic indicators in seven EU states.

[3] Data from the 1999 census show that unemployment among young people whose parents were born in Algeria or Morocco is 40%, compared to a national youth unemployment rate of 20% (see INSEE, *Les immigrés en France*, Edition 2005, p. 130, cited in S. Tebbakh (2007), *Muslims in the EU Cities Report – France: Preliminary Research Report and Literature Survey*, (Open Society Institute, Budapest, p 42 note 122). A survey of French school leavers in 1998 found that after five years the unemployment rate among the North Africans in the cohort was double that of young people whose parents were born in France (see Centre détudes et de recherches sur les qualifications (CEREQ) (1998), Survey ON "Generation 98", Paris; R. Silberman and I. Fournier (2006), "Jeunes issus de l'immigration: une pénalité à l'embauche qui perdure...", *Bref*, No. 226, January, p. 3.

[4] Jochen Blaschke, (2004), "Tolerated but Marginalised – Muslims in Germany", in *State Policies towards Muslim Minorities. Sweden, Great Britain and Germany*, Edition Parabolis Verlagsabteilung im Europäischen Migrationszentrum (EMZ), Kempten, at p. 123.

between two and a half to three times the national average.[5] In Belgium, the unemployment rate among Moroccans and Turks, at 38% is five times the level of national unemployment rate of 7%.[6] In the UK, data from the 2001 census show that, of young people aged 16-24, Muslims have the highest unemployment rate of all groups.[7] Even for those with jobs, employment is over-concentrated in particular sectors. In the UK, 40% of Muslim men in employment were working in the distribution, hotel and restaurant industry, compared with 30% of Christian men.[8] Moreover, 40% of Muslims are in the lowest occupational groups, compared to 30% of Christians.[9] Muslim men are among the least likely to be in managerial or professional jobs and the most likely to be in low-skilled jobs.[10] In France, 40% of Muslims work in factories compared to 21% of the general population.[11] In the Netherlands, the majority of Moroccans and Turks with jobs are employed in 'elementary or low-level' jobs.[12]

---

[5] In the Netherlands the unemployment rate among Moroccans is 29% and for Turks it is 21%; this compares to a national unemployment rate of 9% (see SCP (2006) Hoge (jeud) werkloosheid onder etnische minderheden. Nieuwe bevindingen uit het LAS-onderzoek [High Youth Unemployment among Ethnic Minorities. New Findings from the LAS Study], The Hague: Sociaal en Cultureel Planbureau, cited in Demant et al. *Muslims in the EU Cities Reports – The Netherlands: Preliminary Research Report and Literature Survey*, Budapest, Open Society Institute, 2007, p. 22).

[6] L. Okkerse, and A. Termote (2004), *Etudes statistiques no. 111: Singularité des étrangers sur la marché de l'emploi*, Institut National de la Statistique, Brussels.

[7] 22% are unemployed compared to 11% of Christians. UK Office of National Statistics (2004), *Focus on Religion*, ONS, London, p. 13.

[8] Ibid.

[9] Ibid.

[10] Ibid.

[11] Alberto Lopez and Gwenaëlle Thomas, «L'insertion des jeunes sur le marché du travail: le poids des origines socioculturelles» (The integration of young people into the labour market: The weight of socio-cultural origins), Données sociales, INSEE, édition 2006, pp. 293–305, cited in S. Tebbakh, op. cit.

[12] SCP (2005), Jaarrapport Integratie [Integration Annual Report]. The Hague: Sociaal en Cultureel Planbureau, cited in Demant et al., op. cit.

The impact of poor labour market participation can be felt in other areas of life such as income, housing and health. In the Netherlands, the average income in a Moroccan or Turkish household (€13,600) is one-third below the national average.[13] Muslims in the UK are disproportionately represented in the most deprived urban communities – one-third of the Muslim population lives in the 10% most deprived neighbourhoods.[14] In France, around half of Algerian and Moroccans and over 40% of people of a Turkish and Tunisian background live in social housing. According to Tebbakh, "the strong presence of immigrants in [social housing] can be ascribed to their limited financial means and to a housing shortage in the private sector, which imposed unequal conditions of access and selection".[15] Rates of certain chronic illnesses, particularly cardiovascular diseases, are significantly higher among those of Turkish background than in the general population in both Germany[16] and the Netherlands.[17] In the UK, health data on ethnic minorities show that Pakistanis and Bangladeshis have the highest rate of diagnosed heart disease.[18] Data from the 2001 census on the UK reveals that Muslims reported the highest rates of illness of all faith groups.[19] These findings support the conclusion drawn by the

---

[13] Ibid.

[14] J. Beckford et al. (2006), *Review of the Evidence Based on Faith Communities*, Office of the Deputy Prime Minister, London, p. 39. The census data can be analysed at the level of 'Super Output Areas' which is equivalent to a neighbourhood. These neighbourhoods are classified into 10 deprivation categories based on their score on the ODPM Index of Multiple Deprivation.

[15] S. Tebbakh, op. cit., p. 51

[16] N. Muhe, (2007), *Muslims in the EU Cities Reports – Germany: Preliminary Research Report and Literature Survey*, Open Society Institute, Budapest, p. 36.

[17] Demant et al., p. 26.

[18] While one in six people from ethnic minorities over the age of 40 reported diagnosed heart disease, the figure for Pakistanis and Bangladeshis was one in four. See: J. Nazroo (2001), *Ethnicity, Class and Health*, Policy Studies Institute, London, pp. 74-77.

[19] After taking the age structures of the populations into account, it was found that 13% of Muslim males and 16% of Muslim females reported that their health was "not good", compared to 7% of Christians. Compared to all other faith groups, Muslims had the highest rate of disability, 24% of Muslims females and 21% of Muslim males had a disability, as compared to 15 and 16% of Christian males and

European Union Monitoring on Racism and Xenophobia (EUMC) from its review of existing data on discrimination that "Muslims are often disproportionately represented in areas with poor housing conditions, while their educational achievement falls below average and their unemployment rates are higher than average. Muslims are often employed in jobs that require lower qualifications and as a group they are over represented in low-paying sectors of the economy".[20] In education the picture is more complex. A study by the OECD, measuring performance in mathematics, found that in France, Germany and the Netherlands, there is a significant difference in the performance of 'second generation' children of migrants compared to the national average.[21] When compared to the national average the last few years have seen significant improvements in the attainment levels of Pakistani and Bangladeshi pupils in the UK[22] and Turkish and Moroccan pupils in the Netherlands.[23] In the UK, over half of Muslims aged 16-25 participate in post-compulsory education; this is higher than the national average (42%).[24]

Discrimination in the labour market

While survey data show the levels of disadvantage experienced by some Muslims in Europe, identifying the sources of this disadvantage and the role of discrimination in causing, reinforcing or exacerbating this disadvantage is more difficult.

---

females. See UK Office of National Statistics (2004), *Focus on Religion*, ONS, London, p. 8.

[20] EUMC (European Union Monitoring Centre on Racism and Xenophobia), (2006), *Muslims in the European Union: Discrimination and Islamophobia*, EUMC, Vienna, p. 8.

[21] OECD (2004), *Learning for Tomorrow's World: First Results from PISA 2003*, OECD, Paris.

[22] UK Office of National Statistics (2006), Department for Education and Skills, *National Curriculum Assessment, GCSE* and *Equivalent Attainment and Post-16 Attainment by Pupil Characteristics in England 2005-06* (Provisional), London.

[23] Demant et al. op.cit., p. 18.

[24] S. Hussain (2003), *An Introduction to Muslims in the 2001 National Census*, p. 10. http://www.bristol.ac.uk/sociology/ethnicitycitizenship/intromuslims_census.pdf

If we take the example of the labour market, disadvantage here is the outcome of a variety of interrelated factors including levels of human capital, structural changes in the economy, social networks and place of residence.[25] Fournier and Silberman, for example, suggest that the greater risk of unemployment, in France, among the second generation children of non-EU migrants cannot be accounted for by their educational levels. They suggest that part of the explanation lies in the lower social capital and access to employment in the networks of their children's parents.[26] While it is not possible to gauge with precision the exact role of discrimination in the disadvantage experienced by Muslims, there is evidence that discrimination does play some role. The EUMC notes:

> [T]here is a large body of evidence that demonstrates the persistent scale and dimension of discrimination in employment: derived from controlled experiments in employers' recruitment practices ("discrimination testing"), opinion surveys on discriminatory attitudes, and surveys of perceived discrimination by migrants...The data show that not all migrants are equally exposed to racism and discrimination in employment. Muslims appear to be particularly affected.[27]

In the UK, a report by the government analysing available data on South Asians found that "even after controlling for a range of factors, Sikhs and Indian Muslims remain almost twice as likely to be unemployed as Hindus and that Pakistanis are almost twice as likely to be unemployed". However, the report authors warn against any automatic conclusion that there is a 'religion penalty' at work as "religion may simply be a factor for

---

[25] See Z. Bunglawala (2005), "Muslims in the UK and the Labour Market", in *Muslims in the UK: Policies for Engaged Citizens*, Open Society Institute, Budapest, pp. 193-251.

[26] R. Silberman and I. Fournier (1999), "Immigrants' Children and the Labour Market: The Mechanisms of Selective Discrimination. From one generation to another. How do the immigrants and their children see their position on the labour market?", paper presented at Fourth International MigCities Conference, Lisbon, November.

[27] EUMC (2006), p. 46.

other factors determining employment, like education and fluency".[28] Lindsey's analysis of this same data found that Muslims experience 'some unexplainable employment penalty, relative to other non-white religions, over and above all other characteristics (including ethnic differences and language fluency)'. However, whilst this supports claims that Muslims face religious discrimination, the difference may also conceal further 'unmeasurable variables'.[29]

ILO studies that involve 'situation testing' in employment in Germany and the Netherlands provide evidence of discrimination against some Muslim groups.[30] Situation testing in France found that a person from the Maghreb had five times less chance of receiving a positive reply than other applicants.[31]

Surveys of minority groups can provide an indication of their perceptions of discrimination. In the UK, the 2004 Home Office citizenship survey of those who had been refused a job in the past five years showed that a quarter of Bangladeshis and 12% of Pakistanis cited racial discrimination as the main reason for this. Perceptions of religious discrimination, lower than perceptions of racial discrimination, were highest for Bangladeshi (13%) and Pakistanis (9%). Pakistanis were also the most likely to cite religion as a reason for being refused a promotion in the preceding five years.

---

[28] UK Cabinet Office (2001), *Ethnic Minorities and the Labour Market: Interim Analytical Report*, London, p. 82. See also M. Brown (2000), "Religion and Economic Activity in the South Asian population", *Ethnic and Racial Studies*, 23(6).

[29] J. Lindley (2002), "Race or Religion? The impact of religion on the employment and earnings of Britain's Ethnic communities", *Journal of Ethnic and Migration Studies*, 28(3), p. 429.

[30] A. Goldberg, D. Mourhino and U. Kulke (1997), *Labour market discrimination against foreign workers in Germany*, International Migration Papers 7, ILO, Geneva. F. Bouvenkerk, M.J.I. Gras, D. Ramsoedh, M. Dankoor and A. Havelaar (1995), *Discrimination against migrant workers and ethnic minorities in access to employment in the Netherlands*, ILO, Geneva.

[31] EUMC (2006), op. cit., pp. 44-45.

Discrimination beyond employment

Muslims experience discrimination in a wide range of areas outside employment. One review of NGO and official reports concludes that "direct and indirect discrimination in the housing sector – both public and private – appear to be widespread phenomena".[32] Discrimination can take the form of a refusal to rent or sell, the imposition of extra conditions to secure housing, and the application of discriminatory criteria in the allocation of social housing.[33] Evidence is also emerging of ethnic and religious profiling of Muslims by police and security services in some EU states.[34] The International Helsinki Federation reports that in Germany "since September 11, thousands of Muslims have been subjected to screening for their personal data, houses searches, interrogations, and arrests solely because their profiles have matched certain basic criteria, foremost of which is affiliation to Islam".[35] Other sites where Muslims experience discrimination include 'civic integration' programmes.[36] In Germany, the Gesprächsleitfaden (Interview Guidelines) for examining citizenship applicants produced by the government of Baden-Württemberg provide one example of discrimination:

> Targeting only citizenship applicants from 57 Muslim states, these Gesprächsleitfaden consist of 30 questions that should help determine whether an applicant's formal 'acceptance' of liberal democratic values, which is required by German nationality law, corresponds to his or her 'real convictions'. All questions are formulated in terms of a binary opposition

[32] J. Ringelheim (2006), *Strategic Litigation to Combat Discrimination against Muslims in Europe: "State of Law" Legal Memorandum*, Open Justice Initiative, New York, p. 5.

[33] See V. Amiraux (2002), "The Situation of Muslims in France", in *Monitoring the EU Accession Process: Minority Protection*, Open Society Institute, Budapest, pp. 101-103.

[34] J. Goldstone (2006), *Ethnic Profiling and Counter-Terrorism: Trends, Dangers and Alternatives*, Open Justice Initiative, New York. See also L. Fekete (2004), "Anti-Muslim racism and the European security state", *Race and Class*, 46(1).

[35] IHF (2005), *Intolerance and Discrimination Against Muslims in the EU: Developments since September 11*, March, p. 78.

[36] C. Joppe (2007), "Beyond National Models: Civic Integration Policies for Immigrants in Western Europe", *Western European Politics*, 30(1).

between liberal democracy and a certain idea of Islam, as prescribing or condoning arranged marriage, patriarchy, homophobia, veiling and terrorism (e.g. question 23: 'You heard about the assaults on 11 September 2001 in New York and on 11 March 2004 in Madrid. Were the protagonists in your eyes terrorists or freedom fighters? Elaborate on your statement'). While one may see insult in the transparency of such 'questions' (and correspondingly low intelligence imputed to citizenship candidates), their discriminatory edge consists of 'interpreting … the liberal-democratic order primarily in opposition to the presumed values of a specific group', as a legal evaluation of the Gesprächsleitfaden for the city of Heidelberg put it. In other words, such 'liberalism' is nothing but a device for excluding a specific group, Muslims.[37]

Increasing restrictions on immigration and access to citizenship are perceived by Muslims in Germany and Denmark as being targeted at Muslim migration.[38] In the Netherlands, a new 'integration test' has been introduced for applicants for 'family reunification' that must be taken at a Dutch embassy abroad and passed before a temporary residence permit is even granted. Joppe finds that "most of the family migrants targeted by the Dutch policy are Muslims of Turkish or Moroccan origin" thus, "what began as an immigrant integration policy has…turned into its opposite, a no-immigration policy".[39]

A significant proportion of refugees and asylum-seekers in Europe are Muslim. For this group, their refugee status may be the dominant way in which they experience discrimination in those areas from which refugees are excluded from participation. Similarly, there are significant numbers of Muslims among the population of undocumented migrants.[40] Muhe, for

---

[37] Ibid., p. 15.

[38] T. Choudhury, M. Aziz, D. Izzidien, I. Khireeji and D. Hussain (2006), *Perceptions of Discrimination and Islamophobia: Voices from members of Muslim communities in the European Union*, European Union Monitoring Centre of Racism and Xenophobia, Vienna, pp. 23-24.

[39] Joppe, op. cit., p. 8.

[40] H. Ansari, *'The Infidel Within'* – *Muslims in Britain since 1800*, London, Hurst, 2004, p.172 No. 12 see also S. Tebbakh, *Muslims in the EU City Reports – France:*

example, notes that, 'the one group that has no access at all to health and social protection in Germany is the considerable number of the so-called illegal immigrants, many of whom are Muslims. All persons and institutions that help those 'illegals' are culpable of aiding and abetting illegal entry and illegal residence, and by law every official institution must report any case of illegal residence'.[41]

In European states where the practical exercise of certain religious freedoms requires permission or authorisation by public authorities, the exercise of discretion by public officials provides further arenas in which Muslims can experience discrimination. The most common examples include securing planning permission for mosques or religious burial grounds,[42] the right to slaughter animals in line with religious laws, the wearing of headscarves by women, the state funding of Muslim schools and the recognition of Islam as an 'official religion' by states in which there are institutionalised relations between the state and religious communities.[43]

Preliminary Research and Literature Review, Budapest, Open Society Institute, 2007 (forthcoming).

[41] N. Muhe (2007), *Muslims in the EU Cities Reports – Germany: Preliminary Research Report and Literature Survey*, Open Society Institute, Budapest, p. 7.

[42] R. Gale (2004), "The Multicultural City and the Politics of Religious Architecture: Urban Planning, Mosques and Meaning-making in Birmingham, UK", *Built Environment*, 30(1).

[43] See J. Ringelheim (2006), *Strategic Litigation to Combat Discrimination against Muslims in Europe: "State of Law" Legal Memorandum*, Open Justice Initiative, New York; Choudhury et al. (2006), op. cit., see also J. Rath, R. Penninx, K. Groenendijk and A. Meyer (1999), "The Politics of Recognising Religious Diversity in Europe: Social Reactions to the Institutionalization of Islam in the Netherlands, Belgium and Great Britain", *Netherlands' Journal of Social Sciences*, 35(1), C. Soper and J. Fetzer (2005), "Explaining the Accommodation of Muslim Religious Practices in France, Britain, and Germany", paper for Stream 3, Public Recognition and Secular Democracy, IMSCOE Cluster B6 workshop on Ethnic, Cultural and Religious Diversity, Amsterdam; 26-28 May, and S. Ferrari (2005), "The Secularity of the State and the Shaping of Muslim Representative Organisations in Western Europe", in J. Cesari and S. McLoughlin, (eds), *European Muslims and the Secular State*, Aldershot: Ashgate.

The debate surrounding the right of Muslim women to wear an Islamic headscarf or hijab, illustrates the potential for the public discussion surrounding such issues to reinforce stereotypes and prejudices that further stigmatise Muslims and thereby increase their risk of experiencing discriminatory treatment. The hijab has become a symbolic focus for the discussion of multiculturalism and national identity.[44] In France, where the issue has been under public debate since 1989, national legislation prohibiting the wearing of ostentatious religious symbols in schools by pupils was passed following a National Commission examining the issue.[45] In Germany, while the Federal Supreme Court deemed the ban on wearing the headscarf to be unconstitutional, as the ban did not have sufficient legal basis, it left it open for individual Länder to bring in legislation banning religious symbols in schools.[46] The Court emphasised that regulations introduced by individual states should be non-discriminatory. However, many states have not adhered to this principle. In Baden-Württemberg, for example, the preamble to the legislation made it clear that the regulations were aimed at Islamic headscarves. Furthermore, it provided that the law did not concern the representation of Christian and Western values and traditions. Law-makers relied on state constitutional provisions which require schools to pass Christian values and traditions onto pupils.[47]

---

[44] The issue has also generated considerable literature. See for example, C. El Hamel (2002), "Muslim Diaspora in Western Europe: The Islamic Headscarf, the Media and Muslims' Integration in France", *Citizenship Studies*, 6(3); B. Gökariksel and K. Mitchell (2005), "Veiling, secularism, and the neoliberal subject: national narratives and supranational desires in Turkey and France", *Global Networks* 147, 5(2).

[45] B. Stasi, (2003) Working group (Commission de réflexion) on the application of the principle of laicity. Report to the President of the Republic, La Documentation Française, Paris.

[46] *Ludin,* 2 BvR 1436/02, 24 September 2003. For a discussion of the case see: M. Mahlmann, 'Religious Tolerance, Pluralistic Society and the Neutrality of the State: the Federal Constitutional Court's Decision in the *Headscarf* Case', 4 (11) *German Law Journal* 1099.

[47] I. Gallala, (2006) "The Islamic Headscarf: An Example of Surmountable Conflict between Shari'a and the Fundamental Principles of Europe", *European Law Journal, 12(5),* p. 600.

The issue of the veil has also been addressed by the European Court of Human Rights in cases involving a school teacher in Switzerland[48] and a university medical student in Turkey.[49] The comments of the European Court of Human Rights were particularly unfortunate in reproducing and reinforcing stereotypes about Muslims in the Dahlab case. Here, the Court found that the veil "seemed to be imposed on women" and that it results from a prescription "difficult to reconcile with the principle of equality of the sexes"... furthermore, they found that "it is difficult to reconcile the wearing of the Islamic veil with the message of tolerance, of respect for others and above all of equality and non-discrimination that, in a democratic society, every teacher must transmit to his or her pupils".[50] In France, the President of the French State Commission for Laicity stated that the headscarf was a "sign of the alienation of women" and that Muslim women "wear the headscarf especially because their parents, their older brothers, as well as their religious groups, oblige them to do so. If they do not wear it they are insulted".[51] In both instances, the hijab is inscribed with a single symbolic meaning that excludes alternative interpretation and narratives, whereas the hijab can be a source of empowerment, a way of challenging stereotypes and challenging gender identities.[52] It was left to the dissenting opinion of Judge Tulkens in Sahin to note that "(...) wearing the headscarf has no single meaning; it is a practice that is engaged in for a variety of reasons. It does not necessarily symbolise the submission of women to men and there are those who maintain that, in certain cases, its can be a means of emancipating women."[53] By contrast, the German Federal Constitutional Court, in the Ludin case, accepted that the meaning

---

[48] *Dahlab v Switzerland* (App.42393/98), Admissibility Decision of 15 February 2001.

[49] *Leyla Sahin v Turkey* (App.44774/98), Judgment of 10 November 2005

[50] *Dahlab v Switzerland* (App.42393/98), Admissibility Decision of 15 February 2001.

[51] W. Shadid and Van Koningsveld (2005), "Muslim Dress in Europe: Debates on the Headscarf", *Journal of Islamic Studies*, 16(1), p. 46.

[52] See for example, C. Dwyer (2000), "Negotiating diasporic identities: Young British South Asian Muslim women", *Women's studies international forum*, 23(4), and C. Dwyer (1999), "Veiled meanings: Young British Muslim women and the negotiation of differences", *Gender, place and culture*, 6(1).

[53] *Leyla Sahin v Turkey* (App.44774/98), Judgment of 10 November 2005, dissenting Opinion of Judge Tulkens paragraph 11.

and impact of wearing the veil depends on a complex set of circumstances including not only the individual's intentions but also the general behaviour of the teacher who wears it and the message as it is received by the pupils and parents involved. Therefore, according to the Court, the veil could not just be reduced to a symbol of the social oppression of women.[54] Shadid and van Koningsveld conclude that discussions about the hijab in Europe, by judges, politicians and in the media, perpetuate stereotypes about the women who wear them, about Islam and the attitudes of Muslims towards Western civilisation and their willingness to integrate into its societies.[55] They find that "almost without exception these stereotypes attribute highly negative characteristics to the group concerned" and as such, "they can be considered a form of collective stigmatisation".[56] Even where, as in France, the legal ban is limited to pupils and teachers in schools, research suggests that there are knock-on effects, in terms of discrimination, for women who wear the hijab in other areas of life.[57] Qualitative studies of the experiences of Muslim women comment on the ways in which stereotypes about Muslim women impact on the lives of the women interviewed. Dwyer finds that gendered, class and racialised explanations reinforce the representation of young Muslim women as both oppressed and powerless. Such stereotypes impinged on the lives of those she interviewed. For example, a pupil interviewed for a medical degree was questioned about her commitment to the profession. Others reported that they were often judged on the basis of being representatives of a stereotype rather than as an individual.[58]

The targeting of Muslims, through violence and hate speech directed at individuals because of the groups to which they belong or are perceived

---

[54] I. Gallala (2006), "The Islamic Headscarf: An Example of Surmountable Conflict between Shari'a and the Fundamental Principles of Europe" *European Law Journal*, 12(5), p. 599.

[55] W. Shadid and Van Koningsveld (2005), "Muslim Dress in Europe: Debates on the Headscarf" *Journal of Islamic Studies*, 16(1).

[56] Ibid., p. 43. See also N. Guenif-Souilmas and E. Mace (2004), *Les féministes et le garçon arabe*, Paris: Edition de l'Aube on the stigmatisation or Arab men in France.

[57] T. Choudhury et al. (2006) op. cit.

[58] C. Dwyer (2006), "Negotiating diasporic identities: young British South Asian Muslim women", *Women's studies international forum*, 23(4), p.475.

to belong is a further form of discrimination or 'exclusion'.[59] In the aftermath of the terrorist attacks of September 11, 2001, as well as the killing of Theo Van Gogh in Amsterdam and the Madrid 2004 and London 2005 bombings, there has been a significant increase in the number of attacks on Muslims and those perceived to be Muslims, usually in the days and weeks immediately following such incidents.[60] The majority of attacks take the form of verbal abuse, but there are also cases of severe physical attacks and murders as well as violence aimed at mosques, Islamic schools and cemeteries. In France, the report of the National Consultative Commission on Human Rights for 2004 recorded a rise in anti-Muslim and anti-Arab attacks; 81% of recorded racist or xenophobic violence targeted people of North African or Muslim origin.[61] The EUMC report on Islamophobia in the EU after September 11 noted a significant number of incidents in the Netherlands, including insults, graffiti and threats (53 incidents), and vandalism and acts of aggression against Muslims and Islamic symbols (13 incidents). Following the murder of film director Theo van Gogh, there were attacks on Muslim schools and mosques in the

---

[59] See M. Malik, 'Muslims in the UK: Discrimination, Equality, and Community Cohesion', in *Muslims in the UK: Policies for Engaged Citizens*, Budapest, Open Society Institute, 2005, pp. 69-73, where Iris Marion Young's 'five faces of oppression' – the first of which is oppression through violence – is utilised to provide a framework for understanding the experience of exclusion of Muslins in Britain. She notes that 'Young's definition of violence also encompasses "less severe incidents of harassment, intimidation, or ridicule, simply for the purpose of degrading, humiliating or stigmatising a group member"' see also I. M. Young, *Justice and the Politics of Difference*, p.61, NJ, Princeton University Press, 1990.

[60] See: European Union Monitoring Centre on Racism and Xenophobia, Muslims in the European Union: Discrimination and Islamophobia, Vienna, EUMC, 2006, pp. 66-90; European Union Monitoring Centre on Racism and Xenophobia, *The Impact of 7 July 2005 London Bomb Attacks on Muslim Communities in the EU*, Vienna, EUMC, 2005 and C. Allen and J. Nielsen, *Summary Report on Islamophobia in the European Union after 11 September 2001*, Vienna, European Union Monitoring Centre on Racism and Xenophobia, 2002.

[61] Commission nationale consultative des droits de l'homme (2004), La lutte contre le racisme et la xénophobie.

Netherlands.[62] In 10 opinion polls since 2002, Muslims in the UK have been asked if they have experienced hostility and discrimination. Around 30% of Muslims consistently report experiencing some form of hostility directed at them (the actual figures range from 20-38%). A poll in July 2005 asked Muslims about the kinds of adverse treatment they might experience: 14% said they had experienced verbal abuse; 3% reported physical violence; 5% said they had been stopped and searched by police; 32% felt they had been the object of hostility; and 42% felt they had been the object of suspicion.[63]

The multi-dimensional nature of discrimination

The nature of the discrimination Muslims encounter, the boundaries between different characteristics, race, ethnicity, religion and gender, are less precise and stable than might first appear.[64] Identifying *the* ground of discrimination or even the primary ground may not be possible where a person has more than one characteristic that makes them a target of discrimination. Furthermore, individuals interpret their experiences in ways that allow them to 'mediate' that discrimination.[65] Muslims face

---

[62] Demant et al. (2007), *Muslims in the EU City Reports – The Netherlands: Preliminary Research Report and Literature Review*, Open Society Institute, Budapest, (forthcoming).

[63] A. Blick, T. Choudhury and S. Weir (2006), *The Rules of the Game: Terrorism, Community and Human Rights*, Joseph Rowntree Reform Trust, York, p. 19.

[64] For a discussion of the racialisation of religion, see M. Chon and D. Artz (2005), "Walking While Muslim", *Law and Contemporary Problems*, 68, p. 228, where they note that "Religion is not 'immutable' in the way we understand skin colour to be. Religious affiliation or identity is always a matter of choice. Yet, especially through the war on terror, Islam is acquiring characteristics of immutability, innateness, inevitability, inheritability and, importantly inferiority. In other words religious differences are being 'racialised'".

[65] M. Bying (1998), "Mediating Discrimination: Resisting Oppression Among African-American Muslim Women", *Social Problems*, 45(4), pp. 474-5, "mediation means having the agency to respond to discrimination in ways that resist its power and oppression…human agency is central to mediation: ownership, accountability, self definition, self-determination, and self-evaluation mean that in the face of painful discrimination people maintain their humanity and recognise the humanity of others". Bying's finds that the African-American Muslim women she interviewed "were able to resist the oppression of discrimination by a humanist

different forms of discrimination and experience differing disadvantages depending on a wide range of characteristics including perceptions of race, ethnicity and gender. Across Europe, different ethnic groups are synonymous in the public imagination with Muslims: in France, North Africans; in Germany, Turks; in the Netherlands, Moroccans and Turks, and in the UK, Pakistanis and Bangladeshis. Islam is embedded in the ways in which these groups are racialised in those countries. Thus, being Muslim is significant in structuring the discrimination directed against Turks in Germany but not in London.[66] As with identity, the characteristic that comes into play in the discriminatory treatment is context-sensitive.

Moreover, even when considering discrimination concerning a particular characteristic or religion, the circumstances and experiences of discrimination vary greatly within the Muslim group. For example, race, ethnicity, employment, religious practice and visible signs of religious identity are significant variables in the intensity and frequency of religious discrimination experienced by Muslims.[67] There is no homogenous Muslim experience of religious discrimination.

6.2 The legal and policy tools available to address discrimination

Prohibitions on discrimination in EC Law

This part examines the legal and policy tools that can be mobilised to tackle discrimination experienced by Muslims in Europe. Our focus will be on

---

vision that views discrimination as triggered by difference. Even though these women experience classic cases of discrimination, they maintain the ability of self-definition, determination, and valuation. They define the importance of the experience for themselves and their lives, and thereby are able to mediate discrimination... [They] use their membership in the Muslim community as a self defining and safe social space"'

[66] See for example P. Enneli, T. Modood and H. Bradley (2005), *Young Kurds and Turks: A set of 'invisible' disadvantaged groups*, Joseph Rowntree Foundation, York, p. 41, where young Turkish and Kurdish respondents suggested that religion was not the main for the discrimination targeted at them, but that "negative feelings against Muslims were targeted at Pakistanis".

[67] S. R. Ameli, M. Elahi and A. Merali, *British Muslims' Expectations of Government: social discrimination across the Muslim divide*, Islamic Human Rights Commission, 2004.

action that is possible at the European Union rather than member state level. Discrimination was only a concern of the European Economic Community at its inception in 1957 to the extent that it interfered with market integration. The Treaty of Rome[68] contained only a general prohibition on discrimination on the grounds of nationality,[69] for workers of member states, and a provision on equal pay for men and women, for equal work or work of equal value.[70] Thus, in the Treaty of Rome, "there was something, but it looked like nothing".[71] The Treaty's sparse provisions were not expected to form the basis for developing a far-reaching system of tackling discrimination or promoting equality, their primary purpose was market integration.[72] Yet, over the past 50 years, the EC has become a significant catalyst for anti-discrimination measures in member states, as "the limited conception of non-discrimination which was concealed in the Treaty evolved over the years into a fundamental principle of social policy with constitutional aspirations".[73] The initial expansion of Community measures as confined, by the treaty, to sex discrimination, first in relation to equal pay[74] but then, through invoking Article 308 EC, with

---

[68] Treaty establishing the European Economic Community, 25 March 1957, 298 U.N.T.S. 11 [hereinafter EEC Treaty]

[69] Article 48 EEC, now revised Article 39 EC

[70] Article 119 EEC, now revised Article 141 EC

[71] Perchal, S., 'Equality of Treatment, Non-Discrimination and Social Policy: Achievements in Three Themes' 41 *Common Market Law Review* 533, 2004.

[72] See C. Barnard, "The Economic Objectives of Article 119", in Hervey T., and O'Keeffe (eds.), *Sex Equality Law in the European Union*, 1996.

[73] Perchal, S., 'Equality of Treatment, Non-Discrimination and Social Policy: Achievements in Three Themes' 41 *Common Market Law Review* 533, 2004, at p. 534. See also G. More (1999), "The Principle of Equality Treatment: From Market Unifier to Fundamental Right?", in P. Craig and G. De Búrca (eds), *The Evolution of EU Law*, pp. 517-543.

[74] EC, *Council Directive 75/117 of 10 February 1975 on the approximation of the laws of the Member States relating to the application of the principle of equal pay for men and women*, [1975] O.J.L. 45/19).

respect to equal treatment in access to employment[75] and in social security schemes.[76]

The potential for action in relation to other grounds of discrimination came with the insertion of Article 13 into the Treaty of Rome by the Treaty of Amsterdam.[77] Article 13 provides that the Council, "acting unanimously on a proposal from the Commission and after consulting the European Parliament, may take appropriate action to combat discrimination based on sex, racial or ethnic origin, religion or belief, disability, age or sexual orientation". This dramatic expansion of the grounds of discrimination covered by EC law was the result of determined lobbying and concern for ethnic tension in an enlarged EU.[78] Initial scepticism that the necessary unanimity would be ever be found for passing any measures in the Council was confounded, as the inclusion of the far right Freedom Party in the government of Austria in October 1999 provided the impetus for urgent community action. Two Directives were adopted in 2000. The first, adopted in June, covered discrimination on the grounds of racial or ethnic origin (hereafter the "Race Directive").[79] The second, adopted five months later, prohibited discrimination on the grounds of religion or belief, disability,

---

[75] EC, *Council Directive 76/207 of 9 February 1976 on the implementation of the principle of equal treatment of men and women as regards access to employment, vocational training and promotion, and working conditions*, [1976] O.J.L 39/40.

[76] EC, *Council Directive 79/7 of 19 December 1978 on the progressive implementation of the principle of equal treatment for men and women in matters of social security*, [1979] O.J.L. 6/24; EC, *Council Directive 86/378 of 24 July 1986 on the implementation of the principle of equal treatment for men and women in occupational social security schemes*, [1986] O.J.L 225/40 and EC, *Council Directive 86/613 of 11 December 1986 on the application of the principle of equal treatment between men and women engaged in an activity, including agriculture, in self-employed capacity, and on the protection of self-employed women during pregnancy and motherhood*, [1986] O.J.L. 359/56.

[77] Treaty of Amsterdam, Official Journal C340 of 10 November 1997.

[78] See D. Schiek, "Broadening the Scope of the Norms of EU Gender Equality Law: Towards a Multidimentional Conception of Equality Law", 12(4) *Maastricht Journal of European and Comparative Law*, p. 438 and footnote 40: I. Chopin, "The Starting Line Group: A Harmonised Approach to Fight Racism and to Promote Equal Treatment", 1 *European Journal of Migration and the Law* 111, 1999.

[79] EC, *Council Directive 2000/43 of 29 June 2000 implementing the principle of equal treatment between persons irrespective of racial or ethnic origin*, [2000] O.J.L 180/22.

age or sexual orientation (hereafter the 'Framework Directive).[80] The Framework Directive limits itself to prohibiting discrimination in employment and occupation. The Race Directive goes beyond employment to cover education, social protection including social security and healthcare, social advantage and access to and supply of goods and services. Thus, "touching on areas at the outer limits of Community competence".[81]

The recitals to the Directives suggest that Community action is no longer driven by market integration alone; it recognises that discrimination undermines the achievement of the objectives of the EC Treaty, including the attainment of economic and social cohesion and solidarity.[82] Racial discrimination undermines the European Union's goal of creating an 'area of freedom, security and justice'; moreover, tackling such discrimination, beyond the narrow confines of employment, is needed "to ensure the development of democratic and tolerant societies which allow the participation of all persons irrespective of racial or ethnic origin".[83] Ellis argues that the rationale for adopting Article 13 and its Directives "lies preponderantly in the concepts of fairness, autonomy, human dignity and respect for human rights, the creation of a better society in which the quality of people's lives will be improved".[84] The European Court of Justice in *Mangold v Helm* held that the source of this principle of equal treatment found in the Framework Directive comes from "the various international instruments and in the constitutional traditions common to the Member

---

[80] EC, *Council Directive 2000/78 of 27 November 2000 establishing a general framework for equal treatment in employment and occupation*, [2000] O.J.L 303/16.

[81] C. Barnard (2001), "The Changing Scope of Equality Law?" 46 *McGill Law Review*, p. 967.

[82] Race Directive, recital 9; Framework Directive, recital 11.

[83] Race Directive, recital 12. See M. Bell (2002), "Beyond European Labour Law? Reflections on the EU Racial Equality Directive", 8 *European Law Journal*, p. 387 suggests that the Directive marks a "shift towards a broader conception of European social law".

[84] E. Ellis (2002), "The Principle of non-discrimination in the Post-Nice Era" in Arnull and Wincott (eds.), *Accountability and Legitimacy in the European Union*, Oxford, OUP, 2002, pp. 291-305 at p. 293.

States".[85] Schiek suggests that "the principle of equal treatment of persons irrespective of a set of ascribed characteristics should be accepted as a general principle of law, which is to be applied to all areas of law, irrespective of whether the main actors in the field of law are public or non-state actors".[86] The move from prohibiting discrimination towards achieving equality is further strengthened in the Treaty establishing a Constitution for the European Union[87] and in Charter of Fundamental Rights. The result, it has been suggested, is a model in which the traditional anti-discrimination approach has been joined by a new attachment to substantive equality and a desire to manage diversity.[88] Such a shift, from non-discrimination to equality, leaves the concept of equality unresolved.

The two Directives cover both direct and indirect discrimination[89] – direct discrimination is taken to occur when a person is treated less favourably than another has been or would be treated on the prohibited grounds. Indirect discrimination[90] is taken to occur where an apparently neutral provision, criteria or practice would put a person having a particular relevant characteristic at a particular disadvantage compared with other persons, unless that provision, criteria or practice is objectively justified by a legitimate aim and the means of achieving that aim are appropriate and necessary. They also deem instructions to discriminate[91] and harassment to be forms of discrimination. The latter is defined as unwanted conduct related to the prohibited ground which takes place "with the purpose or effect of violating the dignity of a person and of

---

[85] Case C-144/04 *Mangold v Helm*, 22/11/05.

[86] D. Schiek (xxxx), "Broadening the Scope of the Norms of EU Gender Equality Law: Towards a Multidimensional Conception of Equality Law", 12(4) *Maastricht Journal of European and Comparative Law*, p. 432.

[87] M. Bell (2004), "Equality and the European Constitution", *Industrial Law Journal*, 33.

[88] M. Bell (2003), "The Right to Equality and Non-Discrimination" in T. Hervey and J. Kenner (eds), *Economic and Social Rights under the EC Charter of Fundamental Rights: A Legal Perspective*, Oxford: Hart Publishing.

[89] Race Directive, Article 2(2)(a); Framework Directive, Article 2(2)(a).

[90] Race Directive, Article 2(2)(b); Framework Directive, Article 2(2)(b).

[91] Race Directive, Article 2(4); Framework Directive, Article 2(4).

creating an intimidating, hostile, degrading, humiliating or offensive environment".[92]

Both Directives provide an exemption that allows for discrimination on the basis of a prohibited characteristic where "by reasons of the nature of the particular occupational activities concerned or of the context in which they are carried out, such a characteristic constitutes a genuine and determining occupational requirement, provided that the objective is legitimate and the requirement is proportionate".[93] Furthermore, Article 2(5) of the Framework Directive provides that it "shall be without prejudice to measures laid down by national law which, in a democratic society are necessary for public security, or the maintenance of public order and the prevention of criminal offences, for the protection of public health and for the protection of the rights and freedoms of others". As will be discussed below, the importation of such a broad exemption, mirroring the language of the European Convention on Human Rights may restrict the potential to challenge actions sanctioned by the states which indirectly discriminate.[94] The Framework Directive also provides an exemption from the prohibition on discrimination on the grounds of religion and belief, for organisations with an ethos based on a religion or belief, where, "by reason of the nature of these activities or of the context in which they are carried out, a person's religion or belief constitutes a genuine, legitimate and justified occupational requirement, having regard to the organisation's ethos". Furthermore, such organisations can require individuals working for them to act in good faith and with loyalty to the organisation's ethos.[95]

These Directives lie at the core of the protection that European law offers Muslims in addressing the discrimination they experience. While Article 13 is framed in terms of combating discrimination, several aspects of the Race and Framework Directive appear to entail more substantive

---

[92] Race Directive, Article 2(3); Framework Directive, Article 2(3).

[93] Race Directive, Article 4, Framework Directive, Article 4.

[94] See also P. Skidmore (2001), "EC Framework Directive on Equal Treatment in Employment: Towards a Comprehensive Community Anti-Discrimination Policy?", *Industrial Law Journal*, 30.

[95] Framework Directive Article 4(2).

equality.[96] Firstly, there is the reference to "equal treatment" in the title of the Directives. Furthermore, in contrast to the earlier Directive on Equal Treatment between men and women, in which provisions allowing positive action are framed as exceptions to the principle of equal treatment,[97] the Race and Framework Directive link positive action more clearly to the goal of "ensuring full equality in practice".[98] The inclusion of indirect discrimination among the forms of discrimination encompassed by the Directive provides the greatest potential for using the directives to go beyond formal equality.[99] Two distinct conceptions of the function of indirect discrimination coexist. Under the first conception, indirect discrimination serves to unmask instances of intentional discrimination. Under the second conception, intention is no longer relevant, instead indirect discrimination aims to "permanently revise institutionalized habits and procedures".[100] Thus, indirect discrimination has been identified by Hervey as the "primary legal tool" for tackling structural inequality.[101] However, the potential for achieving structural change is circumscribed as a criterion, provision or practice that has a distinct impact on those within the protected group and remains open to being 'objectively justified' if the

---

[96] The term 'substantive equality' is used here to distinguish it from 'formal equality', that is equality as consistency of treatment. The term remains ambiguous, as it encompasses different conceptions of substantive equality, including equality of result and equality of opportunity. See generally: S. Fredman, *Discrimination Law*, Oxford, Oxford University Press, 2002. For discussion of Fredman's conceptions of equality see also H. Collins, 'Discrimination, Equality and Social Inclusion', 66 *Modern Law Review* 16, 2003, N. Bamforth, 'Conceptions of Anti-Discrimination Law' 24(4) *Oxford Journal of Legal Studies* 693, 2004 and E. Holmes, 'Anti-Discrimination Rights Without Equality' 68(2) *Modern Law Review* 175, 2005.

[97] EC, *Council Directive 76/207 of 9 February 1976 on the implementation of the principle of equal treatment of men and women as regards access to employment, vocational training and promotion, and working conditions*, [1976] O.J.L 39/40.

[98] Race Directive, Article 5; Framework Directive, Article 7. See Perchal.

[99] S. Fredman, *Discrimination Law*, Oxford, Oxford University Press, 2002.

[100] O. De Schutter, *Three Models of Equality and European Anti-Discrimination Law*, (forthcoming)

[101] T. K. Hervey (xxxx), "Thirty Years of EU Sex Equality Law: Looking Backwards, Looking Forwards", *Maastricht Journal of European and Comparative Law*, 12(4).

measure is in pursuit of a legitimate aim and the means of achieving that aim are appropriate and necessary.

The need for a vision of equality for Muslims

The use of indirect discrimination to challenge the structures and institutional settings which discriminate against members of a particular group, is more likely where there is an understanding of why there is protection from discrimination on particular grounds and when there is a general consensus as to what equality for that group looks like, at least in those areas where equality law is being applied. Such understanding and consensus are necessary but not sufficient to cause a shift from using indirect discrimination to address only concealed intentional discrimination, to using it as a tool to permanently revise institutional habits and procedures. In tackling sex discrimination, a growing understanding of the role of stereotyping and the need to change structures that reproduce gender roles is important in developing a clearer vision of what gender equality in the workplace looks like.

The potential for Muslims to utilise the indirect discrimination provisions to "revise institutionalised habits and procedures" is constrained by the absence of any Europe wide consensus over or vision of substantive equality for Muslims. Indirect discrimination provides a tool with which to challenge institutionalised habits and procedures and seek the accommodation of religious practices, such as religious dress, festivals and holidays, prayers and dietary requirements. However, without broad consensus over the vision of religious equality, and agreement over the extent to which religious equality requires such accommodations, using the Directives to challenge societal norms concerning the role of religion in public life will be difficult. This is because, as noted above, any provision, criteria or practice that indirectly discriminates against Muslims, is subject to being objectively justified. Here it is noted that the European Court of Justice has taken a 'bifurcated approach' to justifications in relation to gender discrimination.[102] The Court is willing to question and challenge a justification when it is put forward by an individual employer, subjecting them to a 'robust proportionality test'; however, it grants a broad discretion to justifications put forward by member states where the practice has been

---

[102] Ibid., p. 315.

agreed at the state level and is found in legislation or reflects official state policy.[103] Agreement and consensus around what equality looks like makes it easier for the courts to challenge the justifications put forward by individuals or the state. Furthermore, Article 5(2) of the Framework Directive introduces an extra layer of protection for state-endorsed practices. This exemption echoes the language of the European Convention on Human Rights. In cases taken to the Strasbourg Court by Muslims claiming failures to accommodate manifestations of their religious belief, the Court has shown a readiness to defer, without significant interrogation, to the state's claims that the restrictions on the manifestation of religious belief are justified within the term of Article 8(2) of the ECHR.[104]

Positive action

Alongside indirect discrimination, positive action is an important tool for eliminating structural forms of discrimination. The Race and Framework Directives provide that "with a view to ensuring full equality in practice, the principle of equal treatment shall not prevent any member state from maintaining or adopting specific measures to prevent or compensate for disadvantages linked to the prohibited grounds".[105] The first point to note is that under the Directives, positive action is discretionary rather than mandatory. The Directives do not prevent positive action measures being taken, nor do they require such measures to be taken. The scope of the action that is permissible by the Directives is likely to be interpreted in the light of the ECJ's jurisprudence on positive action in respect of gender. Here, positive action is found to encompass a broad range of measures that aim to benefit women, ranging from mainstreaming through to targets and preferential treatment. The latter is permitted as long as it does not entail an automatic preference.[106] Ambiguity around what constitutes an automatic preference is argued to have a 'chilling effect' on the willingness

---

[103] Ibid.

[104] See *Ahmad v UK* [1981] 4 European Human Rights Reports 126, also *Leyla Sahin v Turkey* (App.44774/98), Judgment of 10 November 2005.

[105] Race Directive, Article 5; Framework Directive, Article 7.

[106] Case 409/95 *Marschall v Land Nordrhein-Westfalen* [1997] ECR I-6363. See also Case 158/97 *Badeck v Hessischer Ministerpresident* [2000] ECR I-1875 and Case 407/98, *Abrahamsson and Andersson v Fogelqvist* [2000] ECR I-5539.

to use forms of preferential treatment where there is a risk that such schemes would be determined to be automatic preferences.[107]

Limitations in the material scope of the Directive

The limited material scope of the Framework Directive places a further constraint on the potential for EU anti-discrimination law to address any discrimination that Muslims face on the grounds of religion. The Framework Directive only prohibits discrimination in employment and occupation. Thus, significant areas in which Muslims face discrimination remain beyond the reach of the Directive. These include health, housing, education and the action of state officials, including law enforcement agencies. Discrimination in some of these areas falls within the scope of the Race Directive. The wider reach of the Race Directive has already provided the impetus for broadening action on gender equality into the provision of goods and services, although not to education.[108] As a first step to rectifying this imbalance, the scope of the Framework Directive needs to be extended to match the reach of the Race Directive. This would still leave areas such as law enforcement and access to citizenship, where there is evidence of discrimination, beyond the reach of European protection. Both the Race and Framework Directive provide that they do not cover differences of treatment based on nationality and are "without prejudice to provisions and conditions relating to the entry into and residence of third-country nationals and state-less persons on the territory of the Member States, and to any treatment which arises from the legal status of the third country nationals and state-less persons concerned".[109] Whether there is room to argue that access to nationality and citizenship – when it is a significant precondition to access to employment – can come within the scope of the

---

[107] C. O'Cinneide (2006), "Positive Action and the Limits of Existing Law" *Maastricht Journal of European and Comparative Law*, 13(3), p. 357.

[108] EC, Council Directive 2004/113 of 13 December 2004 implementing the principle of equal treatment between men and women in the access to and supply of goods and services [2004] O.J.L. 373/37. See: E.C. di Torella (2005), "The Goods and Services Directive: Limitations and Opportunities", *Feminist Legal Studies*, 13, p. 337.

[109] Race Directive, Article 3(2); Framework Directive, Article 3(2).

Directive, if such access is regulated in a discriminatory manner, remains to be tested.

In areas where the Community lacks competence to introduce hard-edged legal frameworks, Community Action may still be possible using softer co-operative governance mechanisms.

A proactive model of equality

The Framework Directive potential to provide the catalyst for the deeper structural changes needed for attaining substantive equality is further limited by its focus on addressing individual instances of discrimination through a negative prohibition of discrimination rather than the positive promotion of equality. Fredman identifies four central difficulties in the individualised discrimination model for achieving equality. First, it is reliant on the individual in bringing an action. It therefore places excessive strain on the individual in terms of resources and personal energy. Secondly, victim-initiated litigation means that the court's intervention is random and ad hoc. The remedy is limited to the individual; it does not create an obligation to change the institutional structure that gives rise to the discrimination. Thirdly, the basis in individual fault means that there must be a proved perpetrator. But discrimination that arises from institutional arrangements is not the result of the fault of any one person. Finally, this approach is adversarial and so instead of viewing equality as a common goal, to be achieved co-operatively, it "becomes a site of conflict and resistance".[110] By contrast the proactive model places the initiative of addressing discrimination on employers and public authorities, institutions and organisations, rather than the individuals facing disadvantage. They are tasked with taking action because they have the power and capacity to do so, not because they are responsible for the discrimination. It ensures that change is systematic rather than random and ad hoc. Action for change does not require the finding of fault or the naming of a perpetrator. The right to equality is available to all not just those able to complain. Finally, this approach provides for the role of civil society in setting and enforcing norms.[111]

---

[110] S. Fredman (2005), "Changing the Norm: Positive Duties in Equal Treatment Legislation", *Maastricht Journal of European and Comparative Law*, 12(4), pp. 372-3.

[111] Ibid.

Protection from violence

Outside the confines of the Article 13 Directives, there are some measures that the EU is attempting to take in response to religiously motivated violence and incitement to religious hatred. On 15 July 1996, the Council adopted a Joint Action concerning action to combat racism and xenophobia on the basis of article K.3 of the EU Treaty (now: Article 31EU).[112] Its main objective was to ensure effective legal cooperation between member states in combating racism and xenophobia. The Joint Action stressed the need to prevent the perpetrators of such offences from benefiting from the fact that they are treated differently in the member states by moving from one country to another to avoid prosecution. In particular, it wanted to address the situation where, under the principle of double criminality, member states may refuse cooperation on the grounds that conduct, though illegal in the state requesting assistance, is not illegal in the requested state. The Joint Action requested member states to ensure that racist and xenophobic behaviour of the type listed, be punishable as criminal offences or, failing that, and pending the adoption of any necessary provisions, to derogate from the principle of double criminality for such behaviours. The Framework Decision on Racism and Xenophobia was developed to take forward the Joint Action programme. The Council Framework Decision on Combating Racism and Xenophobia provide that:

Article 4 Offences concerning racism and xenophobia

Member States shall ensure that the following intentional conduct committed by any means is punishable as a criminal offence:

(a) public incitement to violence or hatred for a racist or xenophobic purpose or to any other racist or xenophobic behaviour which may cause substantial damage to individuals or groups concerned…

---

[112] 96/443/JHA: Joint Action of 15 July 1996 adopted by the Council on the basis of Article K.3 of the Treaty on European Union, concerning action to combat racism and xenophobia, O.J.L. 185, 24 July 1996, p. 5.

Article 5

...that instigating, aiding, abetting or attempting to commit an offence referred to in Article 4 is punishable.[113]

Despite intense negotiations, no agreement was reached by member states on the draft Framework Decision. In February 2005, the Council instructed the working group on substantive criminal law to resume negotiations on the draft Framework Decision. No text was agreed by the time of the Justice and Home Affairs Council Meeting in June 2005. In 2006, the Austrian Presidency hosted a conference to review progress with a view to reopening the discussion on the proposal for a Framework Decision.

Conclusions

The lives of many Muslims in Europe are marked by social and economic exclusion and marginalisation. The absence of systematic data collection on Muslims prevents us from drawing a comprehensive picture of the disadvantages experienced by Muslims; it should not however preclude us from seeing the mounting evidence of their situation. The reasons for these disadvantages are complex and multi-faceted. While it is not possible to identify the precise contribution of discrimination to this situation, it is clear that discrimination plays some role.

Article 13 of the EC Treaty provides the basis for European Union action in addressing discrimination. Weaknesses remain in the legal framework that has developed out of this article. Firstly, the Framework Directive, which covers discrimination on the grounds of religion or belief, does not cover key areas where Muslims continue to experience discrimination, including housing, education, access to goods and services, the actions of public officials particularly, police and immigration officials. Some of these areas – education, housing, the provision of goods and services – will be covered if the scope of the Framework Directive were extended to match that of the Race Directive. Other areas would still remain outside the scope of the Community action.

In those areas covered by the scope of the Directives, the legal tools for challenging embedded structural discrimination are in place, but their

---

[113] COM(2001) 644 final, OJ C 75/E/269 of 26 March 2002.

effective utilisation requires a clear vision and consensus around what religious equality for Muslims looks and feels like. The task of developing such a vision can neither rest on Muslims alone, nor be developed without their contribution. Here, organisations such as the European Union Agency for Fundamental Rights (FRA) and the equal treatment bodies of the member states have an important role in fostering debate and seeking to develop this vision.

Finally, it is important to place discrimination law in the wider policy context. Legal protection from discrimination is only one tool for addressing Islamophobia and anti-Muslim prejudice. Effectively tackling discrimination requires using a broader range of policy tools. Where, for example, discrimination is the result of the reproduction and reinforcement of stereotypes and the perpetuation of prejudices about Muslims, then the solutions lie in empowering Muslims to challenge and disrupt these discourses. There is a role here for arts, media and cultural policies that encourage and support Muslim participation in all areas of cultural reproduction from film, theatre and television to art and journalism.

7. ACCESS TO MEDIA FOR EUROPEAN MUSLIMS

ISABELLE RIGONI

Introduction

Despite its rank as the second-largest religion in several European countries, Islam is facing severe resistance at both state and societal level. Certain conservative political and media discourses associate Islam with violence and fanaticism. For most Muslims, however, their religion is associated with notions of justice and democracy. The conflict between these two conceptualisations of Islam has reinforced defensive attitudes on both sides. While Muslim stereotypes have increased since 9/11, so have the voices in favour of civil liberties for Muslims in Europe. As is argued here, ethnic media (i.e. Muslim media) are playing a major role on both sides of the debate.

These questions are of common concern to many EU member states and associated states and European institutions. They are based on three assumptions. Firstly, new information and communication technology (ICT) has reshaped the media scene, which is now accessible to increasing numbers of people, including exchanges between European countries and third countries. Secondly, the transnational mobilisations are increasingly influenced by ICT, which makes it possible for individuals to travel – both virtually and in reality – between several countries. Thirdly, the representation of the minority or marginalised groups, particularly in the case of Muslims, has become one of the key questions of European socio-political debate, and at the same time can be seen as a test for European democracy.

I would like to propose a historical reading of the representation of Muslims and Islam in the media. It is a question of understanding how media discourse evolved as it did and how and when Muslims are portrayed in the media. Several questions can be raised: How do media technologies influence conditions within both the Muslim community and the mainstream? What are the consequences of national and EU policies for Muslim citizens and their media regarding their social and political inclusion? How do European Muslims aggregate interests in a more effective and efficient way *via* their own media? Do Muslim media advocate social inclusion or pursue narrow interests?

7.1 Problem description

Mainstream media discourse on Islam and Muslims

Much ink has flowed in the Western media on the subject of Islam in the last few years. The audio-visual media were not to be outdone and often broadcast 'debates' related to this topic. Islam is frequently presented as a threat, a danger or a form of subversion.[1] At the very least, it is an 'otherness' and very rarely a legitimate private belief or a freedom of thought guaranteed by a legally constituted state. This tendency was particularly notable around the debate on the Islamic headscarf in French schools,[2] at the time of urban violence in France in October-November 2005,[3] and over the issue of the Danish caricatures, and has become manifest all over Europe, especially in France and the UK.

In France, the subject of religion[4] and, more particularly, that of Islam,[5] became more apparent at the end of the 1990s in media discourse on

---

[1] Open Society Institute (2002), *Monitoring de la protection des minorités dans l'Union européenne: La situation des musulmans en France*, OSI, Budapest.

[2] Isabelle Rigoni (2005), "De hoofddoek ter discussie. Een nieuwe islamitische identiteit voor de vrouw in seculier-burgerlijk Frankrijk" [The Headscarf in Debates. A New Feminine Islamic Identity in Secular France], in Gily Coene and Chia Longman (eds), *Eigen Emancipatie Eerst? Over de rechten en representatie van vrouwen in een multiculturele samenleving* [On Rights and Representation of Women in a Multicultural Society], Gent: Academia Press, pp.95-111.

[3] Isabelle Rigoni (ed) (2007), *Penser l'altérité dans les médias*, La Courneuve: Aux Lieux d'Être (forthcoming).

[4] Pierre Bréchon, Jean-Paul Willaime (eds) (2000), *Media et religions en miroir*, Paris: PUF (coll. Politique d'aujourd'hui).

immigration. However, this was a very gradual phenomenon. In his book *L'Islam imaginaire*, Thomas Deltombe analyses how the dominant media message and political discourse have gradually constructed a frame of reference for French people originating from former colonies: "During the 1980s, with the abandonment of Marxist frames of reference and the emergence of a 'second generation of immigrants' into the public arena, we witness a first evolution: the term 'Islamic' is increasingly employed by the media to talk about 'immigrants' who are no longer, as was the case a decade ago, described first as 'foreign workers'"(our translation). [6] Thus, at a time when 'integration' is placed at the centre of the debates, the recourse to an 'Islamic' reference makes it possible to perpetuate the symbolic remoteness of a segment of the population that is in fact no longer 'foreign'.

If media discourse were seeking to be alarmist, the mainstream media did not need a dramatic topical event to put Islam on the scene.[7] Research shows that generally the French media depict Islam as a threat to the laws of the Republic, secularism, freedom of expression, women's rights and, because of the terrorism with which it is often associated, to the safety of the country or 'the West' as a whole. Cédric Housez stresses that Islam "is often associated with Islamism, which for its part, following the imported rhetoric of American neo-conservatives, and is presented as a new totalitarianism, comparable to Nazism or Stalinism. This analogy rests on (improbable) amalgamations and on a unified vision of Muslim fundamentalism, even of the Muslim world, which denotes a total misunderstanding of Islam" (our translation).[8] The media essay writer and chronicler at *Le Point*, Bernard Henri Lévy, uses the term 'fascislamist' and the leader-writer of *Le Figaro*, Yvan Rioufol, speaks for his part about

---

[5] Thomas Deltombe (2005), *L'islam imaginaire. La construction médiatique de l'islamophobie en France, 1975-2005*, Paris, La Découverte. Rabah Saddek (1998), *L'islam dans le discours médiatique*, Beyrouth, Al-Bouraq. Alain Gresh (1997), *L'Islam dans les media*, Paris, Centre socio-culturel de la rue de Tanger.

[6] Cited on http://www.oumma.com

[7] Mathieu Rigouste (2002), *Les cadres médiatiques, sociaux et mythologiques de l'imaginaire colonial. La représentation de « l'immigration maghrébine » dans la presse française de 1995 à 2002*, Nanterre, Université Paris 10, Mémoire de maîtrise.

[8] Cédric Housez (2006), "L'obsession identitaire des médias français", voltairenet.org, 9 March.

'nazislamist'. The two leader-writers are not the only ones in France to use these word-plays. The satirical weekly magazine *Charlie Hebdo*, now at the forefront of French media in the denunciation of the 'Islamist danger'[9] and which distinguished itself at the time of the scandal of the Danish caricatures, by publishing a proclamation entitled "Together against the new totalitarianism" on 1 March 2006, which also proclaims the amalgamation of Islamism and Nazism.

In Britain, the contribution of Elizabeth Poole[10] provides a systematic and thoroughly researched analysis of the ways in which Muslims are represented in the British national press. Poole shows that coverage is not homogenous, but dissenting voices appear mainly in the margins of the papers "while the bulk of coverage shared the news values, constructions and categorizations of its conservative counterparts".[11] Indeed, since the Rushdie affair, the Gulf and Iraqi wars and 9/11, British journalists have published many articles against Islam. Although some dailies such as *The Guardian* sometimes call on Muslim journalists' cooperation, many of them focus on the debate over whether Islam is a progressive/rational or a barbaric/irrational religion. Media coverage of global terrorism now sits uneasily alongside the views of ordinary British Muslims.

Despite national differences, the mainstream media are acting quite similarly in Western Europe, siding from time to time against Islam and Muslims. Due to the processes involved in its production, news tends to be a limited, conservative and consensual product. Journalistic practices of gathering and selecting news are subject to the organisational constraints shaped by a capitalist system – in other words, their aim is to attract large audiences with sensational issues. Gradually in the Western world, one sees the Manichean image of a bipolar Islam opposing 'the integrated' or 'modern' Muslims. Little by little, the figure of the terrorist joins that of Islamist, legitimising the hardening of immigration policies. Islam is thus one of the prisms through which the populations coming from the old

---

[9] Cédric Housez (2005), "*Charlie Hebdo* et *Prochoix*. Vendre le « choc des civilisations » à la gauche", 30 August, voltairenet.org (voltairenet.com).

[10] Elizabeth Poole (2002), *Reporting Islam. Media Representations of British Muslims*, London: I. B. Tauris. See also Elizabeth Poole (2006), in John E. Richardson (ed.), *Muslims and the News Media*, London: I. B. Tauris.

[11] Ibid (2002), p.249.

colonies are presented, and through which it is possible to stigmatise them as a group.[12]

The rise of a concept: Islamophobia

In view of the foregoing and despite the diversity of membership within Islam, many public discourses promulgated by the Muslim communities themselves would like to show that Muslims form a unique group, are victims of discrimination and inclined to assert certain rights as a minority. The case of the UK is exceptional in Europe for this reason. Attempts by Muslims to preserve their faith and practices have sometimes been interpreted as separatism; a threat to 'traditional British' values, and have led to a questioning of the loyalty of 'Muslims within' Britain's boundaries. This series of questions/responses has in turn considerably sharpened the sense of Muslim identity (or identities), and resulted in the politicisation of Muslims in Britain, who have made numerous claims, including the one to be recognised as a religious minority – like the Jews or Sikhs – rather than as an ethnic minority. Although they enjoy a significant number of rights as an ethnic group, a report by the Runnymede Trust,[13] which gathered data on examples of 'Islamophobia' in the UK, argued that several events beginning in the early 1980s, such as the Rushdie affair, the Honeyford affair and issues such as halal meat in schools and the Gulf War, projected debates about Islam into the national public sphere.

The Runnymede Trust report considered the use of the term Islamophobia, as it has come to be used in English-speaking countries. It has since been imported into other European countries and continues to be the subject of intense political and scientific debate. For about ten years, but mainly after 9/11, European Muslims have complained of unjust treatment as a consequence of educational policies and practices which remain insufficiently sensitive to their culture. This is the case in France, which has more Muslim citizens than any other European country: the arrival of the first Muslim immigrants dates back to the 1920s when 90,000 Muslims came to France. Their numbers have grown rapidly since the 1950s, from 1 million after the War of Independence in Algeria to between 4.5 and 5

---

12 Vincent Geisser (2003), *La nouvelle islamophobie*, Paris : La Découverte.

13 The Runnymede Trust (1997), *Islamophobia. A Challenge for Us All*, Commission on British Muslims and Islamophobia, The Runnymede Trust, London.

million today; that is, 8% of the population. That France is a secular country and a republic poses several complications for Muslim populations. Pupils wearing the hijab have been extensively targeted and have become a 'national problem'.[14] One finds similar examples in the world of work (discrimination in recruitment, in the workplace, in access to training), to which the media give more and more attention. The two French leitmotivs of secularism and integration have led to ambiguous relations with French Muslims in particular, and Islam in general. However, it often remains difficult to provide evidence of the discrimination to which Muslims are subject. Is Islamophobia really visible in social practices, or is there more racism towards the migrants originating in former colonies?

Several studies show that the events of 9/11 caused an increasingly close association between Islam, terrorism and fundamentalism. In several countries of the EU, one can observe a rise in harassment and violence directed against Muslims and those perceived as Muslims, since 9/11. In France, although the number of racist acts has fallen overall, the majority of those that took place were related to 9/11. In Western Europe, racist violence often has a clearly religious dimension: places of worship (mosques and synagogues) are often the targets of attack, of partial or total destruction. The journalistic treatment of the policies regarding the fight against discrimination does not achieve a balance with the often-negative portrayal of Islam through migratory flows (with references to clandestine, *sans-papiers*, refugees), and the suburbs (as zones of urban violence). It is above all the Muslim media that, as we will see, are mobilised against this.

We return to a more detailed consideration of Islamophobia in a later chapter.

---

[14] Isabelle Rigoni (2005), "De hoofddoek ter discussie. Een nieuwe islamitische identiteit voor de vrouw in seculier-burgerlijk Frankrijk", op. cit.; Jocelyne Cesari, "Islam in France: The Shaping of a Religious Minority", in Yvonne Haddad-Yazbek (ed.) (2002), *Muslims in the West, from Sojourners to Citizens*, Oxford: Oxford University Press, pp.36-51; Jocelyne Cesari (1998), *Musulmans et Républicains, les Jeunes, L'islam et la France*, Bruxelles : Complexe and Françoise Gaspard and Farhad Khosrokhavar (1995), *Le foulard et la République*, Paris: La Découverte, "Essais et Documents".

7.2 Policy Alternatives for Europe

Actions in favour of a better representation of visible minorities

The Council of Europe has organised three conferences on the theme of 'Media and Migration': in Tampere in 1983, in Cologne in 1986 and in The Hague in 1988. It has tried to focus attention on the difficulty for television media of taking into account the plurality of society. These meetings have stimulated reflexion at European level and led to several recommendations relating to migrants and the media being adopted by Parliament or the Committee of Ministers of the Council of Europe.[15] Other recommendations aim, in parallel, at the development of 'codes of good conduct' to be adopted by several European television channels in Scandinavia and in the Anglo-Saxon countries.

The positive commitments at supranational level have made it possible to inspire a new dynamic at national level. However, in spite of the increase in debates and exchanges at the European level, at the initiative of governments, intergovernmental authorities or nongovernmental organisations, some European states, for example France, often remain absent from these debates.

Admittedly, policies aiming to take into account the populations of immigrant origin within the media have existed in France for about 30 years.[16] Initially, they were mainly the doing of the *Fonds d'Action Sociale* (FAS). More recently, other public organisations, in particular the *Conseil Supérieur de l'Audiovisuel* (CSA) or the *Haut Conseil à l'Intégration* (HCI), also intervened in this field, often after pressure from civil society organisations. Two major periods characterise the development of the audio-visual policy of the FAS. In its first initiatives, the FAS gave support to programmes known as special-interest (*Mosaic, Rencontres, Premier service*), targeting

---

[15] Conseil de l'Europe, *Recommandation relative aux migrants, aux minorités ethniques et aux médias*, No. 1277, Strasbourg, Conseil de l'Europe, Assemblée parlementaire, June 1995. Conseil de l'Europe, *Recommandation du Comité de ministres aux Etats membres sur les médias et la promotion d'une culture de tolérance*, No. R(97)21, Strasbourg, Conseil de l'Europe, 30 October 1997.

[16] Reynald Blion, Claire Frachon, Alec G. Hargreaves, Catherine Humblot, Isabelle Rigoni, Myria Georgiou, Sirin Dilli (2006), *La représentation des immigrés au sein des media. Bilan des connaissances*, FASILD Rapport, Paris.

immigrants and their families, while also hoping to sensitise mainstream opinion. The participation of the FAS in the financing of the programme *Saga-Cités*, between 1991 and 2002, opened a new strategic era in its televisual policy. As successor to the FAS, the FASILD[17] has since prioritised programmes aimed at a mainstream audience (telefilms, documentaries, etc.) to reinforce the awareness-raising role they can play in relations between the various components of society.

However, the extension of the debate on 'visible' minorities could not have been achieved without the involvement of new actors, initially from civil society, taken up further by other public institutions. Among the first actions undertaken by civil society was a press conference, organised in September 1999 by the *Collectif Egalité*, founded by the female writer Calixthe Beyala, and bringing together mainly artists and intellectuals of African and West-Indian origin. The message was to denounce the 'under-representation' of blacks on television[18] and request the application of quotas. Parallel to the *Collectif Egalité*, and taking it up thereafter, are other claims for a better representation of minorities within the media. The *Club Averroès* also comes into play, with another approach, a key role in the representation of minorities in the media. Created in 1997 and chaired by Amirouche Laïdi, it gathers media professionals from all backgrounds but also elected officials and business leaders. The Club meets the highest leaders of TV channels, launches specific proposals for a different representation in front of and behind the screen. Other movements[19] also make claims for the social and media recognition of minorities in society.

---

[17] The FAS became the *Fonds d'action et de soutien pour l'intégration et la lutte contre les discriminations* (FASILD), and in 2006 the *Agence nationale pour la cohésion sociale et l'égalité des chances* (ANCSEC).

[18] For Marie-France Malonga, there is now an 'overrepresentation' of Blacks on French TV channels: Marie-France Malonga, «La représentation des minorités dans les séries télévisées françaises: entre construction et maintien des frontières ethniques», in Isabelle Rigoni (éd.), Penser l'altérité dans les médias, La Courneuve, Aux Lieux d'Être, to be print in 2007.

[19] The *Collectif des Antillais, Guyanais, Réunionnais* created in 2003 by Patrick Karam; the *Cercle d'Action pour la Promotion et la Diversité en France* (CAPDIV) created the same year by Patrick Lozès to make the voice of Black people heard; the *Club du XXIe siècle*, created in 2004 by important persons of immigrant origin, such as

The *Conseil supérieur de l'audiovisuel* (CSA) evoked, for the first time publicly, the question of the representation of minorities on television in February 1999, largely thanks to the hearing of the *Collectif Egalité* in October 1999. It is on this date that the president of the CSA publicly requested a modification of programming on the public television channels, France 2 and France 3, to encourage them to take account of the multi-ethnic and multicultural reality of French society. In 2000, it made public the results of the study carried out within its services on the representation of visible minorities.[20] The same year, the *Rapport d'activités du CSA* introduced, for the first time, a heading entitled "Representation of minorities". In 2004, the CSA wrote to the TV channels to require them to include their initiatives concerning these new obligations, in their annual report in order to allow the evaluation of their progress compared to experiences abroad. From January 2006, the CSA considered the conditions of adaptation of these new measures to radio, to community or confessional TV channels, to local and overseas television channels, as well as to the current and future channels of digital television. The CSA enjoys alliances with other public organisations, like the *Haut Conseil à l'Intégration*, so that declarations and other decrees are translated into concrete and visible acts. Created in 1989, the *Haut Conseil à l'Intégration* is an authority that formulates policy and proposals and which, at the request of the Prime Minister or interdepartmental committee, gives its opinion on all matters relating to the integration of foreign residents. It is on the initiative of one of its members, Zaïr Kedadouche, that the *Haut Conseil à l'Intégration* became interested in the representativeness of immigrants in the media as a factor for integration in France.[21] In addition, the HCI has invited the government to re-examine legal texts concerning the obligations of public television, since these are considered to be less explicit than those planned for the private channels.

Hakim El-Karoui and Radicha Dati, close adviser of the Minister of Interior, to develop diversity by promoting equal opportunity.

[20] Marie-France Malonga (coord.) (2000), *Présence et représentation des minorités visibles à la télévision française*, Paris, CSA, May.

[21] HCI (2005), *La diversité culturelle et la culture commune dans l'audiovisuel*, Avis du Haut Conseil à l'Intégration au Premier ministre, Paris, 17 March.

The urban violence of November 2005 sparked an increased interest in these media aspects at the highest political level, with little impact however on the media in practice.

Compared to France, the British model is quite different. Its colonial past has shaped policies of migration and integration.[22] Thus, the official ideologies of 'inclusion' and integration have been reflected in a national legislation which has not only allowed, but protected religious and linguistic diversity. In this way, the British model of tolerance and 'inclusion' is very different from the French Jacobin model founded on secularity or from the German model centred on the right to citizenship by 'blood'.[23] The concerns of the British state around the questions of race and ethnicity are reflected in the work of various organisations, public or not (Commission for Racial Equality, the ex-Independent Television Commission, Press Complaints Commission, National Union of Journalists) having, in particular, the aim of promoting actions, for example codes of good practice, aiming at a better representativeness of the ethnic minorities within the media. Whatever their statute, these organisations come up against major obstacles to the development of their actions, and thus to their impact. Indeed, whereas the codes of good practice or the opinions that they formulate influence media practices, none of these tools is constraining enough. However, in 2003, the creation of the OFCOM – new independent organisation to regulate competition in communication sectors and of audio-visual in the UK – represented an evolution of political strategy of the British government in the communications and audio-visual sector. OFCOM has a right to oversee the way in which the media account for the diversity of British society's various ethnic communities. Parallel to this change, the British government supported similar initiatives launched by the media industry itself, for example the Cultural Diversity Network (CDN). Created in 2000 on the initiative of the principal operators of audio-

[22] Charles Husband, Liza Beattie, Lia Markelin (2000), *The key role of minority ethnic media in multiethnic societies: case study, UK*, Bruxelles, The International Media Working Group Against Racism and Xenophobia (IMRAX) and the International Federation of Journalists (IFJ).

[23] Marieke Blommesteijn, Han Entzinger, «Appendix: Report of the Field Studies carried out in France, Italy, the Netherlands, Norway, Portugal and the United Kingdom, 1999», in Christoph Butterwerge, Gudrun Hentges, Fatma Sarigös (eds), *Medien und multikulturelle Gesellschaft*, Opladen, Leske und Budrich Verlag, 1999.

visual media, the CDN aims first to evaluate, and then self-control, the policies and practices of the various audio-visual operators as regards representation of the minorities on the screen. It is the organisation best symbolising the current strategy of the British government. Besides institutional organisations, several independent ones have arisen such as *Migrant Media*, a training centre and a production company created in 1989 by descendants of immigrants.

At the European level an increasing number of non-governmental organisations were created during the 1990s, which have shown a great capacity for initiative and invention concerning the representation of minorities in the media sector. The European network of journalists *OnLine/More Colour in the Media*, has set up specialised training centres and various multicultural organisations in West European countries, with the aim of improving the representativeness of cultural minorities in media programmes. Among other national initiatives one may note the case of the Netherlands: *Mira Media*, an independent organisation created in 1986 by the largest organisation of migrants; *Migrants and the Media*, a working group that intends to ensure a greater diversity of media coverage and which fights for greater recruitment of foreign journalists; *Multiculturele Televisie Nederland* (MTLN), which produces multicultural programmes, etc. In France, the *Panos Paris Institute* is developing the programme Mediam'Rad on 'diasporas and ethnic minorities' media, aiming at a renewed awareness of the European civil societies. Its main objectives are to increase a pluralism of opinion and to reinforce the diversity of standpoints in the media in promoting the diasporas' media and the minorities' media as an alternative source of information and by encouraging lasting partnerships with the mainstream media.

The examples of good practice are numerous. Many European states have adopted various measures in favour of a better representation and representativeness of immigrants in the media, with a major role being played by non-governmental organisations. But all this still mainly concerns immigration, or, with a semantic slip, the 'visible minorities' i.e. naming the various ethnic components of society, but without naming Muslims.

European Muslim media

Alongside the mainstream media, whose positions are often ambiguous to say the least, some Muslim media have been created. Muslim media refers to written media – both online and offline – as well as radio and, when applicable, television programmes targeted at the 'Muslim community'. They are present in Britain more than in any other country in Europe. British Muslim newspapers such as *The Muslim News*, *Q-News*, *Crescent International*, *Impact International* and *Trends*; media committees such as *The Muslim Council of Britain* and the *Forum Against Islamophobia and Racism* (FAIR); or radio stations such as *Radio Umma* and *Radio Ramadan* have taken advantage of emerging communication and information opportunities to produce serious alternative views to the mainstream. While the older generations of immigrants have given Muslim media the benefit of their own experiences, the younger Muslim generation, including women, has brought new blood and new ideas. British Muslim newspapers were established between 1972 and 1992. They contain between 12 and 16 pages each of news and analysis on Muslim issues. They are all written in English although they are also distributed in countries like Pakistan, Nigeria, South Africa, Sri Lanka and Malaysia and sometimes in Canada and the US. In the UK, most of them are distributed free of charge in bookshops and associations. Within the British Muslim media, we can distinguish the community newspapers from the international news magazines. In addition to ideological divisions, the selection of the news differs broadly: while *Crescent International* and *Impact International* are clearly international news magazines, *The Muslim News* combines both national and international news, and *Q-News* attaches the utmost importance to British Muslim issues.

The situation is very different in France where Muslim media as such have developed only very recently. Until the late 1990s, ethnic and religious media were much more oriented towards a community of immigrants (i.e. Algerians, Moroccans, Turkish, etc.) than towards a community of believers.[24] Some Muslim magazines – *Hawwa* and *La Medina*

---

[24] Isabelle Rigoni (2005), "Challenging Notions and Practices: The Muslim Media in Britain and France", *Journal of Ethnic and Migration Studies*, "Media and Minorities in Multicultural Europe", guest-edited by Myria Georgiou & Roger Silverstone, 31(3), pp. 563-580, May.

are the best known; *Réflexions* (Saphir-Médiations group), *Columbus*, *Actualis* (the magazine of the Union of Islamic Organisations in France) – were created between 1998 and 2003 but have all disappeared whereas *La Medina* became a website (sezame.info). Some internet magazines such as *oumma.com*, *Saphirnews.com* or *Aslim Taslam* are still striving to make their voices heard. There are no exclusively Muslim radio stations although some radio stations like *Beur FM* or *Radio Méditerranée* attract large Muslim audiences.

In Germany,[25] the monthly magazine *Die Islamische Zeitung* plays a prominent role in the Muslim media scene. *Die Islamische Zeitung* was created in 1994 mainly by German converts to Islam, such as Abu Bakr Rieger (director) and Sulaiman Wilms (chief editor). As in several other Western European countries, the role of converts is very important for the development of Muslim media.[26] *Die Islamische Zeitung* defends a position often considered as conservative and does not consider Islam as a culture but as a religion for everyone. Its influence on politics appears to be less important than *The Muslim News* in Britain for instance, but it remains one of the leading Muslim media in Germany. Besides associative ones, other Muslim media are *Al-Raid* (Islamischer Informationsdienst e. V.), *Dunia*

---

[25] For an outline of the themes media, migration, Islam in Germany, in the case of people originating in Turkey, see Rainer Geissler, Horst Pöttker (Hrsg.) (2005), *Massenmedien und die Integration ethnischer Minderheiten in Deutschland*, Bielefeld, Transcript. Rüdiger Lohlker (2004), *Islam im Internet. Formen muslimischer Religiosität im Cyberspace*, Hamburg, Deutsches Orient Institut. Kai Hafez (Hrsg.) (2001), *Media and Migration. Ethnicity and Transculturality in the Media Age*, Schwerpunktheft der Zeitschrift NORD-SÜD aktuell 4. Heribert Schatz, Christina Holtz-Bacha, Jörg-Uwe Nieland (Hrsg.) (2000), *Migranten und Medien*, Wiesbaden, Westdeutscher Verlag. Kosnick Kira (2000), "Building Bridges: Media for Migrants and the Public-Service Mission in Germany", *European Journal of Cultural Studies*, No. 3, pp. 319-342.

[26] Monika Wohlrab-Sahr (1999), *Konversion zum Islam in Deutschland und den USA*, Frankfurt/M, Campus. Another significant example, converted Murad Hofmann, former ambassador of Germany in Algeria and in Morocco, and director of the information of NATO, is an important member of the Central Council of the Muslims which supported the recent adoption of the Islamic Charter of the German Muslims.

(Teblig), *Enfal* (Internet Magazine, Turkish language), *Huda* (Netzwerk für muslimische Frauen e. V.).

The young Muslim generation is becoming increasingly involved in the Muslim media in several European countries. They insist on the need to go beyond generational conflicts and national conflicts between Muslims of different backgrounds. They also aim to go beyond matters of post-colonial ideologies, and emphasise dialogue with national and European institutions.

They also seem open to women's participation. In Britain, Muslim women now have access to prominent roles as magazine editors and associations or as conference organisers.[27] Sarah Joseph was the first woman to become editor-in-chief of a Muslim magazine in Britain. She converted to Islam at the age of sixteen and studied religion at university on a scholarship provided by the King Faysal/Prince of Wales Chevening Foundation. After her experience at the helm of *Trends* in the second half of the 1990s, she reoriented her career towards consulting in Islamic affairs and the teaching of training courses. However, she is still a presence in the media, with appearances on televised programmes such as *Panorama* and *Dimbleby*. Other pioneers include Sara Kahn, the president of The Young Muslim Sisters, and Rehana Sadiq, who played a key role in the creation of the female branch of The Young Muslims UK at the end the 1980s, and then became an active member of The Islamic Society of Britain, a lobbying group associated with Muslim media organisations, which broadcasts on the internet. Since then, other young women have risen to production and management positions. Shagufta Yaqub became the editor in chief of the news and analysis monthly magazine *Q-News* in 2000 at the age of 24. She was replaced in 2004 by Fareena Alam, another recent university graduate.

---

[27] The following portraits have been more extensively described and analysed in Isabelle Rigoni (2006), "Women Journalists and Women's Press: Western Europe", *in* Alice Horner & Seteney Shami (ed.), *Encyclopedia of Women and Islamic Cultures*, Leiden, Brill; Isabelle Rigoni (2006), "Islamic Features in French and British Community Media", *in* Elizabeth Poole & John E. Richardson (ed.) (2006), *Muslims and the News Media*, London, I. B. Tauris, pp.74-86; Isabelle Rigoni (2004), "Médias musulmans britanniques. Les voix de la jeune generation", *in* Claire Cossée, Emmanuelle Lada et Isabelle Rigoni (dir.) (2004), *Faire figure d'étranger : regards croisés sur la production de l'altérité*, Paris, Armand Colin, coll. "Sociétales", pp.281-300.

These young women often come from families who emigrated in the 1960s and 1970s. Most of them say they have 'rediscovered' faith during their adolescence or in the transition to adulthood. Their religious commitment is intellectualised and their Islamic practice is reinterpreted. In a Western context and in a country where Islam is not the religion of the majority, the decision to wear the veil, rather than just a headscarf, is an especially strong statement. Some of these young women explain their wearing of the veil in terms of a personal quest for spirituality, others as proof of their political engagement in a world where they consider Islam threatened, and for some, both reasons are equally relevant.

The role of young women in the Muslim media in other European countries is also worth noting, despite a more recent and limited development. In France, the print magazine *Hawwa* specifically targets young Muslim women. Its staff, mostly female, is directed by Dora Mabrouk, a young woman of Maghrebi origin. Launching this media, she intended to create a platform for 'women's struggle'. *Hawwa* addresses women who wish to assert themselves as women, as French citizens and as Muslims. Both 'puritan and rebellious',[28] the young Muslim women discover and promote innovative practices in everyday life.

In Germany, a group of Muslim women, the *Netzwerk für muslimische Frauen e.V.*, started *Huda* magazine, available online at huda.de. In each case, a personal connection to Islam has influenced their professional orientation. While some women mention the difficulties they have faced finding a place in the mainstream media, their strong commitment to and participation in the Muslim media is the result of a personal choice closely tied to their religious activism. This choice does not prevent them from occasionally contributing to the mainstream media, particularly since 9/11. These contributions are considered complementary to their involvement in the Muslim media, and at the same time, serve both pedagogical (i.e., presenting information about Islam) and advertising purposes (i.e., by providing exposure to Muslim media).

The Muslim media have changed the perception of Muslims. They have drawn attention to the involvement of British and French Muslims in the home affairs of these two countries. Most of the Muslim media do

---

[28] Nadine Weibel (2000), *Par-delà le voile, femmes d'islam en Europe*, Bruxelles, Complexe.

indeed show a deep concern for notions and practices relating to citizenship and inclusion in multicultural and multi-religious societies. For young Muslims, the challenge is to show that they can be Muslims and Republicans in France (cf. issues of *La Medina* on 'Islam and the Fifth Republic' and 'Muslim France'), or Muslims and British in the UK. For young Muslim women in particular, the challenge is to show that they can 'fit their citizenship with their femininity', as the journalist Saïda Kada wrote in the French Muslim magazine *Hawwa*.

Ethnic media using NTIC are indeed challenging the boundaries. In Britain in particular, the Muslim media have become skilled at applying significant pressure on the local and national authorities. Civil society, through its actions and claims, notifies its respect for the state.[29] We have learnt from our case-studies that the Muslim media and most of the Muslim solidarity mobilisations are working for full inclusion in the European nation-states. Acting from within, they fully recognise state legitimacy.

Conclusions

There is a need to integrate the problems of the media with those of citizenship, representation and discrimination. It is understood that the representation of people from minority groups in the media influences public opinion, its stereotypes and thus its acceptance of the 'otherness' of society. Conversely, perceptions in public opinion about minority or marginalised groups will influence the representations exchanged in the media about these groups, especially as the professionals of the media (producing, writers, editors, journalists, scenario writers, advertising executives...) are full members of the societies in which they develop their activity.[30]

However the positioning of public opinion, in a democracy, is a determining element in the definition and implementation of public

---

[29] Jürgen Habermas (1997), *Droit et Démocratie: entre faits et normes*, Paris, Gallimard. M.W. Foley and B. Edwards (1996), "The paradox of civil society", *Journal of Democracy*, 7(3), pp. 38-52.

[30] Reynald Blion, Claire Frachon, Alec G. Hargreaves, Catherine Humblot, Isabelle Rigoni, Myria Georgiou, Sirin Dilli, *La représentation des immigrés au sein des media. Bilan des connaissances*, op. cit.

policies. In the field of integration and the fight against discrimination with regard to the people from minority or marginalised groups, public opinion can be a determining factor in the policies implemented. Thus, to modify the perception of opinion relating to minorities can be a positive element contributing to an increase in effectiveness of public policies. The ethnic media, and among them the Muslim media, can for their part influence the individual and collective forms of integration within 'their' community to work in favour of anti-discriminatory practices.

Media have a double responsibility in this direction, on the one hand, they influence the concerns of public opinion by determining the agenda and, on the other hand, they contribute towards creating a perception of reality by this same public opinion. Any policy, any action in the field of integration and the fight against discrimination must therefore include the media. In other words, the media – and in particular ethnic media – are one of the key groups of actors influencing the integration of minority or marginalised people and groups, and thus of their acceptance as belonging to society.

8. THE HEADSCARF QUESTION: WHAT IS REALLY THE ISSUE?

VALÉRIE AMIRAUX

Introduction

Dangerous, scary, intriguing, threatening, intimidating, oppressive, irritating, aggressive, traditional, conservative, reactionary ... These are a few of the adjectives one hears in discussions of what is confusingly called in European contexts not only the headscarf, but also the veil,[1] hijab, nikab, tchador, jilbab, burqa or khimar.[2] All these terms designate a scarf that

---

[1] In French both terms – *voile* (veil) or *foulard* (headscarf) - are used to refer to the Islamic headscarf, bringing more confusion than clarity to the discussion. In this text, I will stick to the use of 'headscarf', which I consider as purely descriptive, while 'veil' brings in a lot of Catholic symbolism that is not relevant to our analysis.

[2] All these words refer to a piece of clothing Muslim women put on when leaving their houses to go outside, but they belong to varying regional traditions. The *hijab* usually refers to a scarf covering the hair, neck and shoulders, and sometimes also the breasts (but in the Koran it refers to piece of cloth that serves more widely to hide, cover or screen an object or a person, therefore not only in the limited sense of headscarf). The *nikab* is a face veil that does not cover the eyes. The *tchador*, *djilbab* or *burqa,* cover the body and not only the head. The *burqa* is a single-piece garment, coloured, cloaking the entire body. The *tchador* (Persian) is a full length scarf, usually a semi-circle piece of cloth, thrown over the head and held by the hand. It goes with the *hijab* (under the *tchador*). Similarly, the *jilbab* (Arabic), which is also referred to in the Koran, designates a long garment, usually a coat, covering the entire body but not head, hands or feet. The use and wear of all these garments vary from one place to the other, from one generation to the other But they also refer to different regions, and do not have the same religious significance

Muslim women wear when outside the home to cover their hair, shoulders and breasts and, in some cases, their entire body including face and hands. The headscarf has become a sensitive issue, giving rise to legal disputes and political controversies in several EU member states, notably France, Belgium, Germany, the Netherlands and the UK.[3] Headscarves, and by definition the Muslim women wearing them, nowadays stand for "everything that is thought to be wrong with Islam".[4] In addition to being obliged to be bare-headed on ID documents as in France, women wearing the headscarf have also been excluded in courts, universities, work places, hospitals and city halls. While the terrain of exclusion is widening, the groups of people affected are also widening to include young girls (adolescents) as well as adults.

In most EU member states, the wearing of the Muslim headscarf is becoming a very awkward issue politically.[5] The religious dress of Muslim women has generated both moral panic[6] and hysteria.[7] In many cases overreaction has led to public obsession, with local incidents occupying national debate and attracting extensive press coverage. The debate surrounding the headscarf tends to touch upon numerous broader issues: the challenge to multiculturalism, the validity of secularism as a way of organising the pacific co-existence of different religions in European contexts, the securitisation of cultural markers and increasing Islamophobia, the loyalty of Muslim European citizens (converted or not) because of their alleged essential differences and 'otherness'. Last but not least, the headscarf controversies bring back to the surface very old

---

[3] With schools having been the primary arena for the explosion of clashes since the mid-1980s.

[4] J. Scott, (2005), "Symptomatic Politics. The Banning of Islamic Headscarves in French Public Schools", *French Politics, Culture & Society*, Vol. 23, 3, pp. 106-127.

[5] N. M. Thomas, (2005), "On Headscarves and Heterogeneity: reflections on the French foulard Affair", *Dialectical Anthropology*, 29, pp. 373-386.

[6] W. Schiffauer, (2006), "Enemies within the gates. The debate about the citizenship of Muslims in Germany", in T. Modood, A. Triandafyllidou and R. Zapata-Barrero (eds), *Multiculturalism, Muslims and Citizenship*, London: Routledge, pp. 94-116.

[7] E. Terray, (2004), "L'hystérie politique", in C. Nordmann (dir.), *Le foulard islamique en questions*, Paris, ed. Amsterdam.

conflicts resulting from the close relationship between states and the church in the EU.

Twenty years after the first controversies appeared on the European stage, much has been written on the headscarf by scholars, journalists, politicians, opinion-makers, religious leaders and others. The most striking aspect of the recent upsurge in debate surrounding the wearing of the Islamic headscarf in European contexts is probably the general feeling that everybody has something to say about it and feels concerned by it. Talking about the headscarf, having something to say about it and even taking a position (for or against) have become an obligation for every EU citizen. An important advantage in writing this kind of paper now rather than ten years ago is that the amount of knowledge has accumulated over the last years, for instance on the motivation of women in wearing a headscarf and the many dimensions of its significance.[8] Public awareness of the complexity of the matter is also much greater than it was twenty years ago.[9]

The dominant trend emerging in EU member states, from a political and legal point of view, is to ban the wearing of the headscarf in public institutions. Beyond the ethnographic data that help to map the differences from one context to the other and that have largely been commented upon, this paper focuses on the subtexts of the European headscarf controversy. How did this very pragmatic issue come, in varying degrees of intensity, to create such passionate national confrontations? Why is it that contrasted regimes of citizenship and traditionally opposed models of integration have given rise to similar public discussions on the Islamic headscarf in the European Union? What do headscarves stand for? Who do they speak for? The following text will try to answer this set of questions by looking at the hidden narratives behind the headscarf controversy, focusing on three elements of the debates: religion, gender and national identity.

---

[8] Not an exhaustive list but recent publications related to some of the contexts mentioned in this paper are Bowen (2006), Amir-Moazami (2007) and Mac Goldrick (2006).

[9] Particularly well-known is the empowering dimension of the wearing of the headscarf in specific contexts; see Göle (1996), El Guindi (1999) and Mahmood (2005).

8.1 The diversity of European headscarf controversies

Headscarf controversies can nowadays be found in many EU contexts. Most EU member states have faced a 'headscarf episode' with varying degrees of impact and types of decision. Most recently, *burqas*, rather than headscarves, have been at the centre of debate in the Netherlands[10] and in Belgium.[11] In France, the headscarf has periodically emerged as an issue since 1989, making the French situation a unique case for its precocity, longevity and intensity.[12] In 2004, the French parliament easily (in the sense that political consensus was reached) passed a law banning the wearing of ostentatious religious symbols from public schools. Part of the surrounding public debate dealt with the way French society defines itself, the confrontation between customary Islamic practices and Republican values being a challenge for French social cohesion and the representation of itself and its principles.[13] The European discussions on the right to wear an

---

[10] "In the course of the last years the term *burka* has been added to the Dutch vocabulary, as happened previously with terms such as *fatwa* and *jihad*". (Moors, 2007: 5).

[11] In Belgium, following the initiative of some members of the Flemish Christian Democrats, some local police regulations now include articles with standard prohibition for *burqas*. It is left to the municipalities to decide whether or not this should be implemented. Local bans on the public wearing of the *burqa* exist in parts of Flemish cities such as Maaseik, with fines being imposed on women continuing to wear it. This echoes the local anti-burqa campaigning organised by the Northern League (Lega Nord) in Italy.

[12] For a perspective on the changing dimensions of the headscarf, see Gaspard & Khosrokhavar (1995) and Lorcerie (2005).

[13] Some observers have noted that the intense headscarf discussions acted as a substitute for other central social difficulties in France (integration, male-female relationships, unemployment) in explaining the abstraction of the discussion and its locus in the "sphère éthérée des grands principes" (ethereal sphere of grand principles) (Terray, 2004: 112). As a matter of fact, the female students were never really an issue, while the symbolic significance of their clothing was. Nor were they seriously interviewed by the different commissions created for the purpose of debating the headscarf (see the Commission created in July 2003 by the French President of the Republic to work on the national conditions of implementation of *laïcité* and the mission of information on the question of religious signs, created by the Parliament created in May 2003).

Islamic headscarf generally focus on abstract principles with the exclusion of central questions like children's rights.[14][15] In her report for the United Nations, Asma Jahangir, for instance, points out one of the paradoxes of the French March 2004 law: although its stated aim is to protect minors from being obliged to wear a headscarf or any other religious symbols, at the same time the law is an obstacle to those who choose freely to wear such a symbol, following their own conviction.[16] In these public discussions, Muslim pupils wearing the headscarf ended up being criticised without ever having a real opportunity to speak.[17] How dare French female citizens display their difference by wearing a sign whose meaning is not culturally part of the national historical trajectory? Before the passing of the March 2004 law, the liberal reading provided by the French Council of State (the highest administrative tribunal) in 1989 was the frame of reference for articulating the neutrality of the state and individual religious freedom, 'public order' being the key notion in deciding whether or not to ban an individual from public schools (whereas, as mentioned earlier, German agencies would have referred to religious pluralism). The Council of State's 1989 decision basically stated that none of the constitutional principles (neutrality and freedom of conscience) could be said to take precedence over the other and that every case should be treated individually in a 'case by case' perspective (Conseil d'Etat, 2004).

The passion – or, it might even be said, the hysteria – involved in the French 2003-04 discussion strongly contrasts with the silence, if not to say the indifference, of other European contexts where accommodations were

---

[14] Nor are the psychological, spiritual and cultural effects of the ban as an assault against women reviewed: the spiritual injury, defilement, silence, denial, shame, guilt, fear, violence, blaming the victim, self-destructive behaviour, 'emotional death'....

[15] E. Brems, (2006), "Above Children's Heads. The headscarf Controversy in European Schools from the Perspective of Children's Rights", *The International Journal of Children's Rights*, 14, pp. 119-136.

[16] Jahangir, A. (2006), *Droits civils et politiques, notamment la question de l'intolérance religieuse. (Additif mission en France)*, Rapport, Commission des droits de l'Homme, ONU, March.

[17] P. Tévanian (2005), *Le voile médiatique. Un faux débat: "l'affaire du foulard"*, Paris, raisons d'agir.

found (as in the UK until autumn 2006), or where distinctions are clearly drawn between users and agents of public services. For instance, in Germany, since 1993 pupils wearing the Islamic headscarf can ask to be exempted from sport lessons (*Bundesverwaltungsgericht*, 25/98/93; InfAuslR1994, 59). In a Constitutional Court decision of September 2003, banning the wearing of the Islamic headscarf for teachers is considered to be constitutional only if motivated by the protection of constitutional values and grounded on a precise legal basis. The central affair in the German context is based on a primary and secondary school teacher named Fereshta Ludin. The Constitutional Court does not give more weight to the obligation of neutrality of a public agent (in this case, respect of parents and children's freedom of belief) than to individual freedom of conscience. Ludin defended herself by arguing that the headscarf was part of her personality and made visible an internal conviction. The ruling of the Constitutional Court overturned the decision by the Administrative Federal Court, which said that the headscarf should not be banned, also to protect religious peace in the country.[18] The Constitutional Court decision opened the way to local legislation. For instance, in January 2007, the Bavarian Constitutional Court upheld a 2004 state law that bans teachers from wearing religious headscarves. This decision follows the initiative of an Islamic association suing the Bavarian state for not respecting the Bavarian constitution and eliminating Muslim symbols from public life. In the German context, headscarves can be banned only by state law, not following an administrative decision. By early 2007, 8 out of 16 Länder had already passed a law banning headscarves.

In the French as in the German contexts, headscarves cannot be taken as 'classic' public policy objects as are the requests for the construction of a mosque or the opening of a private Islamic school. Wearing a headscarf is a private matter, the result of an individual choice. In some contexts (France), it has to be restricted, in other ones (Germany), it has to be protected. Headscarves do not directly relate to worshipping activities, nor are they systematically the result of social coercion by religious authorities, especially in European contexts. They are mostly situated between a private matter (potentially indicating the faith of an individual, but not

---

[18] C. Skach (2006), "Leyla Sahin v. Turkey and 'Teacher Headscarf Case', Case No. 2BvR 1436/02", *American Journal of International Law*, Vol. 100, No. 1, pp. 186-196.

only that) that apparently troubles political authorities and leads them to legislate, and a public issue that attracts conflicting narratives and engages competing public moralities. The argument that integration fails whenever cultural differences become visible is a strong one, in particular if the visible identity markers seem inconsistent with democracy and equality. Differences can only be visible and legitimate in the private sphere, the privatisation of these differences being the most diffused strategy for the good functioning of liberal European democracies (Barry, 2001).[19] In the French context, the discussion about the place to be given to cultural rights was never properly launched as it interferes with the Republican representation of national cohesion through unity.[20]

In the British context, addressing religious diversity in schools has recently become the opening to talk about culture and multiculturalism.[21] The controversy became a nationwide issue after Jack Straw (then leader of the House of Commons) publicly stated his disapproval of the wearing of the veil (i.e. covering all the face except the eyes), giving as his reason that it is an obstacle to good community relations. More generally in the UK, religion today has a similar function in race relations discussions that colour used to have (in the 1960s), race (in the 1970s and 1980s) or ethnicity in the 1990s.[22] In the hijab/djilbab and dress code in public schools debate (2006-07), the central question remains how far schools should be required to go to accommodate the increasingly diverse faiths that now compose British society? The picture is further complicated by the introduction of rules imposed by the EU directives.[23] In the UK, the jilbab became an issue

---

[19] B. Barry (2001), *Culture and Equality: An Egalitarian Critique of Multiculturalism*, Cambridge, MA: Harvard University Press.

[20] V. Amiraux and P. Simon (2006), "'There are no minorities here': Cultures of Scholarship and Public Debate on Immigrants and Integration in France", *International Journal of Comparative Sociology*, 47 (3-4), pp. 191-215.

[21] The traditional way of dealing with dress code issues in the UK context stems from the Mandla v. Dowell Lee affair. This case has established protection for the rights of religious minorities by using provisions of race discrimination legislation.

[22] C. Peach (2006), "Islam, ethnicity and South Asian Religions in the London 2001 census", *Transactions of the Institute of British Geographers*, NS 31(3), pp. 353-370.

[23] In Britain, the discussion focuses very much on compulsory religious education in schools plus a daily act of worship.

after the highly publicised case of S. Begum, defended by the lawyer Cherie Blair (the then Prime Minister's wife). A pupil at a North Luton public school since 2000 (where 80% of the pupils are Muslims), Shabina Begum started wearing the jilbab in 2002, after the school year had started, contravening the school's internal dress code. In a first decision, the breach of Begum's freedom of religion was recognised and the school was asked to reconsider the decision to exclude her (2004). On appeal, the House of Lords took the opposite position, stating there had been no violation of the plaintiff's religious freedom (Article 9 of the European Convention on Human Rights).[24]

As underlined by Lord Bingham of Cornhill, "this case concerns a particular pupil and a particular school in a particular place at a particular time". Like the French Council of State in 1989, the Parliament cannot be asked to decide whether a British school should or should not accept a student wearing Islamic clothes. Relying on the arguments of the ECHR, Lord Bingham goes on to specify that Article 9 rights are not absolute and may even be limited. While sustaining the authority of the head of school, Lord Bingham of Cornhill underlines his awareness of the school's ethnic diversity: the dress code gave the possibility to many students to express their religious distinction by wearing specific clothes "in an inclusive, unthreatening and uncompetitive way" (Lord Bingham of Cornhill, Opinions of the Lords of Appeal, 2006, UKHL 15, §34). S. Begum was excluded because of the breach of the school uniform rules, with no violation of Article 9: the multicultural and multi-faith based school had the right to limit her rights in protection of others' rights. The British decision is consistent with the Sahin decision in the sense that it recognises the interference with one's right to manifest one's religion, and this

---

[24] Article 9 of the European Convention on Human Rights states:

1. Everyone has the right to freedom of thought, conscience and religion; this right includes freedom to change his religion or belief, and freedom, either alone or in community with others and in public or private, to manifest his religion or belief, in worship, teaching, practice and observance.

2. Freedom to manifest one's religion or beliefs shall be subject only to such limitations as are prescribed by law and are necessary in a democratic society in the interests of public safety, for the protection of public order, health or morals, or the protection of the rights and freedoms of others.

interference of the public state authorities is considered legitimate. Her right to education had not been denied in the sense that she could go to alternative schools or be educated at home.[25]

8.2 Religion in secular Europe: what is religious? What is politics?

In secular Europe, the diminishing impact of religion on social behaviour is seen as related to the modernisation processes, in particular to an increased individualisation of religious affiliations (the 'do-it-yourself' perspective) and to its 'privatisation' as the solution to cultural conflicts (Barry, 2001). Politics, culture and social morality are supposed to remain independent of any religious influence. Morality has therefore become a personal concern. Religion is supposed to have a declining influence on society, the authority of the church being diminished. To summarise, the secularisation process goes together with the privatisation of beliefs. European citizens are supposed to relate to society as autonomous, responsible, reflective entities.[26] Given that secularisation refers primarily to the idea that religious values and behaviours are shaped by individuals, it is no surprise that quantitative evidence of secularisation relies mostly on an assessment of personal religiosity. In that context, church attendance illustrates the decline of a more traditional institutional religiosity.[27] But, as pointed out by many authors, different patterns of religious decline should be seen in relation to differences between denominational cultures (Protestants and Catholics): in the Catholic French context for instance, discussion about decline centred on the defence of secularism, while in the Protestant-Catholic German one, it centred on the need to protect religious pluralism. The political horizon contrasts religious pluralism in Germany, the

---

[25] A. Blair and Will Aps (2005), "What not to wear and other stories: Addressing religious diversity in schools", *Education and the Law*, Vol. 17, No. 1-2, March/June, pp. 1-22.

[26] L. Halman and O. Riise (eds), (2003), *Religion in a Secularizing Society: The Europeans' Religion at the End of the 20th Century (European Values Study, 5)*, The Hague: Brill.

[27] Churches have been challenged by the emergence of religious pluralism and voluntarism, exposing them to competition between worldviews, relativisation of their regime of truth, introducing the perspective of a voluntary membership rather than a socially compulsory one.

secularist regime in France,[28] with some German politicians explicitly rejecting all forms of importation of the French secular tradition into the German context. The central role of the Constitution in the German context, on the one hand, tends to restrict individual freedom of religion in the name of the protection of a dominant Christian tradition, and, on the other hand, promotes or protects cultural religious plurality. This last point prevents the headscarf from being perceived as a symbol of cultural political segregation. The principle of *laïcité* was used similarly in France: on the one hand, to motivate the banning of the headscarf; on the other, to defend its authorisation in public schools.

The wearing of an Islamic headscarf is linked to personal religiosity, i.e. the more emotional part of religious commitment.[29] It results from an individual choice and a rather diffuse religiosity, with no consensus from the religious authorities in determining whether there is an obligation or not to wear it. In the headscarf controversies, however, political authorities and grassroots citizens intervene simultaneously to determine whether a religiously motivated gesture can be tolerated or not in European democratic liberal societies. Religious beliefs cease therefore to be a matter of purely personal preference and again become the subject of public argument in political and moral terms. The discussions that took place in different contexts were never really about religion defined as a system of beliefs and practices oriented toward the sacred or supernatural, affecting the way of live of the individual believers. Liberal secularism (radical in its French version, more flexible in the British one) is based on a confessional freedom: people can believe what they want in the private sphere. As a consequence, the public space is a realm based on a cultural consensus that overrides individual liberty and it is based on the idea that practice can be reduced to preferences and choices. But can practices be dissociated from

---

[28] Amir Moazami sees it differently and considers that the reading in terms of civilisational paradigm ('Christian heritage' or 'Christian-Occidental background of German society') restricts the pluralistic character of society and attributes to the Christian hemisphere a monopoly on the secularisation theorem. "While in France the notion of secularity has been interpreted in terms of a rupture from the Christian past, in Germany it has been regarded as implying a continuity of the Christian tradition", (Amir-Moazami, 2005: 271).

[29] This supposes a variety of ways of living one's faith on a scale from religion as a cultural attribute to symbolic identification or normativity guiding everyday life.

convictions (or, in other words, should religion be relegated to the private sphere to make pluralism viable)?

At this stage, we are still left with a series of unanswered questions related to the issue of the "justiciability" (Skach, 2006) of religious freedom in secular contexts (i.e. restricting religious freedom in the name of religious neutrality in EU member states). If religion is a private matter, then why do states care about it? Is cultural distinction a threat to liberal European democracies? From the legal point of view, the claims for equality made by Muslims living in Europe are put forward in a context where religious freedom is no longer absolute. Religions are cultural and historical variables, social and cultural interpretative systems. They are constituents of communities and produce meanings that shape collective as well as individual lives of the members of the community. A belief referring to the personal way one relates to his/her own religion, is probably the easiest term to use in this reflection on 'what is at stake when banning the Islamic headscarf' as it encompasses a wide spectrum of differing worldviews, including non-religious ones. It seems to me, however, that the public controversy on the wearing of the headscarf has completely ignored a more intimate part of belief: that is the 'religiosity' of individuals. I use the term as a reference to the intimate and inventive way in which an individual performs his/her link to a corpus of dogma. In a secular context, the individual is indeed the only reference for the meaning and the justification to give to his/her actions and social behaviours. In a way, religiosity is what makes religion concrete and visible in society: it gives meaning to action, and it may help one to recognise others as well as helping others to recognise you. In that context, the headscarf represents shared identities but also conflicting ones. The idea of a believer performing his religion on a daily basis remains rather exogenous to the discussion even though it is central to the definition of collective identities that signify to members of a group and to the world who they are, what they stand for and what kind of society they hope to create. However, the absence of the voices of the Muslim women wearing headscarves is a shared European characteristic in the national public debate. This has been underlined by Judge Tulkens in the Sahin ECHR judgement: for instance the opinion of Muslim women, both those who wear headscarves and those who don't wear them, is missing in the debate.

The strengthening of public positions towards the wearing of the Islamic headscarf in public circumstances tends to affirm the necessity to limit religious freedom in secular contexts. In some cases, the difference between one system and another (established church, *laicité*, concordate type of church and state relationship) as well as the various definitions of 'disturbances of public order' may become an incentive for European judges to plead for the limitation of the right to wear a headscarf. The European Court of Human Rights (ECHR) at the moment supports the more restrictive member states on this matter (see *Dahlab c. Suisse* in 2001, and more recently *Leyla Sahin c. Turquie* in 2005).[30] According to the ECHR, religious freedom is not absolute and can even be restricted, as in the case of the Islamic headscarf, which does not fit into the European framework of the protection of human rights, public freedoms and public security. Restriction of religious freedom is seen as a necessity in a democratic context. ECHR is, however, extremely cautious in adopting the points made by national authorities. In the Sahin case, the European Court twice points out that there is no violation of freedom of thought, conscience, and religion under Convention article 9 (plus there is no separate question arising from that in conjunction with other Articles of the Convention, for details see Skach, 2006; Bribosia and Rorive, 2004). The ECHR expresses its consideration that the restriction is necessary in democratic societies on the basis that the wearing of the headscarf may impact on others (Blair et al., 2005: 7). The Court adopts a contextual reading of the Turkish case in defending the university president's decision to forbid the wearing of the headscarf on campus.[31] The subsequent decisions by Turkish jurisdictions have since then been validated by this European support: there has been interference with Miss Sahin's individual religious freedom (recognised by the Court), but this is justified by the protection of public order.[32] To a certain extent, the ECHR's position on Sahin interprets the meaning of the

---

[30] Complete references are Dahlab v. Switzerland, App. 42393/98, 15 February 2001; Sahin v. Turkey, App. No. 44774/98 (Eur. Ct. H.R. November 10, 2005) Grand Chamber. All decisions related to religious freedom and article 9 can be found at http://www.echr.coe.int.

[31] The text mentions the challenge of fundamentalism, the need for religious pluralism, highlighting the social dimension of the problem posed by the plaintiff. On the contrary, there is no mention at all of gender equality, a central topic in the equivalent European discussion.

[32] E. Bribosia and I. Rorive (2004), "Le voile à l'école: Une Europe divisée", *Revue trimestrielle des droits de l'homme*, 60, pp. 951-983.

headscarf as political, which is highly arguable in a non-Muslim context.[33] As stated by Baroness Hale of Richmond on S. Begum's jilbab, none of the arguments of the Western feminists describing the Islamic headscarf as a symbol of oppression of whoever chooses to wear it, can be considered as justification for its ban. (Baroness Hale of Richmond, Opinions of the Lords of Appeal, 2006, UKHL 15, §96).

The headscarf controversies in a post 9/11 context are characterised by the culturalisation of socially sensitive issues related to risk and security. Different frames (migration, security, terrorism, secularism) overlap in the public discussion so that Muslim women with headscarves have become new icons in the landscape of enemies of European values. In EU controversies, their headscarf stands for political threat, gender oppression, religious fanaticism, terrorism, political incorrectness, poor socio-economic conditions and illiteracy. The real motivations of young women in wearing the veil are practically irrelevant. For Muslims living in non-Muslim contexts, this specific stigmatisation has increased the social cost of presenting oneself, as Muslim cultural racism is no longer only a discourse, but also leads to acts of discrimination in several areas of social life (employment, education, housing, health). Thus, headscarf controversies do not only operate as a public discussion of symbols, they also imply practices of exclusion of particular bodies performing and speaking from within national societies. A headscarf is not exotic since it is worn within European societies, by European citizens. Women wearing headscarves make things concrete and have confronted public opinion with visible practices as opposed to abstract principles. Moreover, these women have contributed to the awareness of the gendered dimension of national models of cohesion, merging issues of public morality and national unity.

---

[33] This is completely different from the opinion delivered by the United Nations Committee on Human Rights (Rahon Hudiyberganova v. Uzbekistan, 931/2000, 18 January 2005). It recognises the right of a veiled student who was excluded from a State Institute for Oriental languages (Tachkent) because of her headscarf. Article 18 (freedom of thought, conscience and religion) of the International Convention on civil and political rights had been violated. But the Committee did not retain the headscarf as a political symbol.

8.3   Gendered practices and real bodies

Headscarf controversies are complex issues referring to intricate situations in which it is not easy to identify the motives of discrimination and map the boundaries. What is indeed really at stake? Race, ethnicity, religion, gender? Headscarf controversies mix, for instance, gender, race and religious issues (not to mention in some cases the place of residence, and other socio-economic factors). Wearing the headscarf, women become visible twice, first as members of a religious minority (the Muslim believers), second as gendered social actors (women). Women wearing the headscarf therefore experience double discrimination as a result of the combination of their gender and race/religion characteristics. Moreover, women and girls are more subject to dress restrictions than men.[34] Headscarf controversies and related public debates are intricate situations in which nobody knows where the boundaries are, how to classify the discourses and actions or what categories to use to better describe the situation. The category of gender is only partially useful to the understanding of headscarf controversies and it is only recently that specialists of gender issues and feminist theories have entered the discussions on the Islamic headscarf in European societies. The gender perspective is often absent or marginalised. "Where gender is raised, it most often takes the form of a distinction and an opposition between 'the Western/European woman' and 'the other Oriental/migrant woman'".[35] At the European level, the Dahlab v. Switzerland was the first case in which the ECHR explicitly referred to the gender dimension issue, invoking the principle of gender equality as a further justification to ask the Muslim convert teacher to remove her headscarf.

Dress is not only about culture, but is mostly about politics, in religious as well as in secular societies (Mahmood, 2005). "Through the medium of the veil therefore, Muslim women's bodies are gender-coded and form a "cultural text" for the expression of social, political, and

---

[34] Commonly in Europe, the public debate on women's way of dressing reminds us of the imbalance between the political justification for the intervention of authorities in the case of women, while men's clothing is largely ignored.

[35] D. Lyon and D. Spini (2004), "Unveiling the headscarf debate", *Feminist Legal studies*, 12, pp. 333-345.

religious meanings".[36] In the EU context, headscarves are not the only controversial garments inside public schools and universities. In the Dutch context, for example, dress codes ban the headscarf, belly shirt and bomber jacket together, thus addressing and requesting regulation on behalf of the offence some clothes cause to a certain group of the population, to the discrimination of others (Duits and van Zoonen, 2006).[37][38] 'Porno chic' is considered an offence to decency. But decency is never an issue when debating publicly about the Islamic headscarf. Rather, the young woman in a headscarf inside public schools is seen as repressed. However, the discussion on the way certain students dress inappropriately at school is never, as is the case of the headscarf, explicitly mentioning the sexual practices that are associated with it. Clearly, what "holds the two seemingly separate debates about headscarves and porno-chic together is the regulation of girls' sexuality". (Duits, Van Zoonen, 2006: 111, see also 105-108). Thus, maybe debates on such apparently opposite issues (the headscarf on the one hand, porno chic on the other) should be analysed together as "part of a single hegemonic discourse about women's sexuality that transcend this partition". (Duits, van Zoonen, 2006, 104) Indeed, the headscarf is often identified by people who do not wear it (Muslims as well as non-Muslims) as part of a broad-scale system of domination that affects women as a class.

Muslim women with a headscarf living in Europe operate a double detachment: first towards tradition in a double perspective (distance from previous generations, distance towards cultural interpretations of dogma); second, towards European expectations of how they should behave (politically, culturally and sexually). The conformity to a norm of sexual

---

[36] J. Zine (2006), "Unveiled sentiments: Gendered Islamophobia and experiences of Veiling among Muslim Girls in a Canadian Islamic School", *Equity & Excellence in Education*, 39, pp. 239-252.

[37] The connection between decent dress and headscarf is not a newcomer to the debate. I remember the interviews I conducted with followers of Milli Görüs in Germany from 1992 to 1996 and the connection between being authorised to wear a headscarf if others wear a miniskirt was often made by my Muslim interviewees. (Amiraux, 2001).

[38] L. Duits and L. van Zoonen (2006), "Headscarves and Porno-Chic: Disciplining Girls' Bodies in the European Multicultural Society", *European Journal of Women's Studies*, 13, pp. 103-117.

behaviour ends up being central in the agenda of the public discussion on the legitimacy or not of wearing a headscarf in public schools;[39] as is the corollary stigmatisation of deviant sexual behaviours by young male of North African origin. "In order to mask new forms of social and economic domination experienced by working-class young people of non-European origin (i.e. Black and Arab), it has become necessary and sufficient to stigmatise the 'sexual deviance' of Arab boys and thereby invoke the need to impose a 'civilised' sexual norm, the quintessential and most recent expression of an integrationist imperative".[40] This illustrates the spread of racism "through the belief, which is gaining currency in France, that there is an ongoing war between the sexes in the disadvantaged suburbs" (Guénif, 2006: 23). In the French context, the suburbs represent the threat to security and communal existence. Muslim women not wearing the headscarf have played a central part in this process and definitely contributed to the call for the regulation of the appearance and bodies of other women. Through the controversies and the active participation of women from all sides in the condemnation of the headscarf, Islamophobia became gendered. The various public discourses on the headscarf (and on its ban) deny the Muslim female subjects their agency and autonomy by denying them *ex ante* the right to speak up through their headscarf, and participate in a discussion on the meaning of their dress code.

8.4 Promoting equality in religiously and culturally plural societies

In all European member states, headscarf controversies included the issue of personal choice and individual freedom of choice, the protection of the freedom of religion, gender equality, and secularism. Just as there is no European policy on religious matters, there is no consensus concerning the way national states should cooperate on the policy towards Islam and Muslims. Wearing the headscarf in public schools is therefore still an issue on which there is no convergence between EU member states. The absence of a common attitude on this specific subject is no surprise as there are

---

[39] N. Guenif-Souilmas and E. Macé (2004), *Les féministes et le garçon arabe*, Paris: De l'Aube.

[40] N. Guénif-Souilamas (2006), "The Other French exception. Virtuous Racism and the War of the Sexes in Postcolonial France", *French Politics, Culture and Society*, Vol. 24, 3, pp. 23-41.

different patterns of secularisation coexisting in Europe. Secularisation was either implemented as a consequence of political confrontation, or as an outcome of the differentiation of roles amongst institutions. This brings us back to the validity of the contextual approach: general principles need to be looked at in their interpretation and application in very specific contexts.[41]

Two main positions can be identified in the EU member states' domestic discussion of the legitimacy of wearing a headscarf as a female Muslim European citizen. First, the accommodating position (dominant in the '80s but decreasing since the '90s) of public authorities towards the request by Muslim women to wear a headscarf in their lives as European citizens,[42] and second, the position adopted by those who wish to ban this behaviour from certain parts of the public sphere. Theoretically, European legal receptiveness to religious and cultural diversity would be grounded in the public neutrality of liberal states. This does not fit with the current tendency of national models that move back towards more restrictive definitions of cohesive citizenship. In a culturally plural society, the fight against discrimination is a central element of the organisation of pacified coexistence between competing interpretative systems (as in the case of religions) or between conflicting values (as in neutrality of the state versus individual freedom of religion). For instance, in the Dutch case, prohibiting the wearing of the headscarf cannot be justified in the sense that it would contravene anti-discrimination law and such a move would constitute a case for direct discrimination.[43] This Commission on Equal Treatment view was exceptionally not respected when the safety of the individuals was at

---

[41] J. Carens (2004), The weight of context: Headscarfs in Holland, Journal of Ethical Theory and Moral Practice, Springer Netherlands, Volume 7, No. 2, April.

[42] The situation of Muslim police officers is well known. For instance, in January 2000, a discussion took place in the Netherlands about whether or not to maintain the accommodation making it possible to wear a headscarf in all police departments except in the mobile force for reasons of security. In 2001, the new police uniform did not include 'blue police' headscarf. Here accommodation of religious and ethnic specific requests was motivated by practical, pragmatic motivations and awareness of the impact of such a decision on public opinion. (Verhaar & Saharso, 2004).

[43] S. Saharso and O. Verhaar (2006), "Headscarves in the Police force and the Court: Does Context Matter?", *Acta Politica*, 41, pp. 68-86.

stake. For similar 'no discrimination' motives, the French decision on the banning of the headscarf in public schools (March 2004 Law) does not mention any specific item but refers to "ostentatious signs of religious belonging". In the British context, until December 2003 it was somehow 'lawful' to discriminate against Muslims as Muslims because the courts did not accept that Muslims are an ethnic group. Then an offence of religious discrimination was created but confined to employment (in respect of the EU's Equality in Employment Directive), and Muslims are now protected as members of an ethnic group.

From one context to another in the European Union, similar fundamental rights are being challenged (freedom of expression, freedom of religion versus neutrality, freedom of 'the other' and public order), but the reactions of member states range from a complete ban (French law 2004-228 of March, 2004) to public discussion with no legal decision (as in Italy). There is no consensus on the way to approach the meaning of the headscarf: is it an individual free choice? Is it a religious obligation related to specific circumstances? In the German context, the headscarf was qualified as a sign of 'cultural segregation'.[44] Discussions are accelerating in the Netherlands in the sense of a ban of the *burqa* (facial veil) worn by a tiny minority of women, mostly Dutch converts, even if the new Integration Minister, Ella Vogelaar, recently declared that such a ban would be stigmatising and counter-productive.[45] One of the claims made by the supporters of a ban in the UK suggested this practice has consequences on the integration of women (access to the job market). This claim seems to be quite popular in other contexts: in a poll by IPSOS Mori for ITV (October, 2006), 61% of the British interviewees declared that Muslim women are segregating themselves by wearing a headscarf. Different forms of anti-discrimination legislation are, however, insufficient. Equality before the

---

[44] S. Amir-Moazami (2005), "Muslim Challenges to the Secular Consensus: A German Case Study", *Journal of Contemporary European Studies*, Vol. 13, No. 3, pp. 267-286.

[45] Face covering is also a problem in Muslim contexts. See, for instance, the declaration in January 2007 by the Egyptian Minister of Culture qualifying the wearing of the headscarf of obscurantism. Full face cover (the niqab) is denied for public officers.

law is a major but insufficient achievement and deep-seated discriminatory structures survive.

What do school authorities aim to prevent by regulating the wearing of the headscarf or, more broadly as in the French law, the wearing of symbols that express religious belonging? The answer includes peace inside schools, the emancipation of girls not wearing the headscarf and protection of them vis-à-vis more 'orthodox' members of the same community of belief. What dominates in the European contexts is deductive reasoning setting up hierarchies between values as a result of the confrontation of competing principles. Almost no space is left for proper consideration of the context, or for the cultural norms eventually framing them. The problem in deciding whether or not an agent of any public institution (police, education, hospital, prisons) could be seen with a specific religious symbol (headscarf) is related to the fact that these individuals represent the public face of authority and thus must be must be impartial and neutral and recognised as such. The classification of the different values/principles that are said to be brought into discussion by the fact that women living in Europe still wish to wear a headscarf varies from one country to the other. Usually, the principle of freedom of religion is assessed as non-absolute. This is reflected in the body of European case-law governing the freedom of religion (and the right to manifest one's own religion).

Concluding remarks and questions

The exclusion of Muslim women wearing the headscarf from specific public functions and institutions seems likely to become an increasingly general rule. Given both the intensity (sometimes almost hysteria) and confusion surrounding these issues in many European countries, I conclude with some suggestions as to how to calm public discussion about Islamic headscarves.

Firstly, most of the political and legal reasoning related to the headscarf affairs adopts a deductive approach that confronts normative principles explaining the opposition of the parties (in most cases, the neutrality of the state, sexual equality versus freedom of religion and non-discrimination). Considering the different constitutional court (or equivalent) decisions when they were asked to give their opinion on this matter, it seems impossible to make a final decision on the basis of pure abstract reasoning principles (see *Conseil d'Etat* or *Bundesverfassungsgsericht*). It seems therefore essential to insist on the need to understand principles systematically in relation to local and individual situations. Any case is specific and needs to be considered in relation to the context of its emergence.

Secondly, less politicisation and more 'juridicisation' of the headscarf controversies may be a provisional solution to solve conflict. By 'juridicisation' I hereby refer to the use, by individuals, of juridical tools and arenas (courts) to seek satisfaction of their needs and answers to their complaints. This would of course give principles, norms and values a central place, but it would also give importance to the narratives brought by the victims (the Muslim women). National decisions in the headscarf controversies lack accountability. A better and more systematic use of legal resources would constitute a step towards accountability in the equal treatment of Muslim citizens in the enlarged EU.

Thirdly, the role of international bodies is central in this search for accountability. ECHR's decisions and suggestions have stated that religious freedom is not an absolute value. It can be restricted on conditions that these restrictions are motivated and argued. Considering the passionate nature of national discussions, the ECHR can be seen as a central arbiter of citizens and state interactions. More precisely, in the European context of promotion of equality, neutrality should not disproportionately disadvantage minority groups and non-national institutions could be the guarantors of the respect for different principles and fundamental rights framing the lives of individual citizens.

Fourthly, headscarf controversies reveal the porosity of borders that have been taken for granted, the border between private and public as well as of that between religious and secular spheres of social activities. While some theories of secularisation have claimed that religion would disappear from public life through the individual emancipation of citizens, the religious part of the political functioning of society returns to the domestic agenda by addressing the issues of national cohesion and unity. Policy-makers and decision-makers should elaborate more on what is unsaid about religion in European liberal democracies, as a priority at the local level, on the basis of deliberation and public discussion with citizens.

Fifthly and finally, new maps of inequality and experiences of injustice are becoming visible, in particular for individuals embedded in the complex and intersectional context of oppression and discrimination. The headscarf is not only about symbols. It is not only the headscarf that is being excluded; it is individuals and their bodies too.

9. ISLAMOPHOBIA AND ITS CONSEQUENCES

CHRIS ALLEN

Introduction

"Islamophobia is the shorthand way of referring to dread or hatred of Islam – and, therefore, to fear or dislike of all or most Muslims",[1] wrote the Commission on British Muslims and Islamophobia in the Runnymede report a decade ago. Widely accepted as the definition of Islamophobia, and given the report's impact, it might come as some surprise that only five years ago, the term and concept of Islamophobia had little discursive relevance or value beyond the UK.

Today, the situation is completely changed. Nowadays, Islamophobia emerges from many bi-polar extremes: from those who denounce any criticism of Muslims or Islam whatsoever as Islamophobic, to those who actively and openly espouse a vitriolic hatred of Islam and Muslims founded upon various ideological justifications. Consequently, little clear thinking or expression rarely – if indeed ever – comes into the equation as regards its usage or understanding. From the high-profile murder of Theo van Gogh in the Netherlands and the ensuing backlash against Muslims, to complaints about irresponsible parking during Friday prayers, these disparate and myriad events are indiscriminately incorporated into the discourse of Islamophobia. Islamophobia in many ways therefore remains an undifferentiated and bland term, employed to satisfy or appease in numerous and to various degrees.

---

[1] Runnymede Trust (1997), Commission on British Muslims and Islamophobia, *Islamophobia: a challenge for us all: report of the Runnymede Trust Commission on British Muslims and Islamophobia*, London: Runnymede Trust, p. 1.

With the term now being much more widely used, Islamophobia has since found a resonance or presence in the increasingly mediatised societies that we inhabit. At the same time the media is being earmarked as one of the most virulent producers of those stereotypical misunderstandings of Muslims and Islam that allegedly underpin such discourses and understandings. In the political sphere, remarks that continue to invoke Huntington's 'clash of civilisations' thesis abound, from Berlusconi's now infamous remarks about Islam being a backward 'civilisation' to the wide-ranging debates currently raging in France, the UK and the Netherlands surrounding the wearing of the hijab, niqab and burqa respectively. In each setting, allegations also abound that such apparel constitute a barrier to integration and in some ways, a barrier to being French, British and Dutch respectively. It is not only in those countries where large Muslim communities are present but so too in Belgium, where headscarves and other forms of Muslim dress have been banned at the local level in many schools.[2] And so, quite irrespective of geographical or national settings, it would be unlikely that in the past five years some claim or counter-claim regarding Islamophobia had not been played out through the media, political or public spaces in most parts of Europe. Few would have been able to avoid the allegations of the growing menace that either Islam or Muslims are said to present or, from an alternative perspective, the growing prevalence of Europe's Islamophobia. Either way, one's perspective remains always subjective and open to disagreement.

One possible consequence of this has been the intense scrutiny and interrogation of the roles and responsibilities of Europe's Muslim communities. Beyond the mainstream political spaces – and in some circumstances even within them – this has been the catalyst for a more virulent and open discourse about Muslims and Islam to emerge. At the same time, evidence might also point towards a more willing and receptive audience to such a discourse. The rise of the British National Party (BNP) in the UK is an example of the type of protagonists promoting such a discourse, the ever-widening concerns about 'security' and 'anti-terror' forming the backdrop against which a greater receptivity is grounded. At the same time, numerous legislative measures, political debates, policy recommendations and cultural awareness programmes have sought to

---

[2] IHF (2005), Intolerance and Discrimination against Muslims in the EU: Developments since September 11, March.

challenge and potentially halt what is seen by some to be a downward spiralling acceptance of such discourses. The situation is therefore far from one-sided and one cannot apportion blame against all Europeans and their governments, as indeed some commentators and agitators have attempted. From within some Muslim communities themselves also, a two-pronged response has also begun to emerge. If security sources are to be believed, a shift towards a greater radicalisation of Muslim youth has occurred; in the opposite direction some Muslim communities have begun to respond much more positively and directly to Islamophobia. In the UK, an annual awards ceremony for the 'Islamophobe of the Year'[3] has been initiated to increase awareness of Islamophobia through satire and comedy, whilst the Forum against Islamophobia & Racism (FAIR) was established to tackle Islamophobia and its consequences.[4] In the past five years therefore, the situation affecting and informing the European landscape has undoubtedly changed.

Yet despite or maybe even because of these changes, Islamophobia remains a contested concept.[5] Underpinning all of the various discourses – both for and against Islamophobia - has been a highly protean and largely inconsistent phenomenon. As Marcel Maussen puts it:[6]

> 'Islamophobia' groups together all kinds of different forms of discourse, speech and acts, by suggesting that they all emanate from an identical ideological core, which is an "irrational fear" (a phobia) of Islam.[7]

Encompassing so many varied events, activities, actions and attitudes, the simplified terminologies and definitions have failed to

---

[3] The Annual Islamophobia Awards have been recently established by the Islamic Human Rights Commission. For more information see http://www.ihrc.org.uk.

[4] The Forum against Islamophobia and Racism (FAIR). See http://www.fairuk.org for further information about the organisation and its activities.

[5] Christopher Allen (2006), "Islamophobia: contested concept in the public space", Ph.D dissertation, University of Birmingham.

[6] M. Maussen, "Anti-Muslim sentiments and mobilization in the Netherlands: discourse, policies and violence", in Cesari (2006).

[7] Jocelyne Cesari (2006), *Securitization and religious divides in Europe: Muslims in Western Europe after 9/11 – Why the term Islamophobia is more a predicament than an explanation*, Paris: Challenge, p. 6.

understand or explain a phenomenon that has had such a dramatic impact in such a relatively short space of time. At the same time, it might also be argued that the same failings have not convinced a largely sceptical audience of the reality of Islamophobia, given that the past five years have been one of unprecedented and undeniably eventful history. So despite there being signs of anti-Muslim, anti-Islamic phenomena, there also appears to be some contestation about what it is, where it is and where it comes from.

A lack of clear meaning, interpretation and ownership first became apparent with the researches of the European Monitoring Centre for Racism and Xenophobia's (EUMC) *Summary report into Islamophobia in the EU following 11 September 2001*.[8] Despite having asked each of the then fifteen national focus points employed by the EUMC to define 'Islamophobia', for many it was something that was seriously problematic, meaning that the end result was inconclusive. This is brought into context by the findings of a defining exercise undertaken by the EUMC prior to 9/11.[9] In attempting to establish operable EU-wide definitions for racism, anti-Semitism and Islamophobia, Clayton sought a range of definitions that could be codified into a universally accepted standard to be employed primarily politically and legislatively but also socially. The project found that in seven of the fifteen member states, no clear or known definition of Islamophobia was operable.[10] Of the rest, two noted that the term was non-

[8] Christopher Allen and Jorgen Nielsen (2002), *Summary report on Islamophobia in the EU after 11 September 2001*, European Monitoring Centre on Racism and Xenophobia (EUMC), Vienna.

[9] Named the RAREN 3 data collection project, this project was undertaken in late 2001 and early 2002 and sought to establish universally accepted definitions for 'racism', 'xenophobia', 'Anti-Semitism' and 'Islamophobia'. Overseen by Dimitria Clayton on behalf of the EUMC, the findings of this report were distributed to those participants of the RAXEN NFP meeting held in Vienna on 24-25 June 2002. Further developments of this project and the problems experienced in trying to establish a universally accepted definition were explored in Dimitria Clayton, "Data comparability, definitions and the challenges for data collection on the phenomenon of racism, xenophobia, anti-Semitism and Islamophobia in the European Union", *European Monitoring Centre on Racism and Xenophobia Colloque*, EUMC, Vienna, 25 June 2002. Neither the findings of the RAREN 3 project nor Clayton's paper were published.

[10] Denmark, Finland, Germany, Greece, Italy, Luxembourg and Portugal.

operational but were able to provide a definition;[11] three referenced the UK's Runnymede model (something we will come onto shortly);[12] whilst the others offered different if sometimes correlative definitions.[13] So whilst 'Islamophobia' had been afforded United Nations recognition at the World Conference against Racism, Racial Discrimination, Xenophobia and Related Intolerance in Durban – an event 'lost' in the aftermath of 9/11 – little clarity or consensus existed about exactly what this was.

9.1   Context

The word Islamophobia appears to have been coined as an analogy to xenophobia, but exactly when, where and by whom, remains uncertain.[14] The French word *Islamophobie* was recorded in print in the 1920s and again in the 1970s, but in both instances, it referred to disputes and differences within Islam rather than as a phenomenon against Muslims. More specifically, it referred to the rejection of aspects of the tradition by people born into the Islamic faith especially in the late 1970s by those feminists and liberals who were 'fearful' of the adoption of a more traditional way of life following the revolution in Iran. It is possible, though highly unlikely, that whoever first used the word in English was simply translating a French word that was already in existence, merely applying it to the hostile attitudes and actions of non-Muslims towards Muslims. There is some evidence to suggest that certain British Muslim organisations translated the term into a much more overtly 'anti-Muslim' and 'anti-Islam' context. Nonetheless, it would seem more likely that the English word was a new coining.

As regards its first use in print contemporarily, there is some debate about whether it was in an edition of the December 1991 American journal *Insight* or in a book review by Tariq Modood in *The Independent* newspaper around the same time.[15] Whilst Modood used the term twice, on neither occasion was there the slightest indication that it needed explanation or

---

[11] France and the Netherlands.

[12] Austria, Ireland and the UK.

[13] Belgium, Spain and Sweden.

[14] The discussion of the origins of the term and concept of Islamophobia are derived primarily from Allen, op. cit.

[15] 16 December 1991.

definition, or that it was a word that he himself had coined. It is clear though that it did not appear in the book he was reviewing, *Sacrilege and Civility: Muslim perspectives on The Satanic Verses affair.*[16] The word was again used without explanation in the 1993 report of the Runnymede Trust Commission on Anti-Semitism,[17] which led to the establishment of the Commission on British Muslims and Islamophobia three years later. Whilst the Commission published a number of reports and pamphlets between 1997 and 2004 about Islamophobia, it was its 1997 report *Islamophobia: a challenge for us all*[18] that was most influential. As with the RAREN 3 exercise referred to previously, its model – definition and concept – of Islamophobia has helped shape the wider definitions and conceptualisations of the phenomenon, informing what we allege to know about Islamophobia as well as how it manifests itself. Islamophobia is therefore typically understood to be (as quoted at the beginning) the "shorthand way of referring to dread or hatred of Islam – and, by extension, to fear or dislike of all or most Muslims".[19]

However both the report and its model have failed to stand the test of time and a detailed analysis highlights a number of serious flaws.[20] The most obvious disadvantage of the term is that it is understood to be a 'phobia'. As phobias are irrational, such an accusation makes people defensive and defiant, in turn making reflective dialogue all but impossible. Likewise, Islamophobia as a separate and stand-alone concept implies that prejudice against Muslims is unrelated to other forms of prejudice, for example prejudice based around physical appearance and skin colour; prejudice against immigrants; prejudice against military, religious or economic rivals; and prejudices around class, power and status. The separateness of the concept can also imply that Muslims themselves

---

[16] Muhammad Aanazir Ahsan & Abdul Raheem Kidwai, *Sacrilege versus civility: Muslim perspectives on the Satanic Verses affair*, Leicester: Islamic Foundation, 1991.

[17] Runnymede Commission on Anti-Semitism (1994), *A very light sleeper: the persistence and dangers of anti-Semitism*, London: Runnymede Trust.

[18] Runnymede Trust: Commission on British Muslims and Islamophobia (1997), *Islamophobia: a challenge for us all: report of the Runnymede Trust Commission on British Muslims and Islamophobia*, London: Runnymede Trust.

[19] Ibid., p. 1.

[20] Allen, op. cit.

want to be 'separate' or 'different' even, thereby failing to recognise or accept the 'similarities' and 'overlaps' that also exist. Relevant to the contemporary climate in particular is that the continued use or over-use of the term prevents – either inadvertently or deliberately, depending upon the sources in question, legitimate criticisms of Muslims being voiced, let alone attended to. Elsewhere it has been used far too indiscriminately and inappropriately, failing to differentiate between opinions that are anti-religion per se from those that are specifically anti-Islam. For example, 'I am an Islamophobe, yes,' said Polly Toynbee in the *Guardian* newspaper, 'But I am a Christophobe and Judeophobe too'.[21] As Halliday has argued, the key phenomenon to be addressed is an anti-Muslim hostility directed at an ethno-religious identity rather than the tenets of a religion.[22] In terms of the Runnymede model and Rokeach's Dogmatism Scale upon which it was based therefore, "the instrument does not measure up to the theory".[23]

As regards Islamophobia per se, the same is blatantly true: the instruments we have to define, identify and explain it neither measure up to the theory nor are they entirely bias-free. Despite being able to identify incidents, events and expressions of what we might simplistically suggest as being 'Islamophobia', as the EUMC 9/11 report noted, "these were not necessarily in themselves the reason for any attacks...". Islamophobia seemed to be the "...stimulant" underpinning them.[24] Consequently, what was thought to be known about Islamophobia failed to provide any insight or explanation as to why Islamophobic retaliatory acts ensued or why such a phenomenon exists. Consequently, we are trying to locate something that we maybe do not adequately understand, hence Maussen's comments. Nonetheless, the EUMC's 9/11 report does offer some respite from this lack of clarity. As it stated:

> [N]either exhaustive nor conclusive...[it did] clarify some of the common trends and themes that were apparent in the wake of September 11. No single explanation can completely account for

[21] *The Guardian*, 5 October 2001.

[22] See chapters 4 & 6 in Fred Halliday (1999), *Islam and the myth of confrontation: religion and politics in the Middle East*, London: IB Tauris.

[23] Jacques-Philippe Leyens et al. (1994), *Stereotypes and social cognition*, London: Sage, p. 37.

[24] Ibid., p. 34.

the events that followed those in the US, but this does allow an insight into a certain identifiable phenomenon…[25]

Most important therefore is the report's categorical and justifiable conclusion that a "certain identifiable phenomenon" was evident.[26] In doing so, and in contrast to the Runnymede model, the report differentiated the manifestations – the 'common trends and themes' – from what it saw as the phenomenon of Islamophobia itself, neither concluding nor making the assumption that the manifestations or forms of that 'certain identifiable phenomenon' were either that which constituted it or defined it.

9.2   Conditions

Whether or not it is clear what this 'certain identifiable phenomenon' is, it is this very phenomenon that impacts upon real people in their everyday lives and has also spread as a conceptual and/or social construct. The question to ask therefore is what are, or indeed have been, the conditions upon which this spread of Islamophobia occurred. To do so we must consider the backdrop of the past five years, punctuated as they have been by various terrorist atrocities, the mediatisation of knowledge and understanding, and the burgeoning hyper-reality of the 'war on terror'. It has been a backdrop of hyperbolic overstatement, where mythological intent and evidential reality become both obscured and distorted as in Baudrillard's 'close-up photography' analogy:

> [W]hen we get 'too close' to an object, we sometimes have trouble even distinguishing what the object is. In that sense, we cannot say that we have a grasp on the 'real' object in front of us. The hyperreal, in relation to this analogy, is like the extreme close-up and an extreme long-distance photograph at the same time. That is to say, there is no longer a third, normative position of realistic perspective. The notion of total involvement or immersion combined with alienating detachment is also perceived".[27]

---

[25] Ibid., 49.

[26] Allen & Nielsen (2002), p. 49, op. cit.

[27] Richard J. Lane (2001), *Jean Baudrillard*, London: Routledge, p. 98.

To some extent, the condition for this emergent and developing Islamophobia has been one where there has been a collapse of perspectival space, contextualised and informed by an eventful history and a climate of fear but without the necessary focus. Historically, Muslims and Islam have appeared as external, distant and essentially 'out there', both physically and conceptually. In recent years this critical – and possibly safe – distance has been eradicated. In such conditions, Muslims are no longer the enemy 'other' but much more contemporarily, the enemy 'within'. This of course does not explain why some EU citizens felt the need to exact revenge or engage in some retaliatory act but given the contemporary context with international tensions and uncertainties relating to the ongoing 'war on terrorism' being high in the consciousness of many in the West, it is clearly a possible catalyst. In fact, these feelings have continued and arguably intensified for a further five years, such that the conditions – a seedbed for Islamophobia perhaps – can begin to be seen to be taking shape. Because of these factors, "Islamophobia and anti-Muslim sentiments will continue to be founded for the foreseeable future".[28]

It is also worth noting how these are the same conditions governing the response to Islamophobia. If one considers this response at the pan-European level, these conditions have prompted various reports and monitoring projects, such as those produced by the EUMC following 9/11 and 7/7. This is not an entirely negative process however because it is these reports that have helped generalise and attribute both the term and concept of Islamophobia at the European level with some much needed legitimacy and credibility. It is also worth noting the flipside, however and acknowledge how – at the pan-European level at least – activities that have been proactive towards overcoming Islamophobia have been almost non-existent. To compound the problem, rarely, whether socially or politically, has the concept of Islamophobia been dealt with in such a way as to allow the emergence of a critical analysis, a criticism that might – to some degree – also be levelled against academia.

9.3 Consequences

Having begun to identify the contexts and conditions pertaining to Islamophobia it is essential to consider some of the consequences: the

---

[28] Allen & Nielsen (2002), p. 37, op. cit.

events and incidents that impinge upon the lives of real people in real ways. Such consequences range from verbal abuse and being spat on in the street, through to firebombs and hate-crimes, from politicians stoking the fears already directed towards isolated and excluded communities, through to racial profiling and the tightening of security measures to contain, restrain and at times, ban. To better highlight the breadth of these consequences, it is necessary to offer some differentiation. In this way, a better panoramic landscape is set out at the European level. It is important to stress however that these consequences are in themselves Islamophobic but more importantly that that they are possibly informed or initiated by ideological meanings or motivations. For example, the act of spitting on someone is far from Islamophobic in itself but spitting on someone because they are Muslim would be more than likely based on some anti-Muslim ideological premise. It is therefore the recognition of 'Muslim-ness' or 'Islamic-ness' and a response to that which is Islamophobic and nothing more. This distinction is necessary as it offers the required differentiation that the more literalist Runnymede model fails to provide.

Erosion of the multicultural model

The growing presence, or more importantly, the recognition of the presence of Muslims has meant that the issue of integration has become a recurrent feature of the discourse surrounding Muslims and Islam. This has led to questions being asked about the 'place' of Muslims in Europe, or the Muslims of Europe. Besides Muslims themselves, the most significant victim of these debates has been the previously upheld social model of multiculturalism, something that is particularly relevant in the British and Dutch contexts. Broadly speaking, arguments against the ongoing validity of the multiculturalism model have suggested that its continuation will dilute or even eradicate notions of European identity, something increasingly framed in terms of being white and Christian. This can be seen in the rhetoric of both the Austrian Freedom Party leader, Jorg Haider and the Flemish separatist Vlaams Blok (now Vlaams Belang) and might also underlie the rhetoric surrounding Turkey's accession into the EU.

In the UK, the recognition of the perpetrators of 7/7 being 'homegrown bombers' – not incidentally a new phenomenon in the UK given decades of 'homegrown' Northern Irish-born individuals participating in terrorist activities both in the province and on the mainland – has resulted in a complete overhaul of thinking about multiculturalism.

One consequence is the rhetorical question of whether it is possible to be both 'British' and 'Muslim'. In some ways, many of the recent attacks on multiculturalism have been little more than a thinly veiled attack on Muslims and their identity. In the Netherlands – a model of liberal multiculturalism that until recently was routinely touted as an exemplar for the UK to emulate – the focus has seen a much greater emphasis being placed on cultural assimilation where 'good citizenship' and 'civic integration' have become key policy goals.[29] The fears, anxieties and perceived threats that have been associated with this discourse have nowhere been as articulately voiced as by the assassinated Pim Fortuyn. Being vociferous about the need to maintain the liberal values and ethics of the Netherlands, Fortuyn directed much of his rhetoric towards Muslims and the religion of Islam. As he put it, "if it were legally possible, I'd say no more Muslims will get in here". For Fortuyn, Islam both theologically and culturally had failed to undergo the necessary process of modernisation that was required if Muslims were to ever be fully Dutch. For him, this meant that both lacked either the ability or possibly even the willingness to accept certain tenets of a Western society. Regarding multiculturalism, his position was possibly most persuasively put when in a 2002 televised debate an imam taunted him for his homosexuality. As the imam eventually exploded in a rage of homophobia, Fortuyn calmly turned to the camera and addressing viewers directly, told them "this is the kind of Trojan horse of intolerance the Dutch are inviting into their society in the name of multiculturalism".[30] Having been posthumously voted the greatest ever Dutch man in 2004, his words and views have had a resonance across Europe and in many ways, encapsulate many of the debates which have and indeed continue to rage about the presence of Muslims.

Anti-terrorism and security laws

The tightening and implementation of anti-terror and security legislation has thrown a long shadow of suspicion over Muslims across Europe. In this context, issues relating to anti-terror and security have far too often been equated with issues relating to immigration where internal and external security policies have become conflated or even interchangeable with each

---

[29] Cesari (2006), op. cit.

[30] Rod Dreher (2002), "Murder in Holland", *National Review*, 7, May.

other. Because of this, Muslims have become understood in frames that both acknowledge and perpetuate an ongoing 'otherness'; one that is inherently foreign, alien, enemy and regularly interchanged with populist notions of Muslims as 'terrorists' and 'fifth columnists', amongst others. Since 9/11, the nations of the EU have arrested more than twenty times the number of terrorist suspects as the US (but maybe because Europe has more of them).[31] In the UK, two high profile shooting incidents can offer some insight. The first resulted in the death of the innocent Jean Charles de Menezes, a Brazilian national who was shot in the head seven times at point blank range on the basis that Metropolitan Police officers thought he might have been a suicide bomber. There has been much debate since about how he possibly 'looked' Muslim and what impact this had. Yet despite his killing, justifications have been put forward by the police, politicians and members of the general public to suggest that such mistakes are necessary and unavoidable if security and safety are to be priorities. The second shooting resulted in the innocent Mohammed Abdul Kahar, a British Muslim living in London, being shot in his home following a security raid that it is alleged involved up to 250 police officers, many of whom were wearing chemical warfare outfits. Despite such a large-scale operation and another shooting – Kahar was only wounded – the same justifications were aired, including some that seemingly blamed the innocent victims. Increasingly mediatised 'terror raids' have since become something of a recurrent feature in Britain. Similar events have occurred in both Germany and Italy also. Interestingly, despite populist attitudes to the contrary, terrorism in much of Europe since 9/11 has had a much less 'Islamic' persona. In France and Spain for example, many more Basque nationalists have been arrested than Islamists: of 358 inmates accused of terrorism in France, only 94 are Muslim.[32]

Under increased legislation that is on one level identified as being vital to increase security and protect the homeland and its people, other impacting consequences have also ensued. In Britain, legislation has made indirect incitement and the glorification of terrorism criminal offences, whilst the length of time terror suspects can be held without charge or trial has also increased. Similarly in Germany, where not only a number of

---

31 Cesari (2006).

32 Alexandre Caeiro, "French report", in Cesari (2006), p. 203.

organisations have been banned but mosques are also searched with little justification and new data-mining techniques have been introduced to identify the 'quiet' radicals.[33] Three significant consequences therefore appear to have emerged from this situation; first, increased surveillance and police activity; second, the banning of various Muslim/Islamic groups; and finally, the growing deportation of those deemed radical or extremist. Each of these has affected Muslim communities more than any other community.

Immigration policies

Likewise, it has also been commonplace for immigration procedures to be tightened, sometimes where the overlap with security issues has not always been fully distinguishable. In Germany and France for example, the prospect of high numbers of low skill migrants is highly politicised and socially untenable. In response, they have sought to address this 'problem' by putting policies in place that make it easier for highly skilled immigrants to enter the countries at the same time as reducing this possibility by making immigration more difficult for others. Nicolas Sarkozy's call for a more selective immigration policy has since been followed up with policies and legislation being introduced in May 2005. In highlighting the blurring of boundaries that exists between immigration and security, Sarkozy has quite openly referred to Muslims in his rhetorical justifications, arguing that any new migrants to France must, for example, be willing to accept the publication of religious cartoons in newspapers and women should have identity photographs taken without wearing the *hijab* or *niqab*. Similarly, he also referred to the riots of 2005 as part of his arguments about the roles and responsibilities of Muslims.[34]

It has also been noted how the gap between the right and left of the political spectrum has shifted markedly closer since the events of 9/11 in their views and discourse about Islam.[35] In France it has been noted how those from the left have contributed to the debates about Islam, especially

---

[33] Yasemin Karakasoglu et al., "German report", in Cesari (2006), pp. 148-149.

[34] Caeiro (2006), p. 198.

[35] Christopher Allen (2005), "From race to religion: the new face of discrimination", in Tahir Abbas (ed.), *Muslim Britain: communities under pressure*, London: Zed Books.

the issue of gender, as with the ex-president of the anti-racism organisation SOS-Racisme and prominent member of the Socialist Party Malek Boutih, who defended a policy of immigration with 'laïcité' and the acceptance of gender equality as a precondition for migration.[36] From an equally liberal perspective, the Dutch Ministry of Aliens Affairs and Integration recently produced a film which is intended to assist with the screening of suitable immigrants by showing them the 'norms' of Dutch gender relations and sexuality, including images of naked beachgoers, public homosexuality and assertive female characters.[37] Citizenship tests have also become *de rigueur* if somewhat less controversial. So in the German state of Baden-Wurttemberg for example, moral questions have been raised to ensure that all children participate in swimming lessons. In the UK, questions have been devised as part of a 'British-ness' test that is aimed at providing immigrants with the opportunity to respect and share in Britain's values and traditions.[38] As Spain and Italy have only recently introduced newly developed immigration policies, it is too early to determine whether or indeed how these might affect Muslims as opposed to all immigrants. In Spain the spokesman of the Association of Moroccan Immigrant Workers (ATIME), Mustafa Mrabet, highlighted the apparent disparity between the 52% acceptance of citizenship applications from Moroccans compared to more than 80% of Latin Americans.[39] It is important to point out that in many settings, changes to immigration legislation and the perceptions associated with this should be understood in the wider context, where perceptions and attitudes to immigration are rapidly changing. This change is not Muslim-exclusive and in the UK for example, much recent debate has been about the widening of the EU and the influx of migrants from Bulgaria, Poland and Romania.

---

[36] Caeiro (2006), p. 197.

[37] Marcel Maussen, "Anti-Muslim sentiments and mobilization in the Netherlands: discourse, policies and violence", in Cesari (2006), p. 122.

[38] http://news.bbc.co.uk/1/hi/uk_politics/4393172.stm.

[39] Jose Maria Ortuno Aix, "Report on Islamophobia in Spain", in Cesari (2006), p. 253.

Physical and material abuses and attacks

In 2002, the EUMC noted how "across the entire spectrum of the EU member states, incidents were identified where a negative or discriminatory act was perpetrated against Muslims or an entity that was associated with Islam".[40] However, due to the lack of reliable and effective national and Europe-wide monitoring systems, it is difficult to determine the actual scale or nature of the violence, damage and discrimination that was or has since been directed against Muslims. This is a problem that is further compounded by the fact that it is not only difficult to determine the motivation for such acts but that there is a widespread unwillingness amongst Muslim communities – seemingly irrespective of location – to report such crimes. Consequently, evidence tends to be largely anecdotal and thus easily refuted. Because of this, there is little value in detailing long lists of those attacks and abuses as they may not accurately reflect the true depth and breadth of the situation.

However as noted after 9/11, events or incidents identified as 'Muslim' or 'Islamic' do seem to act as a catalyst for a rise in retaliatory attacks and responses. Following 9/11 for example, Muslim women in Austria and Ireland became targets of verbal and physical abuse whilst in Denmark, a Muslim woman was thrown from a moving taxi for being nothing more than 'Muslim'. Similar incidents – though varying in number and intensity – have also been recorded in other less obvious locations including Belgium, Finland and Luxembourg, among others. Likewise, following the death of Theo van Gogh in 2004, more than eighty incidents against Muslims were recorded in the Netherlands, including a bomb being placed at a Muslim school, an arson attack on a place of worship in Helden, started by neo-Nazis.[41] Following the atrocities of 7/7, similar events were seen in the UK, apparent from police records in the northern city of Sheffield. Note that from the beginning of the year to 6 July 2005 only one 'Islamophobic' incident was reported, in the two weeks following 7/7 more than 30 were recorded.[42] Figures have since returned to 'normal' despite 'street' tensions remaining.

---

[40] Allen & Nielsen (2002), p. 33, op. cit.

[41] Maussen (2006), op. cit.

[42] Unpublished resources acquired from West Yorkshire Police Force (Sheffield), November 2006.

Role of political leaders and political parties

Possibly as a consequence of the political pressure applied by such issues as terrorism, immigration and the widening of the EU's boundaries, a growing incidence of right-wing and nationalistic rhetoric and discourse has also emerged. An Austrian source has noted, "resentments, fears and constructions of the enemy ... [have] now come to the surface" where the attacks of 9/11 and the ongoing 'war on terror' "confirm old prejudices".[43] It is not only Islamophobia that has ensued as a result of this shift, but so too other forms of discrimination and hate-speech including racism by colour and anti-Semitism.[44]

Numerous examples of this can be seen, for example, in Italy, where representatives of Forza Nuova have laid claim to the fact that Italy is, by history and nature, essentially Catholic. The argument continues, as Muslims are not Catholic, then Muslims cannot either be or indeed ever be Italian. Consequently, Muslims should not be allowed to be citizens as they will never be 'good' citizens.[45] Elsewhere the Lega Nord has switched its rhetoric to take advantage of the current climate, deploying slightly modified versions of traditional anti-Semitism against Islam. In Denmark – a country placed under the spotlight by the publication of cartoons of the Prophet Muhammad – a similar shift can also be seen. With its Prime Minister having publicly criticised Muslims for unnecessarily taking up to 'four' [sic] prayer breaks at work each day, Denmark was also the first European country to have governmental elections following the 9/11 attacks. Maybe unsurprisingly, political capital was sought by focusing on the presence and role of Muslims in Denmark via debates about immigration, terrorism, security and the role of 'foreigners', a term that has become increasingly equated in the Danish vernacular with 'Muslims'. With the Dansk Folkeparti being reported to the police for hate speech crimes, the Danish political spaces were dominated by tests of loyalty, the requirement for Muslims to pledge their allegiance to the Danish constitution over and above the Koran, the legal restrictions on Danish

---

[43] Unpublished document as part of the EUMC monitoring programme into Islamophobia following 11 September 2001 from the Austrian National Focal Point.

[44] European Monitoring Centre on Racism & Xenophobia (2006), *Antisemitism - Summary overview of the situation in the European Union 2001-05*, Vienna: EUMC.

[45] Mirna Liguori, "Report on Islamophobia", in Cesari (2006), pp. 308-309.

citizens or residents to bring spouses into the country from elsewhere, and the need for all immigrants to pursue a strong cultural connection to Denmark rather than anywhere else. Without exploring debates about the cartoons issue at this particular juncture, what is interesting is that one year after the original publication of the cartoons, members of the Dansk Folkeparti's youth movement were shown in a secret video taking part in a competition to draw insulting pictures of Muhammad.

A shift towards populist right wing politics, albeit localised, can be seen in the growing popularity of the British National Party (BNP) and its Islamophobic campaigns. Emerging from the 2001 Bradford disturbances - originally presented as being racial rather than religious, 'Asian' as opposed to 'Muslim' – the BNP and indeed others began to re-interpret and re-evaluate who those 'Asians' were, subsequently substituting 'Asian' with 'Muslim-ness' and the 'problems' of Islam.[46] Through a variety of campaigns including 'I.S.L.A.M.: Intolerance, Slaughter, Looting, Arson and Molestation of Women', 'Islam out of Britain' and 'Islam Referendum Day', so the BNP has in just five years gone from an extremely marginal far-right movement to a minor political party that has been able to make significant gains in a number of areas. Targeting those areas where poverty is high amongst white communities, the BNP have made in-roads in municipal elections where they currently hold 43 council seats including Barking and Dagenham in London, where it won 11 out of the 13 seats it contested in May 2006. With growing localised support and the intention to stand in future European Parliamentary elections they have enlisted fringe Sikh and Hindu allies in their anti-Muslim campaign, exacerbating the intra-Asian tensions that exist: a uniquely dramatic shift away from traditional racist and xenophobic strategies.

Such examples are indicative of the profound changes that have occurred across Europe in the past few years. Without a doubt, it is now possible to make anti-Muslim, anti-Islamic and anti-immigrant statements and put forward associated ideas which five years ago would have been entirely inappropriate and unacceptable. Politically however, two other trends are worthy of note. The first is the increasing differentiation between 'good' and 'bad' Islam increasingly couched in terms of 'mainstream' or

---

[46] Christopher Allen (2003), *Fair justice: the Bradford disturbances, the sentencing and the impact*, London: FAIR.

'moderate' and 'extremist' or 'radical' respectively.[47] Rarely in any political setting are the terms Islam or Muslim used neutrally. Given that the distinctions of 'good', 'moderate', 'mainstream', 'true' and others are regularly made, underlying this is the assumption that Muslims and Islam are inherently and normatively problematic and that stressing their 'good', 'moderate' or other similar characteristics is therefore a necessity. The second is the increasing deployment of Muslim voices to air criticisms of Islam and Muslims. Reflecting the BNP's employment of Sikhs and Hindus as 'Asians' to denounce other types of 'Asians', the deployment of Muslim voices also provides a similar justification by speaking from the 'inside'. Possibly the most notorious of these is Ayaan Hirsi Ali. Questionably established as an 'expert' on Islam, she has moved her political leanings from left to right as her prominence has increased. Throughout she has decried moderate expressions of Islam as fundamentally incompatible with liberal democracies and most controversially, the Prophet Muhammad 'a paedophile' and 'perverse tyrant'.[48]

Media coverage of Islam

As with much of the underlying meaning in political spheres, the same applies in the media where Muslims and Islam are without doubt increasingly problematised, framed in discourses of violence, terrorism and misogyny, amongst others.[49] To illustrate this, Geisser's study of the French media notes how it typically prefers to adopt populist public attitudes and prejudices rather than trying to be informative and balanced. Similarly, Tévanian shows how the media helped construct the 'problem of the hijab' by deciding which voices should be included in the debate: all social scientists, feminists, teachers, and civil actors not opposed to the hijab being excluded, thus leaving the ensuing debate to be played out between stereotypically bearded foreign Muslim men on the one side and secular male intellectuals on the other.[50] In Spain, a similar climate exists where the

---

[47] Laurent Bonnefoy (2003), "Public institutions and Islam: a new stigmatization?", *International Institute for the study of Islam in the Modern World* No.13, December, pp. 22-23.

[48] Maussen (2006), ibid, p. 128.

[49] For a detailed treatment see the chapter by Isabelle Rigoni.

[50] Caeiro (2006), pp. 208-209.

media recurrently constructs Muslims as an "internal enemy",[51] whilst in Italy those such as Gritti have noted how the vast majority of the country's media coverage is built around "the myth of Islamic martyrdom and national fanatics".[52]

Two incidents in particular best highlight the role of the media. The first is the decision by the British *Daily Star* to run a spoof of itself entitled the *Daily Fatwa* that included an editorial column that was blank and stamped 'censored' alongside semi-nude female models as part of its 'Burqa Babes' special. The *Daily Fatwa* also ran under the headline "How your favourite paper would look under Muslim law".[53] Before printing however, the National Union of Journalists blocked its publication. Yet within a few days, men's magazine – or 'lad's mag' – *Zoo* had taken up the mantle and printed a double-page spread featuring headlines such as "Public stonings!", "Beheadings!" and "Absolutely nobody having any fun whatsoever". It also featured a full-page picture of a woman in a niqab alongside the headline, "A girl! As you've never seen her before...Pending approval under shariah law". The article went on:

> [M]aybe sharia law isn't so controversial after all...Muslims who practise it to the letter are able to divorce their wives (up to four allowed) by text message. Wives are banned from being in a car with a man who is not a blood relative. And - common sense a-go-go - women aren't allowed to drive cars anyway! And hey, maybe the stricter Muslim woman is happy to hide her face and fleshy bits from public view? Been getting it all wrong with bikini-wearing babes, all-seeing Sex-Ray Specs and the pro-flesh Hot List? So for one week only, we proudly present your all-new, veil-friendly Zoo...[54]

---

[51] Jose Maria Ortuno Aix, "Report on Islamophobia in Spain", in Cesari (2006), p. 253.

[52] R. Gritti da 'Torri crollanti. Comunicazioni, media e nuovi terrorismi dopo l'11 settembre', Rome: Fillenzi, pp. 278-279.

[53] Socialist Worker (London, 21 October 2006). The article can also be retrieved from: (http://www.socialistworker.co.uk/article.php?article_id=9977).

[54] AIM (London, 21 October 2006). This article can also be retrieved from: (http://www.asiansinmedia.org/diary/?p=15).

The second is the decision by the *Jyllands Posten* to print cartoons of the Prophet Muhammad. Whilst various conspiracy stories are circulating about why the cartoons were published, it was the ensuing debates about freedom of speech that spread across Europe and indeed the world that were important. With the newspaper being accused of abusing freedom of speech by various Muslim groups and certain non-Muslim Danes, many also sought to defend the newspaper. For many, this epitomised the 'clash of civilisations' thesis: an unavoidable clash of values, practices, beliefs, ethics and most importantly, a clash of Muslims against the secular West. Beyond the confines of Europe, the controversy resulted in the withdrawal of the ambassadors of Libya, Saudi Arabia and Syria from Denmark, as well as consumer boycotts by Muslims of Danish products. Various Danish embassies were firebombed and numerous violent protests worldwide became international news. Despite apologising to Muslims, the newspaper maintained its right to print the cartoons, arguing that Islamic 'fundamentalism' must not be able to dictate what newspapers can and cannot print. An interesting development however emerged in April 2003, when a different editor of the newspaper rejected a set of unsolicited Jesus cartoons on the grounds that they might provoke a public outcry. For many who opposed the printing of the Prophet cartoons, this was merely evidence that the newspaper – and indeed for many, the West – applied double-standards when it came to Islam.

These examples are useful in that they reinforce the observation set out in the EUMC 9/11 report. In the first instance, whilst distasteful to Muslims, it is unclear whether such incidents in reality initiate or promote Islamophobia in their audience. In the second, whilst the number of incidents against Muslims rose in Denmark, it is again difficult to establish whether these were as a result of the cartoons being printed or whether because this was another 'Muslim' incident that merely reinforced views and attitudes already in circulation. The EUMC report therefore remains pertinent:

> To try and explain the media's role therefore remains difficult. None of the reports suggested that the media directly caused or, indeed, were responsible for any reported or identified act of aggression or significant change in attitude. However, this is not to dismiss their impact in any way, and despite there being no direct evidence to suggest otherwise, the media continue to play a major role in the formulation and establishment of popular perceptions in the public sphere. So when certain

media were identified as representing Muslims both negatively and stereotypically – sometimes as an almost necessary part of the reporting process – in a situation that was volatile, a greater willingness to be responsible and accountable would have been welcomed. However, some media sectors were responsible and accountable, while others sought to remain balanced and objective, and for this those sources should be congratulated. So whilst no evidence exists to suggest that media are influentially causal, they also cannot be completely dismissed either.[55]

9.4   Anti-Islamophobia initiatives

The conditions that have initiated a greater receptivity towards Islamophobia and anti-Muslim attitudes have also been the same conditions that have informed efforts to tackle Islamophobia. At the political level therefore, various politicians have at some time or another called for people to clearly differentiate between Muslims and Islam and what might in some settings be referred to as 'Islamism', 'fundamentalism' and so on. For those such as former British Prime Minister Tony Blair and the Irish Taoiseach Bertie Ahern amongst others, some political leaders have tried to make 'goodwill' gestures towards Muslims within their national contexts.[56] Whether this has been successful, however, remains open to debate, especially when derogatory or negative comments about Islam and Muslims – for example Berlusconi's comments – have been reported as frames that are of European concern and importance, cutting across national borders. Maybe this says more about the media though than it does about politicians.

Other efforts to combat Islamophobia have begun to emerge across a number of European countries, albeit locally focused and largely exempted from state or other governmental influence. This is not so in the UK where the state has acknowledged in varying degrees the need for the misconceptions and misunderstandings about Islam and Muslims to be challenged by both Muslims and non-Muslims. This has taken numerous forms, from how different police forces have begun trying to prevent any backlash or retaliatory attacks on Muslims at the same time as trying to

---

[55] Allen & Nielsen (2002), pp. 52-53.

[56] Allen & Nielsen (2002).

reduce the sense of threat felt by many Muslims themselves. In various locations, police patrols have been stepped up around mosques and Islamic centres, and senior officers have sought to liaise with community leaders. One such project has been the collaboration between the London Metropolitan Police and the Muslim communities in the London borough of Southwark. Here 58 different Muslim voluntary and community organisations participated in meetings to establish a dedicated telephone line to record crimes against Muslims and indeed any other community that is targeted or attacked. In Scotland, Lothian and Borders Police Chief Constable, Sir Roy Cameron, called upon all communities to root out racism following a fire attack on a mosque in Edinburgh whilst the Scottish Executive gave mosques and other places of 'ethnic community worship' £1 million to improve security.

As for Muslim communities, the response has been equally as wide-ranging in the UK. These have included the Muslim Council of Britain (MCB),[57] meeting regularly with different governmental offices including both the Foreign Minister and Prime Minister, with the backing of around 250 affiliate organisations. A year after 9/11 it also published a collection of reflective writings by both Muslims and non-Muslims entitled, *The quest for sanity: reflections on September 11 and its aftermath*.[58] Shortly after the Madrid train bombing atrocities, it also sent a letter to more than a thousand mosques urging imams to promote peace and harmony. Other organisations have included the Islamic Human Rights Commission (IHRC), which issued safety tips for the Muslim community and FAIR, which, amongst other things, organised a University of Westminster conference entitled: Exploring Islamophobia: Deepening Our Understanding of Islam and Muslims.[59] Elsewhere the Islamic Foundation[60] has provided cultural awareness and diversity training for non-Muslim professionals whilst the Islamic Society of Britain (ISB) has been organising

---

[57] For more information, see the MCB website (http://www.mcb.org.uk).

[58] Abdul Wahid Hamid (2002), *The quest for sanity: reflections on September 11 and its aftermath*, London: MCB.

[59] 29 September 2001.

[60] For more information, see http://www.islamic-foundation.org.uk.

its annual Islam Awareness Week since 1994, albeit with more vigour since 9/11.[61]

Outside the UK, Muslim communities have been strengthening their organisations not only to monitor and keep records of Islamophobic incidents but to also aid their push towards official recognition. One such example has been the establishment of the Islamic Anti-Defamation League of Italy in 2005.[62] Most notable have been the many different initiatives that have emanated from within other faith groups and communities, identifiable particularly in the growth and development of inter-faith dialogue initiatives between Muslims and Christians. These have been both important and influential, as in Greece where Archbishop Christodoulos, the head of the Church of Greece, quickly brought together leading figures from the Abrahamic traditions as a show of solidarity soon after 9/11. Similarly, the Orthodox Ecumenical Patriarchate organised an inter-faith summit in Brussels to challenge the legacy of historical enmity in shaping the way in which people view each other contemporarily.[63] Many other initiatives include those such as the multi-faith prayer events held in Senate's Square, Helsinki and the oration for peace organised by the Pax Christi in Lisbon.[64]

Inter-faith initiatives have provided invaluable opportunities for communities to come together and challenge misconceptions. The *Christlich-Islamische Gesellschaft* in Germany is a national organisation that sponsors such dialogue and has established groups in various cities across Germany.[65] Likewise, the *Deutsches Islamforum* has begun to mediate between Muslims and non-Muslims whilst the Central Council of German Muslims has declared 3 October – German reunification day – as Open Mosque Day also, thereby providing people the opportunity to visit a mosque and speak with Muslims. A similar initiative also occurs in Austria at the same time.[66] What with the overlap between 'Muslims' and

---

[61] For more details about the Islamic Society of Britain, see http://www.isb.org.uk. For more information about Islam Awareness Week, see http://www.iaw.org.uk.

[62] Liguori M. (2006), "Report on Islamofobia" in Cesari (2006).

[63] Allen & Nielsen (2002).

[64] Ibid.

[65] Karakasoglu et al. (2006), "German Report" in Cesari (2006).

[66] Allen & Nielsen (2002).

'immigrants', in Spain a council has been established to give advice to the Spanish government about questions of integration, whilst the Spanish Observatory on Racism and Xenophobia was set up to monitor and report on a range of issues including Islamophobia, albeit not explicitly.[67] In the Netherlands, a Commission on Equal Treatment has been established to help implement the 1994 Equal Treatment Law whilst a National Bureau Against Racial Discrimination provides the expertise to prevent the growth of racial – and by default, religious – discrimination.[68]

Conclusions

Understanding Islamophobia is neither easy nor straightforward. Whilst a decade might have passed since the Runnymede report noted how Islamophobia was becoming 'more explicit', it may be that since then, the reverse has occurred, with links to debates, events, and incidents that are seemingly unconnected to earlier concepts of Islamophobia. Many of the examples set out here may not therefore be overtly Islamophobic. But underpinning them – sometimes in a relatively invisible way – there seem to be an anti-Muslim, anti-Islamic ideology that informs, explains and causes these and many other consequences to ensue. Despite the failings of the term and the lack of clarity about the phenomenon, Islamophobia is without doubt here to stay and can no longer be discarded from the European lexicon. The task now is to set out more clearly what Islamophobia is and importantly, what it is not – about which there is little consensus at present. Nonetheless, a 'certain identifiable phenomenon' does continue to exist and further research is needed. Despite being something of an unknown term less than five years ago, the spread of Islamophobia both discursively and conceptually in the public and political arena has meant that Islamophobia is now a social reality. It has been transformed into an increasingly important and urgent issue, demanding our attention and action. This paper has attempted to identify the significant changes that have occurred in Europe and to show how far-reaching these have been. At this particular juncture, however, it is impossible to even begin to speculate on where Europe and its Islamophobia will be at the end of its second decade in 2017.

---

[67] Ortuno Aix (2006).

[68] Maussen (2006).

PART C

INSTITUTIONALISATION

10. MUSLIM INSTITUTIONS AND POLITICAL MOBILISATION

SARA SILVESTRI

Introduction

In Europe, and most of the Western world, Muslim presence in the public sphere is a recent phenomenon that characterised the last decade of the 20th century and has deeply marked the beginning of the 21st. This visible presence, which amounts to something between 15 and 20 million individuals, can best be analysed if dissected into a number of components. The first part of this chapter illustrates where, when and why organised Muslim voices and institutions have emerged in Europe, and which actors have been involved. The second part is more schematic and analytical, in that it seeks to identify from these dynamics the process through which Muslims become political actors and how they relate to other, often in competing political forces and priorities. It does so by observing the objectives and the variety of strategies that Muslims have adopted in order to articulate their concerns vis-à-vis different contexts and interlocutors. The conclusions offer an initial evaluation of the impact and of the consequences of Muslim mobilisation and institution-formation for European society and policy-making.

10.1 Background[1]

We are witnessing the increasingly assertive emergence of a universal and transnational religion – Islam – in the European public sphere. And yet, this

---

[1] Some paragraphs in the second half of this section draw on and re-elaborate Silvestri, S. (2007), Regards croisés sur l.institutionnalisation de l'islam au niveau national et européen, in F. Foret (ed.), L'Europe à l.épreuve du religieux, Bruxelles: Etudes européennes series, Editions de l'Université Libre de Bruxelles.

is happening in a rather disorganised way and across an umma (the global community of the faithful) that is fractured. This is because, as with Protestantism, Islam is a faith focused on the direct relationship between the believer and God, and without significant intermediary figures and hierarchical structures comparable to those of the Catholic or Orthodox churches. Moreover, the Prophet Muhammad left no instructions as to how to select his successor to lead Muslims after his death.[2]

In the absence of Muslim institutions with a wide recognition and legitimacy from across the variety of Muslim communities, European governments have experienced considerable difficulty in relating to and addressing the needs of their Muslim populations. The nature of these difficulties is rooted in a combination of legal, structural and political issues, as well as perceptions. The socio-political dominance exercised by the Church in Europe throughout the centuries, combined with Enlightenment-driven notions of secularism, has also shaped the way bureaucracies, public authorities and legal systems all over the continent have dealt with, and still relate to, religion in general and with Islam more specifically. On the one hand, European states enthusiastically support equality and religious freedom whilst operating within the framework of the separation between private and public sphere. On the other hand, the way states have developed their relations with religious groups is still shaped by corporatist models and by the traditional pattern of church-state relations, which still reflects, if anything in this very terminology, the privileged position enjoyed until recently by the Christian churches in this part of the world.[3]

The lack of formal Muslim leaders and institutions in Europe has led European governments and EU institutions to push for an 'artificial' creation of Muslim councils that would fit into the standard pattern of

---

[2] I have expanded on this in Silvestri, S. (2005), .Institutionalising British and Italian Islam: Attitudes and Policies., forthcoming as a chapter in H. Yilmaz and C. Aykac (eds), Rethinking Europe through Rethinking Islam, proceedings of conference held at Bogazici University, Istanbul, December.

[3] On church-state relations, see G. Robbers (ed.) (2005), *State and Church in the European Union*, Baden Baden: Nomos. On corporatist approaches to institutionalising Islam in France see for instance W. Safran (2004), "Ethno-religious Politics in France", *West European Politics*, 27/3, May, pp. 423-251.

religion-state relations. But before looking at the implications of the process of 'institutionalisation of Islam' in the sense of 'official recognition by state agencies', it is important to provide an overview of the evolution of Muslim political mobilisation in Europe.

The first instances of Muslim mobilisation in the European public sphere appeared in the 1970s – with a couple of earlier exceptions – and coincided with the establishment of places of worship, and of religious, cultural and educational associations.[4] In the mid 1970s there were already examples of grassroots mobilisation to create basic points of reference and institutions for the Muslim communities of Europe. Mosques and cultural centres were often established by and/or controlled by Muslim states or by Muslim transnational networks such as the Muslim Brotherhood or the Jamaat-i-Islami. Originating respectively in South Asia and North Africa and the Middle East, these two movements are known for having an Islamist agenda, i.e. they actively want to bring Islamic values and interests (and eventually sharia law) into the political sphere. In Europe they are organised by diasporas and political exiles that often antagonise the governments of their own countries. Although the Islamists' politico-religious project has provoked a great deal of suspicion and fear on the part of the establishments (especially but not only the secular ones), both in Europe and in the Muslim world, de facto these movements do not offer any exact picture, in practical terms, of what society and political process would look like in the event of them obtaining power. Most of the Islamist movements are focused on agenda of political reform rooted in social justice, which explains, on the one hand, their success amongst the masses and lower classes and, on the other hand, the hostility of the establishments that feel threatened by these 'revolutionary' forces. From the outset, the scenario of Muslim political mobilisation in the European public sphere is marked by competing forces: the 'Islam of the states', Islamist and diaspora networks, and more informal and more local groupings. The expression 'Islam of the states' refers to attempts on the part of the governments and diplomatic seats of prominent Muslim countries such as Saudi Arabia, Algeria, Morocco and Turkey to organise religious and cultural activities, language courses and to sponsor the creation of Islamic institutions for

---

[4] J. Nielsen (2005), *Muslims in Western Europe*, Edinburgh University Press.

Muslims living in Europe, 'in line' with the official version of Islam that these states support.

Muslim activism took on a more independent and political nature at the time of and after the 'Rushdie affair' and the 'veil affair' (which exploded in the UK and France respectively in 1989) and intensified exponentially throughout the 1990s. The close of the century saw a considerable growth and diversification of Muslim mobilisation in Europe; this was the consequence of the gradual settlement of Muslims here, first as long-term residents and then as citizens.

Increasing political awareness was provoked inter alia by the first Gulf War against Saddam Hussein in 1991. Communication and mobilisation were also facilitated by the spread of the internet. A number of Muslim associations providing counselling and social services (and primarily concerned with health, housing, English language and vocational training) also appeared in the same period, together with Muslim professional networks, advocacy groups, and Muslim print and broadcast media. Muslims became more and more vocal in their claims concerning religious practices and freedom in the public domain, religious education, discrimination and Islamophobia.[5] As this 'civil society Islam' spread, the 'Islam of the states' gradually lost influence over the Muslim population of Europe.

Before the presence of an increasingly strong, and yet multiform, unstructured and acephalous Islam in the public sphere, European states became faced with two choices. Either they had to rethink the way they relate (through their legal and administrative provisions) to this growing minority religion or they had to demand the establishment of Muslim institutions. There is an expectation that such institutions should be created if Muslims want to 'earn' a place in the complex mechanisms of governance in EU institutions and member states. This is primarily because Muslims are perceived – and often tend to present themselves – as a bloc, as a

---

[5] See also the chapter by Chris Allen for a detailed treatment of Islamophobia. A good study of Muslim claims in Europe has been conducted by Ruud Koopmans and Paul Statham and their colleagues. See P. Statham, R. Koopmans, M. Giugni and F. Passy (2005), "Resilient or Adaptable Islam? Multiculturalism, Religion and Migrants' Claims-making for Group Demands in Britain, the Netherlands and France", *Ethnicities*, 5/4, pp. 427-459.

community sharing fundamental values, sensitivities, and perspectives which are often discriminated against or ignored. Second, a structural problem comes into play when we talk of Muslim engagement and representation with European states and societies; that is, the idea that Islam should 'fit in' with the criteria that regulate relations with the dominant faith groups. Such criteria are rooted in at least three basic expectations: 1) that Islam should behave like an 'organised' belief, with mechanisms of representation and religious leaders in clear positions of power. This is based on the assumption that the traditional church-state model within the secular framework of the separation between public and private sphere would work for Islam too, 2) there is a somewhat abstract notion of 'integration' which de facto differs between various multicultural, 'assimilationist' or mixed practices adopted by European states, 3) Muslim organisations should be representative both of the demographic and of the doctrinal characteristics of the Muslim populations of Europe.

In short, Muslim communities are implicitly expected to adapt to and to adopt the existing pattern of relations between the state and ethnic and religious communities in order to engage with the social and political context in which they live. As a consequence, new forms of institutionalisation of Islam (other than mosques and Islamic schools) have begun to appear in Europe, often through the direct intervention of European governments. Elsewhere I have illustrated the emergence of a particular instance, 'national Muslim councils'.[6] These bodies are created with the expectation that they constitute official interlocutors available for consultation and capable of representing the Muslim community and acting as bridges between the grassroots level and the state. This process inaugurates a 'domestication' or 'normalisation' of a European version of Islam shaped around the idea that a 'moderate' (and artificial) form of Islam should be supported in order to do justice to Muslim minorities, but also to stem radicalisation.[7]

---

[6] S. Silvestri, "The Situation of Muslim Immigrants in Europe in the Twenty-first century: The creation of National Muslim Councils", in H. Henke (ed.) (2005), *Crossing Over: Comparing Recent Migration in Europe and the United States*, Lanham, MD: Lexington, pp.101-129.

[7] Cf. S. Silvestri, "Institutionalising British and Italian Islam..."; A. Caeiro, "Religious Authorities or Political Actors? The Muslim Leaders of the French

The two decades bridging the 20th and 21st centuries have witnessed the establishment and spreading of this common pattern of institutionalisation of Islam within the borders of the EU. As described in more detail in the chapter by Bernard Godard, this has been mainly a top-down, state-driven dynamic, although a mutual interest in formalising relations is clearly visible among many Muslim groups and individuals living in Europe too.[8] There are various motivations behind this move and security concerns are certainly top of the list. However, beside the necessity to maintain law and order and to counter terrorism (i.e. to 'control' specific social, ethnic and religious groups at risk of 'radicalisation'), there is also a genuine intention to facilitate communication between state institutions and Muslim individuals in order to do justice to the principles of freedom of religion and non-discrimination. In this way, the state seeks – or at least claims to be able – to respond better to the needs of European Muslims and to 'protect' them from abuse and discrimination. Muslim individuals and organisations, for their part, though critical of the security aspect of this exercise and of the continuous use of the words 'moderate' and 'Islamic extremism' and 'Islamic terrorism' seem to welcome the prospect of a platform (with money and public visibility attached to it) to channel their concerns.

Whereas the motivations for becoming involved in the institutionalisation of Islam are pretty similar across the various EU member states, in practical terms the strategies adopted by each country present certain differences.[9] Factors that determine these differences include: the variety of versions of Islam that exist across Europe, ideologies, the socio-economic circumstances of the local Muslim population, cultural and historical features that characterise specific European countries and their approach to secularisation, national and EU provisions concerning

---

Representative Body of Islam", in J. Cesari and S. Mcloughlin (eds), *European Muslims and the Secular State*, Aldershot: Ashgate, pp. 71-84.

[8] This common pattern is examined in S. Silvestri, "The Situation of Muslim Immigrants...", S. Silvestri, "Institutionalising British and Italian Islam...".

[9] These differences are addressed in detail, especially from a legal perspective, in S. Ferrari (ed.) (1996), *L'Islam in Europa. Lo statuto giuridico delle comunità musulmane*, Bologna: il Mulino, and in R. Aluffi and G. Zincone (eds) (2004), *The legal treatment of Islamic minorities in Europe*, Leuven: Peeters.

immigration and citizenship, church-state relations and attitudes towards foreigners and minorities in individual countries.

10.2 The EU, Islam, Muslim networks and institutions

As far as the EU is concerned, there are a number of policy dimensions connected to Islam and Muslim communities.[10] Social affairs is the policy area concerned with social cohesion and which, in 2000, put forth legislation condemning discrimination in the work place on religious grounds. Initiatives around immigration are also very likely to have an impact on the Muslim populations of Europe because many Muslims are still immigrants, not citizens, of the EU. Since 2000, when the Charter of Fundamental Rights was signed at Nice, the EU has also stressed its commitment to protect fundamental rights, including religious freedom and the rights of minorities. At least since 1999, when at the Council in Tampere the EU member states announced their determination to go ahead with the development of common immigration and asylum policies and stressed the importance of integration, the EU has also prioritised the need to accompany immigration control with measures to facilitate the integration of migrants. The fight against terrorism and radicalisation conducted in the field of Justice, Security and Freedom has also to deal with thorny issues of Islamic principles being monopolised by terrorists for violent purposes. One aspect of EU external relations, the Euro-Mediterranean Partnership, also places considerable emphasis on the importance of establishing social and cultural exchanges across the two shores of the Mediterranean, and includes intercultural relations and interfaith relations. Moreover we cannot leave out the EU's ambivalent relations with Turkey and with other Muslim political actors across the Mediterranean. More than the religious identity of the majority of the country's population, it is perhaps the recent re-Islamisation of Turkey's politics – first with the Refah party and now with Erdogan's Justice and Development Party, and the prominent role that Turkey is playing in the

---

[10] These are spelt out more in detail in S. Silvestri (2005), "EU relations with Islam in the context of the EMP's cultural dialogue", *Mediterranean Politics*, 10/3, November, and in S. Silvestri, "Europe and Political Islam: Encounters of the 20th and 21st century", in T. Abbas (ed.) (2007), *Islamic Political Radicalism: A European Comparative Perspective*, Edinburgh University Press, pp. 57-70.

Organisation of the Islamic Conference – that constitutes a cause for concern for at least some parts of the EU. Finally, the EU has initiated an internal process of institutionalisation of Islam which seems to fit the same framework of the national Muslim councils described above. In the mid 1990s the Commission set up the Muslim Council of Cooperation in Europe (MCCE), whose story I have told elsewhere.[11] Even if the MCCE were not successful, the idea of creating a supranational Muslim interlocutor, for and promoted by the EU institutions, remained alive. So, the 2004 Constitutional Treaty contains article I-52 which spells out the important contributions that the Churches and other religious and philosophical groups could make to the Union and outlines a flexible form of regular and transparent consultation between the religious groups of Europe and the EU institutions. As a matter of fact such a consultation has only happened a couple of times since the summer of 2005, when Commission President Barroso convened an emergency meeting in the aftermath of the London bombings.[12] This shows that the way the European Union (EU) has explicitly conceptualised and made space for engagement with religious groups is in the context of civil society. This approach, which falls under the corporatist mentality described above for the national level, indicates a preference for dialogue with formal, organised groups rather than with individual citizens. It has been criticised for being elitist, restricting democratic participation and missing out the real contribution of individual citizens or organisations that do not have the resources to coordinate their interests very effectively.[13] The origin and mobilisation strategies of the only two pan-European Muslim pressure groups that were established in the mid 1990s and based in Brussels (the Federation of European Muslim Youth Organisations, FEMYSO, and the Federation of Islamic Organisations in Europe, FIOE) proves that this criticism is not unfounded. As with any lobby group, the conditions upon which these organisations can subsist and be successful are a combination of factors:

---

[11] Cf. S. Silvestri, "Regards croisés…".

[12] On article I-52, see S. Silvestri, "Regards croisés…"; P. Schlesinger and F. Foret (2006), "Political Roof and Sacred Canopy? Religion and the EU Constitution", *European Journal of Social Theory*, 9.

[13] Cf. P. Magnette (2003), "European Governance and Civic Participation: Beyond Elitist Citizenship?", *Political Studies*, 51/1, p. 150.

motivation, availability of economic and human resources and some form of institutional structure. Perhaps in this case the motivation is the crucial factor that triggers the rest. They are staffed mainly by volunteers, who are moderately to highly educated, extremely mobile and confident individuals, often university students and professionals, who have at some point been involved in grassroots work. FEMYSO and FIOE appear to be the EU branches of two networks of local associations, mosques and cultural centres across the EU with some remote ties to the Islamist discourse of the Jamaat-i-Islami and the Muslim Brotherhood.[14]

10.3 Analysing the dynamics

The points made above show that Muslim mobilisation has taken place on two levels, the national and the transnational, i.e. either locally, inside the individual nation states of the EU or across and beyond the EU member states. It is mainly directed towards the articulation of identity politics and can take more or less organised – or even institutionalised – forms. Sometimes the objective of the mobilisation itself is the creation of Muslim authorities and institutions. In order to simplify the picture and to grasp the relationship between its components, this mobilisation can be reduced to three broad typologies:

1. Religious institutions in a traditional sense, such as mosques and schools.

2. Grassroots and civil society organisations, which in turn can be divided into a) community associations devoted to cultural and educational projects, support networks and the provision of aid and social services, and b) advocacy and pressure groups, which tend to be of a more political nature.

3. Muslim states trying to help ('interfere with' would perhaps be a more accurate term) their own diasporas by providing moral guidance and economic support through the funding of mosques and cultural centres or by appointing imams and teachers of Arabic.

---

[14] A more detailed analysis of these organisations and their transnational connections and work within and beyond Europe is offered in S. Silvestri (2006), *Muslim Political Mobilisation in Europe and the EU Response*, PhD thesis, Cambridge University, Cambridge.

These three 'formats' of Muslim assertiveness and engagement with the public sphere seem to be 'spontaneous' in character, i.e. to originate from within a Muslim context. The main differences are that 1) and 2) tend to be instances coming from 'inside' Europe, whereas 3) comes from outside, and 2) is more informal than 1) and 3). Both 1) and 2) though, are often exposed to external influences, not directly of states but of transnational movements – for instance the missionary movement Tablighi Jamaat or the Islamist Jamaat-i-Islami and Muslim Brotherhood – if not established Islamic parties.

Even if the involvement of elite groups were crucial to the establishment of associations and institutions such as those described under 1) and 2), these forms of mobilisation could be regarded as 'bottom-up' because they are part of the variegated world of civil society. On the other hand, even if 3) supposedly includes 'genuinely Muslim' initiatives, it should still be classified as 'top-down' because in this case governments, not civil society groups, take the initiative to impose-propose the establishment of religious, cultural and educational institutions with a specific and restrictive agenda concerning Muslim articulation of identity and political participation in Europe.

As far as the dynamics between and among Muslim organisations in Europe and their relationship with European states are concerned, more often than not we see competition between Muslim organisations for access to resources, visibility and power. The search for authority and legitimisation happens on two levels: on the one hand, those individuals and groups that are involved in the articulation of a Muslim voice and in the establishment of Muslim institutions seek the support of the largest number of fellow Muslims; on the other hand, they keep a constant eye on the priorities and attitudes of the state and government where they reside and which they try to please.[15] Fragmentation and rivalries within the umma are perceived and lived as real problems by Muslims all over the world. This is especially so in the European context when they hinder the interaction of Muslim communities with the rest of European society, thus creating obstacles to the development of a public policy that takes into account the needs and claims of this conspicuous religious minority.

---

[15] I have expanded on the internal power struggle of European Islam in S. Silvestri, "Institutionalising British and Italian Islam…".

When it comes to the motivations behind Muslim engagement in identity politics and institution-building, we can detect several reasons that are at times separate and at other times are combined. First there can be the genuine desire to give a voice to and improve the plight of Muslim individuals, alongside the pursuit of personal gain and political opportunism. Secondly, political structures and culture, and the juridical context of each country, as well as varying notions of the relationship between citizens and the state that Muslim individuals might have inherited from their place of origin, also determine how, if at all, Muslim political participation can materialise in Europe. For instance, in many European countries, the legal status of 'immigrant' versus that of 'citizen' can make a lot of a difference when translated into civil and political rights exercised by any individual, from the right to vote in national elections to the right to establish legally recognised associations. Finally, Muslim mobilisation is often a response to a country's attitude to religion and secularism, as well as to its internal and external policies.

This latter point has raised considerable concern among several academic and policy circles. There is almost an obsession with 'Muslim attitudes' to British and American foreign policy. To a certain degree this concern is justified since one of the bombers of 7 July 2005 left a statement explicitly telling that he was fighting because he disapproved of British foreign policy. But reducing Muslim claims, feelings and concerns to their views of Western foreign policy is too much of a reductive exercise. Their political opinions and changing modes of political participation and association should not be observed in isolation, but seen in light of the changing attitudes, the dissatisfaction, the frustrations and the changing modes of participation in democratic politics of the wider European population. While participation in traditional party politics and voting are in decline, transnational social movements and interest groups of any sort – not just Muslim – are thriving.

Conclusions

Any discussion of the prospect of systematising Muslim political participation into the creation of Muslim representative bodies – as something in-between a church, an interest group and a corporatist model that brings together the stakeholders in a particular field – ought to be conducted with caution. More importantly, the question of whether and how the state should have a role in this process of institutionalisation should be thought through very carefully. States have an interest in maintaining peace and stability within their borders and for this reason provide the 'rules of the game' that will enable their inhabitants to coexist peacefully and respectfully of each other. From a certain point of view one could consider the attempts to regulate and institutionalise relations with Muslim communities as merely another application and extension of these rules to a relatively new community. This process would be acceptable if it were limited to providing the framework for creating a dynamic representative body. The fear is that it constrains free expression into an institution, paradoxically at a time when individuals are reclaiming their independence, and that its representative members are cherry-picked from above, rather than agreed upon by the community. Indeed the few examples of state-promoted Muslim consultative bodies that exist in France, Belgium and Great Britain have gone through legitimacy crises, confrontations and fierce criticism from within their own Muslim communities. Often, and this is perhaps more explicit in the case of Spain and Italy, the creation of these institutions seems reduced to a PR exercise on the part of the government.

In general, political participation in Western democracies can take place at the level of the individual and/or can be articulated through a group (e.g. a political party, a community association, a social movement, a lobbying organisation). In order to examine Muslim attitudes to political participation and patterns of mobilisation in the public sphere, we should therefore treat them as ordinary individuals, and not isolate them from the rest of the picture, as if 'Muslim' was a special new socio-political category. There are, indeed, Muslim individuals who prefer to articulate their identity primarily as 'Muslim', and there are also people who have voluntarily decided to be active in political life as 'Muslims'. From the examples mentioned above, though, we ought to be cautious and not jump to the conclusion that the Muslims of Europe 'need' expressly 'Muslim' institutions in order to be active citizens, or simply to convey their concerns. Furthermore, channelling Muslim voices into the formation of institutions that are shaped around the structure of the Christian churches (what scholars including Roy have called the 'churchification' of Islam)[16] seems not only a constraint on a religion that has no hierarchy, but is also

---

[16] O. Roy (2004), *Globalised Islam*, London: Hurst.

rather anachronistic at a time when people's connection to and trust in institutions is declining. They prefer to 'believe' without belonging.[17]

Humankind is very diverse and, regardless of the legal status of a person (i.e. whether s/he is a national citizen or an immigrant), individuals range from apathetic types to people with a discreet degree of interest in political affairs, to others who are more passionate and willing to engage with – and perhaps have the ambition to impact on – the political process. Among those persons of Islamic faith who feel that they ought to engage in public life, it is not automatic that they would opt for 'Muslim' channels in order to voice their concerns. Some might find it more appropriate to express their political choices simply through casting a vote, or maybe by becoming actively involved with a political party, or with a non-denominational NGO... People might regularly go to a mosque and even financially support it, without nevertheless wishing to be represented in public life by its director or by the imam.

So, faced with the vocal presence of Islam in the public sphere, European states are compelled to rethink the way they relate to minority religious communities such as Islam. Muslim communities, for their part, can decide whether to adapt to the existing pattern of religion-state relations in order to engage with the social and political context where they live, or whether to adopt the more market-driven and perhaps more effective path of remaining 'disestablished' actors in the world of pressure groups, which is perhaps the option that would give them more leeway. We should also always remember that Islam in Europe is a plural entity, and that the possibility of disagreement between the Muslim actors is high. Hence the scenario of Muslims splitting into two or more strands, some working through the state, some remaining independent associations, and both claiming and fighting for authority and recognition, is not unthinkable.

Should the preferred path be that of institutionalising Islam through the state, both the state and the Muslim communities involved should be aware of the following considerations: 1) evaluate the feasibility of the enterprise, in terms of economic and human resources; 2) be aware of and reflect on the complex variety of interpretations that exist in Islam within and outside Europe and the influence of transnational movements; 3)

---

[17] G. Davie (2000), *Religion in Modern Europe*, Oxford: Oxford University Press.

remember that governments and coalitions wax and wane and that the priorities and approaches (including towards Islam) of political parties can also change. But, above all, the short and long term benefits as well as the consequences of establishing such an institution should be taken into consideration. To summarise, the crucial questions are: what is the ultimate purpose of these Muslim institutions? What are the consequences of establishing them? Once governments have created these institutions and raised expectations among Muslims to be able to influence the political process, will governments be able to listen to and to stand the weight of the empowered Muslim bodies that they have produced?

11. OFFICIAL RECOGNITION OF ISLAM

BERNARD GODARD

Introduction

The establishment of Islam in European countries came about in a variety of ways, giving rise initially to quite contrasting policies, in particular with respect to the setting up of representative bodies of this faith. Furthermore, in the European Union the status of churches has always been the exclusive domain of the member states (as was confirmed by article I-52 of the (non-ratified) Constitution.

Those countries with a colonial tradition, such as France and the UK, or with an imperial tradition, such as Austria with Bosnia, or Greece or Bulgaria within the Ottoman empire, have policies of recognition that are closely linked to their history and to the manner in which they have nurtured ties to the populations they have known over a long period of time. A second category of country, such as Spain, Italy or Germany has only known this migratory phenomenon relatively recently. In the case of Italy and Germany, the recognition of a Muslim representation has been linked to the 'non-domestic' character of this new religious actor. Other countries, notably Denmark and Sweden, are mostly dealing with Muslim populations who have fled their countries as a result of pressure or political problems. The overall proportion of Muslims also plays a decisive role: the greater the number of Muslims, the greater the recognition by the state of a representative body.

Geographical origins, as we will see, also determine a certain relational modus operandi with the state: the mosaic of populations of diverse origins (mainly Maghrebi, African, and Turk) in France has influenced state intervention over the last twenty years, resulting in a representative body. Conversely, in Germany, the relative ethnic-religious homogeneity of the immigrant community, with a majority of associations and mosques falling under the authority of the Turkish state and other Turkish associations, meant a rather delayed interest in promoting the emergence of a representative body.

The particular history of relations between the state and religions, and the juridical arrangements governing the life of these religions over the centuries, constitute a third element determining the make-up of the institutional representation of Islam. Conceptions range from the very secular, as in France, to a view that accords a great deal of space to religious bodies for their participation in the life of society. The reinforcement of the process of secularisation, however, is what characterises recent trends in Europe the most, especially compared to the rest of the world. And no matter what legislative forms these relations between the state and religions take, this drive towards secularisation touches the countries with state religions such as Denmark, Greece or the UK as much as the 'concordat' countries, namely Spain and Italy. Those countries that had developed a clearly 'culturalist' vision, like the Netherlands, in particular through the policy 'pillars' of Catholic, Protestant and humanistic doctrines, now seem to be returning to a more distanced policy with regard to different faiths. One could even advance the view that the presence of Islam has necessitated this distance, and some people now consider that this new religion cannot be too closely associated with public life. Policies that favour the expression of the Muslim faith could appear to contradict the declared neutrality of the state. For example, the very active support of the state for the establishment of the French Muslim Council was vehemently attacked in France as being contrary to Republican principles.

And finally, the concerns engendered by radicalisation, in particular terrorism, have certainly accelerated the processes of recognising official bodies representing the Muslim faith. The British example is indicative of this, with the government shifting in 2005 from a very neutral, distant position to a desire to almost manage these bodies.

In order to illustrate these points, we will examine the different processes that have been tried out to provide Muslims with a representative structure in France, Germany, Belgium, Netherlands, Spain, Italy, UK, Austria, Greece and Bulgaria and, secondarily, the public policies that have aimed to develop training curricula for imams.

France

France has the largest Muslim population in Europe. People of Algerian origin make up more than a third of the five million Muslims in France today. People of Moroccan origin are the second and more recent community. The Turkish community, along with those of Senegalese and Mali origin, make up the other main communities.

The law of December 1905, which settled the scission of the Catholic Church from the state, was not applied in Algeria. This exception to the law weighed heavily on subsequent relations between the state and Islam. The Mosque of Paris was long considered to be the centre of institutional Islam and, since 1926, the symbol of French Islam's presence in Paris. It represented the repatriated Algerians in 1962, but the state waited until 1989 to begin dialogue with all the representatives of the Muslim community. The specificity of France's secularism forbad the evocation of any questions other than those directly relating to worship. Indeed, all questions concerning the integration of Muslims at the social, cultural or political level could on no account be brought up as a religious subject. Otherwise Muslims could use the common law to constitute associations.

In view of the tense international climate, and with the increasing presence of a more marked Islamic activism, in 1989 the Minister for the Interior proposed the creation of an official study group *(Conseil de Reflexion)* on Islam. This was to be a strictly consultative organ that studied particular dossiers, including mosques, imams and halal food. Fifteen renowned individuals were invited as either representatives of organisations or of mosques. But this process failed.

It was only in 1999, following an attempt to restore the Mosque of Paris to a central role in the organisation of the Islam of France, that a new initiative was launched, that was to lead to the *Conseil Français du Culte Musulman* (CFCM - French Council of the Muslim Faith). This initiative came about in a calmer context than in the previous decade. France had known two terrorists waves, in 1985 and in 1995, which delayed the recognition of the Muslim faith in acceptable forms. The necessity of satisfying the aspirations of Muslims at the religious level had become evident. From the year 2000 onwards, France began to disconnect the notion of Islam as a source of international tension from the need to recognise the full citizenship of Muslims. As all over Europe, the most significant level of intervention to facilitate the practice of the Muslim faith took place at the local level. Policies of blocking the building of mosques gave way to a very active indirect assistance on the part of municipalities to build mosques and arrange for Muslim cemeteries.

But, as the main organisations of traditional Islam and the reformists agreed to deal with the state, organisations close to young Muslims refused any such masked 'allegiance'. This was illustrated in 2000 when the signature by participating organisations of a kind of charter was sought. The principle of this 'charter', which features the main points of the 1905 law on secularism, was rejected by young Muslims, mainly those born in France and of French nationality, whereas most of the participants in the consultative process were born abroad and later naturalised.

However, after three years of talks, agreement was reached on the charter creating the CFCM in 2003, following considerable efforts on the part of the Ministry of Interior. The mosques still lack organisational unity and are often autonomous and divided by national and doctrinal differences, which in turn hinder the functioning of the CFCM. Nevertheless, there continues to be headway in the recognition of Muslim practices, in particular at the local level.

On a more polemical issue, in 2003 the government tried to find a negotiated solution at the statutory level to limit the wearing of the 'voile' (headscarf)[1] in schools. Considerable pressure from the political class and the conclusions of a report (the Stasi report) resulted in the law of March 2004 banning religious symbols in public places (a de facto ban on the headscarf). From then on, organisations present in the CFCM, while regretting this decision, did not urge refusal to respect the law, but turned instead to the opening of private schools.

Despite the fact that the government does not provide support for imam training courses in France, it has been concerned with this issue for more than fifty years. There was a failed attempt to create a curriculum in which the French universities would provide certain courses, especially history, law, social sciences and French, with the Mosque of Paris. Professors refused to give specific courses to imams. There are no curricula defined by CFCM, though the government has asked to it to agree on an

---

[1] As recounted in the chapter by Valerie Amiraux, the semantics of the veil are highly confusing as between the French 'voile', which is understood to comprehend the 'foulard' (headscarf), whereas the English 'veil' always covers the face, and is quite distinct from the headscarf.

official definition of the imam and its training. Attempts to give courses on teaching the French language, on a regional basis, failed too. The FASILD, a public organisation in charge of this curriculum, claimed that the regional offices of CFCM were not able to mobilise the imams.

Germany

Since the Weimar constitution of 1919, freedom of conscience and religion has been definitively established. The social function of religion is widely recognised and support for religious instruction is compulsory for the different Länder. Religious institutions are organised at least as associations or, going one step further, as corporations under public law. The major religions and others more recently seen in Germany enjoy the legal capacity granted to these corporations, in particular that of tax-raising powers (8-10% depending on the Land, deducted at source), to appoint prison chaplains or teachers of the Muslim faith within the *Länder* education systems. However German Islam and Muslim groups are still evolving in a rather precarious legal context, and has so far not attained the status of corporation under public law.

The 3.5 million Muslims in Germany are for the most part of Turkish origin, then to a lesser degree of Bosnian, Iranian and Moroccan origin. This Turkish omnipresence, the legacy of traditional links between Turkey and Germany without post-colonial condescension, is combined with the notion of *gästarbeiter*, or guests. However the increasing acquisition of German nationality, only made legally possible in 2000, has brought to the fore the recurring issues we see in the rest of Europe, such as unemployment and discrimination, in particular for young people.

The federal system leaves to the *Länder* the main task of relations with Muslims. Moreover the strong German sense of religious identity, essentially to the Catholic and Protestant faiths, made it quite natural to virtually 'delegate' religious affairs to the *Diyanet Işleri Türk-Islam Birliği* (DİTİB), (Turkish Islamic Union for Religious Affairs), which is one of the largest Islamic organisations in Germany, and the German branch of the Turkish government's *Diyanet İşleri Başkanlığı* (Presidency of Religious Affairs). The situation has evolved in recent years with several cases concerning the veil in certain *Länder*, in particular involving teachers and civil servants, taken to the constitutional court in Karlsruhe, and which now obliges Germany to consider Islam as a domestic religion.

If the federal state cannot take a position on the theological foundations of a faith, the *Bundesamt für Verfassungschutz* (Federal Office for the Protection of the Constitution) is allowed a certain margin of operation to limit the activities of certain religious organisations. Interest in Islam has remained essentially at the level of the *Länder*. The majority tendencies of each *Land* – the Bavarian conservative Catholicism, the Rheinish more social Catholicism, the Protestantism of the northern Länder, or the lesser religious inclinations of the new eastern *Länder* – have generated different approaches towards relations with Islam. The policy of integration of Muslims in Rhineland-Westphalia, where more than a third of all Muslims in Germany live, is exemplary in this respect. Four of the most important Muslim organisations, the Islamrat, the Suleymanci, the DITIB and the Zentralrat reside in this region. The government of the *Land* is keen to ensure the education of Islam in schools as it does for the other religions, to allow Islam to enjoy advantages of the corporations of public law, in particular for tax collection, to train imams and to allow the building of mosques. In Duisburg and Cologne it has launched a pilot project to define religious instruction curricula in agreement with a representative body. A sort of Turkish and German 'joint management' seems to be the rule.

In the middle of 2006 the federal government took the initiative of organising a meeting with the *Deutsche Islam Konferenz* (DIK), which is expected to bring about changes in a comprehensive attempt to resolve outstanding issues. In addressing the German parliament on the subject of the DIK in September 2006, Wolfgang Schäuble, Minister for the Interior, argued that Muslims needed the framework of an appropriate process in order to gain the same advantages as the other religions. Defined as a meeting intended for the "Muslims in Germany and German Muslims", it is a project of high ambition. It was proposed that the DIK be based on the five main Muslim organisations (five of them, among which four Turkish) and ten individuals from civil society. The five organisations are: the Council of Islam (*Islamrat)* held by Milli Görüs; the Union of the Islamic Cultural Centres of Suleymanci; the official DITIB of Ankara; the Alévie community and the Muslim Central Council (*Zentralrat*). The Zentralrat is more multi-ethnic, and the only one that indicates its respect for the German Constitution in its charter of 2002, and the freedom to change religion, or to have none. The ten individuals, three women of Turkish origin committed to the defence of the rights of the Muslim women, and seven men of Turkish, Iranian, Lebanese and Afghan origins, are all engaged openly in the political or intellectual life of their country, and will be a significant counterweight to traditionalist or Islamist organisations, (the exception here being the Alevi community, known for its liberal vision of the Muslim faith).

The question of the compatibility of Islam with the constitution (*Grundgesetz*) was presented by the German Minister as the core of forthcoming conversations, as the choice of four working topics shows:

The German social order and the consensus on its values: equality of human rights and women's rights, training in political representation, the family, education, self-determination of youth, the acceptance of the variety of the democratic cultures, secularisation.

Questions of religion within the framework of the constitution: basic principle of the separation of the church and the state, the use of religious symbols, the building of mosques, the education of Islam in German under the control of the *Länder*, learning the German language, equal rights for girls and boys, joint education in sports, sex education, training of the imams and the study of Islam in higher education.

The media and the economy as a bridge: the question of young people on the labour market, upgrading qualifications, policy to remove the prejudices in the Turkish and German media.

Security and Islam: this group, more closed and secretive, should tackle questions of internal security, in particular to warn against and prevent violent acts against the democratic order.

The subject matters here far exceed a strictly religious context. The main Muslim organisations were surprised at first. However in September 2006, following the invitation, they issued a joint statement agreeing to participate, in spite of certain reservations. The next two years will reveal if this exhaustive approach to the question of citizenship for German Muslims will prove successful.

Belgium

The migratory streams of the 1960s brought mainly Moroccan and Turkish populations to Belgium. Today there are over 400,000 foreigners or Belgians of Muslim culture. The Belgian state maintains neutrality with regard to the faiths and the organisation of worship. It nevertheless recognises the public utility of churches, which leads to a certain interventionism. The Muslim faith was recognised in 1974. The state finances the confessional educational networks, provides for the salaries of the clergy and professors of religion and their accommodation. Buildings dedicated to worship are tax-exempt. Subsidies for the maintenance of places of worship are within the competence of three regions: Flanders, Wallonia and Brussels.

As elsewhere in Europe the question of the recognition of the leadership of the Muslim faith has proved extremely difficult to accommodate in the traditional legal framework. However, at the end of the 1990s Belgium initiated a highly original process. The state co-organised elections in mosques to the *Assemblée générale des Musulmans de Belgique* (AGMB - General Assembly of Muslims of Belgium), which in turn elects the *Executif des Musulmans de Belgique* (EMB - Executive of Belgian Muslims). This has led to the creation of elected colleges with ethnic character, differentiating Turks, Moroccans and converts, and then also between Flemish and French speakers. The officials of this body were elected in 1998 and again in 2005. Nevertheless, various difficulties, including the obligatory 'screening' of the elected members by the security services, have partly compromised the credibility of the EMB. A royal order of October 2005 recognised 17 new members of the EMB as proposed by the AGMB. Turkish activism resulted in the presidency going to a Turk, although the Moroccans are superior in number in Belgian society. Many Moroccans were incited to boycott the elections. As a result the state withheld certain advantages granted to a recognised religion, in particular that of the payment for the Ministers of the faith. The Flemish region seems more advanced that the two others in the approval of religious communities. For the training of the imams, the region has planned curricula at a high level, where instruction on the knowledge of Belgian society has been included.

Netherlands

The Muslim population totals almost 1 million, with the largest communities coming from Turkey, Morocco and Surinam. In the past five years, Islam has become a subject of intense controversy in the Netherlands, as dramatically symbolised by the murder of the film director Theo van Gogh. This and other events have prompted intense debate over the question of compatibility of Islam with democratic values in the Netherlands. A recent inquiry of June 2006,[2] revealed a disturbing account

---

[2] *Radicalen democraten*, Institute of Migrations and entitled Ethnic Studies (IMES).

of the views of young people of Moroccan origin. 40% reject the values of Western democracy and 6-7% says they are ready to resort to violence to defend their religion. The development of racism and the recent obligation to follow lessons in Dutch civilisation and language also contribute to a climate of insecurity among immigrants of Muslim origin. This tension, also illustrated also by the segregation into ethnic districts, contradicts the Dutch tradition of liberal tolerance. The birth of an Islamic party – the Muslim Democratic Party (MDP) - based in Belgium, contributes to the tension.

Until the end of the sixties the principle of 'pillarisation' prevailed, allowing for the real organisation of communities. A recent project proposed in this vein was for the construction of an Islamic hospital in Rotterdam, where the food would be halal, where men would be separated from women, and where an imam would live permanently, but this was rejected by right-wing officials within the municipal council.

People from immigrant communities have easy access to Dutch citizenship. As a result there are now more than 200 elected members of Muslim origin in municipalities, numerous elected members in the provincial advisory bodies, and ten members in the lower chamber of the parliament.

Since 1983 subsidies to churches have been cut, in particular the salaries and pensions of the clergy. However tax advantages remain, for example for the repair of mosques and the financing of chaplains in the army. But various subsidies of a cultural and social character are allocated to Muslim communities more as ethnic than religious minorities. Public funds allow the financing of private schools (*bizondere scholen*): 37 primary schools and three Muslim secondary schools have been established. But as in all other European states, it is the local level that is most involved. The municipality of Rotterdam finances Islamic education in its public schools, while Utrecht opposes this.

It is only at the end of 2004 and the beginning of 2005 that the government gave official recognition to organisations already widely implanted in the Netherlands. The *Contactorgaan Moslims in Overheid* (CMO) represents the majority of sunnis, with all the Turkish tendencies (DITIB, Milli Görüs and Suleymanci) except Alévis, and also the Moroccans close to the authorities in Rabat. The *Contactgroep Islam* (CGI) includes the other minorities including those from Surinam, Pakistan and Turkish alevis. This recognition was preceded by a close examination of their real representativeness.

The major preoccupation of the Dutch authorities remains the prevention of Islamic radicalisation. A debate within the lower chamber of the parliament in April 2005 gave way to a government plan entitled *Prevention of radicalisation in the context of integration policy*. The conclusions of this memorandum proposed actions to promote citizenship, social cohesion and integration (intensification of the values of the Dutch society and the means to combat discrimination). It recommended that practising Muslims be assisted to convince young people not to give in to radical Islamist temptations. Educational activities for Muslim populations were also proposed, including discussion forums, a sort of positive action for young people to get into university, and help to young Muslims to become emancipated.

There has also been an active policy for the training of imams and the leaders of mosques. The University of Amsterdam (VU) opened its doors in September 2005 with 40 students, receiving an annual grant of €250,000 for six years for this special course. Leiden University was chosen for a course on Islamic theology, with a grant of €2.35 million for 2006-10. Both universities plan to develop masters courses. Further training for imams, spiritual advisors and chaplains is undertaken by the Hogeschool Inholland, and in November 2005 received declarations of intent from five organisations of the CMO. Apart from theology, these initiatives teach knowledge of Dutch Islam and pastoral care. A central question remains over the legitimacy of a Protestant university to teach Muslim religious staff. Neither the VU nor Leiden received an explicit mandate from the Muslim organisations. The Hogeschool has had a programme in Islamic studies since 1995 for Islamic teachers in secondary schools. While the Milli Görüs accepted this programme, the DITIB was more reticent and continues to send imams from Turkey. Overall this is a unique experiment in Europe, as an attempt to provide Muslim theological education in a western university with Muslim and non-Muslim teachers.

Spain

Islam has been present in Spain since the Moorish invasion of the 8th century. There is a clear consciousness on the part of the Spanish people that the Muslim religion is one of the spiritual faiths that is rooted in Spanish history and one that is still present today. The more recent presence of Muslims in Spain has increased to around 600-800,000 in a relatively short space of time. They are first and foremost of Moroccan origin, with many working in the big farming exploitations in the south east. Other communities, namely Algerian and Syrian, are less numerous but complete the ethnic landscape.

The first institutional appearance of the Muslims in Spain was with the *Asociacion Muslmana de Espana* in 1971, whose first president was Ryay Tatari from Syria. By 1968 Islamic associations had been created in the Spanish enclaves in Morocco, Ceuta and Melilla. In June 1968 the first law on the freedom of religion was adopted, which opened the way for Muslims to establish themselves as religious entities. From the 1980s onwards, more than forty entities had appeared. The first association participated actively in the preparation of the Organic Law on the freedom of religion of July 1980, aimed at Islam and other religions.

In 1992 the Spanish government signed agreements with organisations representing Muslims, Jews and Protestants. And so the *Comision Islamica de Espana* (CIE) was born, comprising two unions, the *Federacion Espanola de Entitades Religiosas Islamicas* (FEERI) and the *Union of Communidades Islamicas of Espana* (UCIDE). The CIE signed its agreement of cooperation in April 1992. Among dossiers opened with the Spanish government appear religious education in schools, the registration regime of imams with the social security system, and the appointment of clergy in prisons. As regards financing, a foundation, *Fundacion Pluralismo y Convivencia,* was created in 2005. This foundation aims to help the poorest minority faiths with grant subsidies, but not for religious activities. In 2007, its budget of €4.5 million is allocated by the state.

In March 2006, the president of the CIE, Ryay Tatari, made a very critical assessment of relations between his organisation and the state[3] on all accounts. The CIE criticised difficulties in opening and maintaining mosques. Responsibility for mosques is held first and foremost by the municipalities, and their decisions can be very diverse. The pervading Islamophobia, according to the CIE, tends to limit the building of mosques. No new cemeteries have been opened. In spite of the registrations of certain associations as religious entities, the tax authorities refuse to grant them the exemptions to which they are entitled. The appointment of the clergy in

---

[3] Two years with the new administration of the State, IslamHispania.org.

prisons and hospitals has only been 'exceptional'. Only 35 professors of religion have been appointed; despite the best efforts of the government, they were obstructed by the provincial educational services. It has been difficult to clarify the programme for Muslim religious education in schools. In 2006 however, a book *Descubrir el Islam* was edited with the help of a Catholic editor and the funds of the foundation *Pluralismo convivencia*. There are difficulties in the application of the law for religious holidays. Although it is stated in the agreement of 1992 that Muslims would be actively involved in the management of the Spanish-Muslim heritage, the CIE complains that it is excluded from this management.

Concerning the wearing of the headscarf, the only recorded case of refusal was at a private school. In this case a public school welcomed the pupil.

Italy

The presence of Muslims in Italy is relatively recent, in spite of the history of Sicily and the South of Italy with its rich exchanges with Islam during the Middle Ages. The precise number of Muslims in Italy now is difficult to gauge, but is believed to be around 700,000. The great ethnic variety of immigrants, albeit with numerous Moroccan and Albanian communities, has impeded the constitution of representative entities capable of dialogue with the Italian government. As in Spain and France, the Catholic influence prevails, with a trend towards secularisation. The legal Italian regime for relations with the faiths is driven, according to the Constitution of 1948, by agreements (*intesas*) between churches and the Italian state, which settles the terms for the practice of each faith. If a certain number of religions have sealed such agreements, it was not the case for the Muslims until 2005, when the Italian authorities began discussions with a group of Muslim individuals. As all over Europe, the lack of dialogue between the state authorities and the myriad Muslim associations was often compensated by local policies. As a result about 200 mosques were built over the last fifteen years. Nevertheless, certain tensions persist. Certain intellectuals and even the Catholic church take a critical view of the presence of Muslims, and feelings of rejection on the part of the immigrants, of which Islam is supposed to be the symbol, also remain.

In spite of these obstacles, a '*Consulta*', between Muslim individuals and the Ministry of the Interior, was organised by a decree of September 2005. Previously, the services of the Minister had inquired about the functioning of France's *Consultation* with its Muslim communities. Throughout the declarations and the reports of the activities of the *Consulta*, the 'immigrant' character of the Muslim religion is asserted. This consultation is placed under the presidency of the Minister of Interior. The secretariat is assured by a civil servant of the Ministry of Interior and the agenda fixed in advance by the Minister. Participants are individual personalities rather than organisations, selected by virtue of their support for republican values and principles. Contrary to the other European countries, Italy refrained from dealing with organisations, but nonetheless includes representatives of the Ismailia community, the converts of the Religious Community of Italy, the World Islamic League and the World Islamic Mission. The inclusion of Mohamed Nour Dahan, president of the Union of the Community and the Islamic Organisations in Italy (UCOII) was the object of debates because of his closeness to the Muslim Brotherhood, although his organisation is the biggest in Italy. Among the 16 Muslim members of the *Consulta*, all the communities are represented, with three Moroccans, four women and two journalists. Working groups are constituted around different subjects, including the status of mosques, religious holidays, programmes in koranic schools, the Islamic veil, the training of imams, marriage and halal, among others.

In March 2006, at the conclusion of the second meeting of the *Consulta*, 11 of the 16 Muslim members presented a "Manifesto of Islam of Italy". This manifesto emphasises the desire to integrate into Italian society. They underline their wish to respect the constitution, condemn fundamentalism and terrorism, and to live together within the framework of a secular and pluralistic society. They reject radical ideologies; condemn anti-Christian and anti-Western preaching and evoke the right of Israel to security and the Palestinians to a state. They propose that imams deliver their sermons in Italian in places of worship, favouring integration into Italian society. They propose the posting by the mosques of their annual balance sheet and accounts. The necessity of knowing Italian, its culture and its fundamental values, is reaffirmed for all Muslims. Concerning schooling, the manifesto speaks of the superiority of public schools in advancing integration, with a possibility of optional education in Islam. It goes as far as cautioning against the creation of "Islamic school ghettos" by authorising Muslim private schools. Moreover it requests control over the curricula taught in koranic schools, to verify their compliance with the law. In the university field, it asks for the creation of exchanges between Italian universities and those of the Muslim world, and the creation of a doctoral programme in religion for imams. Finally, family values and the equality of the sexes are reaffirmed.

UCOII and its president, alone with an Algerian imam of Salerno, refused the manifesto, and presented a counter-proposal. Closer to the demands of the religious order, this counter-proposal asks inter alia for halal on the menus of schools and companies, for the implementation of chaplaincies, for the control of school curricula in their presentation of Islam, tax allowances for the building and maintenance of mosques and a whole swathe of measures to improve the integration of immigrants. As we can see this more 'militant' Islam, as elsewhere in Europe, has the advantage of being closer to the strictly religious demands of Muslims, whereas the Muslims disconnected from the practice of their faith are more concerned with promoting their harmonious integration into the society in which they live. Overall, dialogue in the *Consulta* appears to advance very slowly.

United Kingdom

In the British system the practice of worship is placed under the regime of freedom. Some official assistance for religion exists, however, as in other European countries, with tax exemption for places of worship and remuneration of the clergy. Subsidies for social, cultural, educational or charitable activities are widely used. The status of charitable activities allows for the promotion of religion. Registration is required with the Charity Commission, directed by a nominee of the Home Secretary. The diverse activities of a mosque can be supported in this way by public funds. The role of the state in dealings with religions is organised via the Ministerial Department of Communities and Local Government, but only recently were these accorded a full office. Previously, it was the responsibility of the Office of Race Relations. A technical guide, called *Working together: consultation between government and faith communities*, published in October 2003, describes the approach of central government towards consultation arrangements.

A real umbrella for the Muslim community, the Muslim Council of Britain (MCB), appeared only in 1997 in the UK, following the election to power of the Labour government and the fact that many constituencies had large Muslim populations. This was eight years after the publication of Salmon Rushdie's Satanic Verses had shaken the indifference of British society to the separate development of the Muslim community. 1997 was also the year when state funds were awarded to private Muslim schools.

The terrorist attacks of 9/11 in New York and Washington, and of 7/7 in London contributed in a short space of time to radically change the approach towards Islam by the government. Today, they are seven state Muslim schools in England and five more are recommended for public funding. The then Prime Minister seemed to want to bring more of the 150 private Muslim schools into the state sector. By comparison with other religions the Catholics have 2,041 state supported schools and the Church of England 4,646. However there are now complaints that faith schools divide society rather than promote social cohesion. And the obligation for these faith schools to reserve a quarter of their places for non-believers or children of other faiths is seen by Muslims as an unjust measure. Concerning the Islamic veil, several MPs, and specially Shahid Malik, the Labour MP of Dewsbury, expressed disapproval of a Muslim teaching assistant who refused to remove her veil in school. This case came after Jack Straw, the former foreign minister, asked Muslim women visiting his constituency surgery to remove their veils.

There are other initiatives to help the Muslim community. The involvement of the public authority in banking is an example, where the Financial Services Authority (FSA) responsible for banking regulation fosters the development of Islamic finance in the UK with an invitation to bankers from the Middle East to create an Islamic bank. This led to the Islamic Bank of Britain. The government has created a working group with members of the Muslim community, the banks and the FSA to discuss how the regulatory system could oversee new Islamic financial products. And UK banking and taxation laws have been modified to promote this new system.

Shortly after the 7/7 attacks in 2005 the British authorities organised consultations, called *Preventing Extremism Together (PET)*, which for the first time drew up a comprehensive review of the state of Muslim worship. This was the first step in a longer term partnership between the government and the Muslim communities, resulting in several important initiatives, and notably the creation of the Mosques and Imams National Advisory Board (MINAB). A steering group of Muslim leaders is working, consulting mosques and imams, on matters such as the accreditation of imams, better governance of mosques and interfaith activity. The affair of the Finsbury Park mosque in London, closely involved in international terrorism networks, is cited as an example of the inadequate governance in mosques. Concerning imams, MINAB provides guidelines on the accreditation of imams and to ensure that the profession of imam attracts young English-born Muslims. As elsewhere in Europe, the issue of foreign imams is always present, despite the 22 seminaries in UK that are supposed to train imams. There are Muslim universities like the Leicester Institute and the Markfield Institute of Higher Education also has a module for the management of mosques.

The government asked MINAB to ensure that mosques and imams play a role in community cohesion and combating extremism. An attempt to directly involve MCB with denouncing suspects of terrorism, however, was rejected by all Muslim leaders. Muslim forums against extremism and islamophobia have been created with 6 regional forums. Country-wide 'road shows' of influential and popular personalities have been organised, with influential international Muslim scholars and thinkers to speak to audiences of 18-30 years old British Muslims.

Nobody knows if this 'voluntarist' policy will succeed. But very substantial means have been devoted to it.

And on the international level, the UK also wants to play a role. An international conference was organised in 2006 in Istanbul by the Foreign Office and the British Council together with the Turkish government. This was led by 12 individuals living in Europe (seven from the UK, including Tariq Ramadan, two from Turkey, the general secretary of French UOIF, one for Germany and the Mufti of Bosnia, Mustafa Ceric). The conference addressed issues of identity and citizenship, and resistance of the European Muslim community to extremism. 200 individuals attended this conference, most of them having been contacted by the European Muslim Brotherhood. The final declaration presented some recommendations – one can find the same elements presented in other forums, such as work for the full application of EU legislation on positive migration, freedom to practise religion, recognition of existing establishments and the creation of new academic institutions, to ensure that imams are educated appropriately and are familiar with European culture and support the development of European fatwa bodies.

Austria

Religious communities are treated as public law corporations. But, unlike in Germany, Austrian Muslims have own their official body, the Islamic

Religious Community (*Islamische Glaubengemeinschaft in Österreich* – IGGÖ). Islam is one of the thirteen religions recognised. This formal recognition came about in 1912, after the recognition of the Muslim majority of Bosnia, which was annexed in 1898. The originality, if compared with the other EU member states, is that membership of this official body is limited to the individual; organisations are not represented. Hence, Turkish DITIB and Milli Görüs are not supposed to participate. Conditions of membership are three years of residence, Austrian citizenship and payment of membership fees. Members vote in four voting districts to elect a leader and a board. They send representatives to a Shira Council, which in turn elects the Supreme Council and there is a Grand Mufti.

The biggest communities are those of Turkish origin followed by the Bosnians. The president of IGGÖ, Anas Shakfe, is a Syrian-born Austrian. The long-established recognition of Islamic worship in Austria has also resulted in the establishment of an institute in Vienna (*Islamisches Religion pädagogisches Akademie* – IRPA), to train teachers who know the fundamentals of Islam, are German speakers and are supposed to be able to explain and enter into discussion about Islam in the context of life in Austria. The IGGÖ and the IRPA are the official partners of the government and leaders of both bodies are proud to train teachers to use theological arguments against extremism. Nevertheless, if Islamic education is provided in public schools by teachers under the control of IRPA and IGGÖ, a large number of Muslim students avoid religious education. Parents, especially of Turkish origin, prefer to send their children to the school's mosque. For the moment, students finish with a technical school diploma in the IRPA, but this will be changed to a BA; IRPA will be established as an *Urschule* (founding school) in Islamic Education in 2007. And efforts continue to strengthen the Centre of Research into Islamic Pedagogy of Vienna, situated inside the Faculty of Philosophy and of Sciences of Education and providing a masters diploma. There are no special training courses for imams. The majority come, as in the other countries, from the Turkish universities, under the control of DITIB (Turkish Islamic Union for Religious Affairs).

The Austrian foreign ministry twice helped IGGÖ to hold an international meeting of imams in Vienna. The first time was in 2003 and the second in April 2006, under the Austrian presidency of Europe. Chancellor Schüssel welcomed the second session where more than 200 imams and Muslim religious leaders attended. The final declaration, like three months later in Istanbul at another conference (see above in the chapter on the UK) claimed: "Islam is a real component of the European identity through the accomplishments of its grand scientific and cultural heritage". To thank the guest country the conference concluded: "Consequently, the model of the status of recognition for Islam, as it exists in Austria, is actually especially suitable, because it brings with it, beyond the emotional level of belonging, an institutionalised dialogue".

During this meeting, the idea emerged for a sort of European Council of Fatwa, which can prevent "having to fall back on foreign experts' opinions" because it will "grow from the local Muslim community". This was interesting considering that this body is supposed to exist already: there is a European Council of the Fatwa and Research, located in Dublin and directed by Muslim Brotherhood leaders. As we can see, Austria, like the UK, wishes to play a role in promoting European Islam.

Greece

The particular history of Greece, given the weight of the Orthodox Church and the old conflicts with Turkey, leads to a rather problematic recognition of the rights of Muslims. According to the Treaty of Lausanne, a community of 120,000 Turkish-speakers lives in Thrace under a special arrangement. Three Muftis have the power to control family affairs according to Muslim legislation (but since 1991 decisions have to be confirmed by a civil court) and the freedom to practise and teach the Turkish language. Immigration, mostly from Albania and then from Arab countries (200,000 in Athens), incites Greece to consider Muslims as full citizens, not as a local minority. Even for the Turkish minority, problems still remain. As in Bulgaria, the government does not let the Muslim community elect their Muftis. The Greek government was twice sentenced by the European Court of Human Rights (1999 and 2006) for having chosen a Mufti. Another conflict concerns the identity of the Thracian Muslims. Yet in 1990, the first independent Turkish Member of Parliament, Ahmet Sadiq, was elected. But he was then disqualified and sentenced to 18 months in jail because he said that the Muslims of Thrace were Turkish instead of, according to Greek law, Greek Muslim.

This complicates matters for other Muslims. The affair of the Athens mosque has been outstanding for years. Greek citizens and the Orthodox church, which can give advice on the state management of religion, were opposed to the building of a mosque. After several years, it seems that the problem will be solved. Other problems persist like cemeteries encountering opposition from local authorities to let Muslims and other non-orthodox religions practise their faiths.

Bulgaria

One legacy of the Ottoman Empire is that most of the more than one million Muslims in Bulgaria (Muslims claim a higher number) are ethnic Turks, followed by ethnic Roma and then ethnic Slavs (Pomaks). They are mostly Bulgarian born and live in particular areas. The Muslims have seen their situation change progressively since 1990, when the communist system fell. Before this date, from 1946 to 1989, a tough campaign of assimilation was imposed. In 2002 a religious Act was passed requiring religious groups to register with the state, which included Muslims. However the Orthodox Church, as the only traditional religion, was not obliged to register. An official directorate plays a role as a kind of religious police force. As in Greece, they have a sort of minority status, but are not defined by any treaty with Turkey. With 1,150 mosques, 150 built since 1989, three Muslim primary and secondary schools and a higher education institute in Sofia, the representation of Muslim interests has been progressing. Muslims are influential with a party, the Movement for Rights and Freedom, which is the third party in the country.

The National Muslim Conference represents the community. But problems have appeared since the return to democracy. As in Greece, the state has imposed a mufti against the will of the Muslim community, and has been also been condemned by the European Court of Human rights for intervening in the religious affairs of the community. Another issue concerns the return of properties confiscated by the communist regime. Refusals to build new mosques are also a symbol of the resistance on the part of the local authorities to admit Muslim worship. Tensions have increased since 9/11 and fear of radicalisation has exacerbated the situation, (Ayman Al Zawahiri, al Qaeda operative 'No. 2', was said to be a resident in Sofia in the 1990s).

Conclusions

This paper has described how the governments of some European countries have been trying to resolve issues surrounding the recognition of Muslims in their respective societies. There is no European Union policy on matters of religion. Yet the comparison of these various experiences, for example on questions of Islamic education or institutionalisation, can be helpful.

It is clear that the situation has changed over the last five years. If the international context has become increasingly difficult, new trends can be observed towards a greater control by the state over the organisation of the Muslim community. In fact all European countries seem to be moving in the same direction here. Even France, considered as the most secular of European countries, has begun an active policy of a kind of 'recognition' of the Islamic religion. All countries' policies tend towards more inclusive citizenship as an antidote to the dangers of racism and Islamophobia.

Religious affairs are not still European affairs, but a competence reserved for the member states. The European Court of Human Rights remains very prudent, each President of the Commission has his own project, and each country has its point of view on how to arrange the place of religion in our societies. There are nonetheless common themes and concerns.[4] Islam can no longer be considered as another ethnic or cultural system that has nothing to do with European culture. It is necessary to consider that Muslims have the same rights and the same duties as people of other religions.

It is also necessary to disconnect the inclusion of the Muslim religion within European countries from European policy towards the wider Muslim world. Policies towards the Euro-Mediterranean dialogue or the entry of Turkey into the European Union cannot replace or cancel progress in relations with European Muslim communities. Even if radicalism and terrorism are very weighty problems that have to be confronted, they cannot justify not allowing Muslims the liberty to practise their faith. The obligation to denounce 'extremists' to security services is not appropriate. But, on the contrary, asking to them to form their own 'police' is necessary.

What is called 'islamophobia' is not the rejection of a religion, but a refusal to include people whose skins and names are not 'European'. Discrimination at the level of religious identity merely gives support to extremist Muslim groups. Before being Muslim, they are citizens, with their political opinions, and every element constituting their personality.

---

[4] At the practical level European Union directives on the subjects of discrimination in the labour market and race relations are highly relevant to the concerns of the Muslim community (as the chapter by Tufyal Choudhury explained).

The issues of worship are mostly local. Each state has to improve communications between local and national levels to help the Muslim community.

Supervision of youngsters and the creation of training centres for imams, teachers of religion or chaplains appear to be urgent. Delays over the control of teaching materials used in the koranic schools are dangerous. Muslim religious education has to be considered as the first challenge.

It could be useful to create a steering group at the European level to study all the means to create a European dynamic for concerted policies towards the Muslim community. It is difficult for the moment to unify a policy, Islam being a religion like any other religion. But reflection about religions in general and the ways in which non-traditional religions can be allowed to establish themselves in Europe could begin with the Muslim case.

REFERENCES AND FURTHER READING

Ahsan, M. A. and A. R. Kidwai, *Sacrilege versus civility: Muslim perspectives on the Satanic Verses affair*, Leicester: Islamic Foundation, 1991.

AIM (Asians in Media online magazine), "Burqa Babes in Zoo", London, 21 October 2006: (retrivable at: http://www.asiansinmedia.org/diary/ ?p=15).

Akgonul, S. (2006), "Millî Görüs: institution religieuse minoritaire et mouvement politique transnational (France et Allemagne)", in Samir Amghar (dir.), *Islamismes d'Occident. État des lieux et perspectives*, Paris, Lignes de Reperes.

Allen, C. (2003), *Fair justice: the Bradford disturbances, the sentencing and the impact*, London: FAIR.

Allen, C. (2005), "From race to religion: the new face of discrimination", in Tahir Abbas (ed.), Muslim Britain: communities under pressure, London: Zed Books.

Allen, C. (2006), "Islamophobia: contested concept in the public space", Ph.D dissertation, University of Birmingham.

Allen, C. and J. Nielsen (2002), *Summary Report on Islamophobia in the European Union after 11 September 2001*, European Union Monitoring Centre on Racism and Xenophobia (EUMC), Vienna.

Al Hussani, A. (2005), *Islamophobia in Europe*, ENAR Shadow Report, European Network Against Racism, Brussels.

Al-Rasheed, M. (2007), *Contesting the Saudi State: Islamic Voices from a New Generation*, Cambridge: Cambridge University Press.

Aluffi, R. and G. Zincone (eds) (2004), *The legal treatment of Islamic minorities in Europe*, Leuven: Peeters.

Al-Zawahiri, A. (2002), «Al wala'wa al-baraa», September.

Ameli, S. R., M. Elahi and A. Merali (2004), *British Muslims' Expectations of Government: Social discrimination across the Muslim divide*, Islamic Human Rights Commission, London.

Amghar, S. (2006), «Les trois âges du discours des frères musulmans en Europe», in Samir Amghar (dir.), *Islamismes d'Occident: perspectives et enjeux*, Lignes de Repères.

Amghar, S. (2006), "Le salafisme en Europe: la mouvance polymorphe d'une radicalisation", *Politique étrangère*, 1.

Amghar, S. (2005), «Le paysage Islamique français: acteurs et enjeu» in J.F. Dortier and L. Testot, *La religion. Unité et Diversité*, Paris, Sciences humaines.

Amghar, S. (2005), "Les salafistes français: une nouvelle aristocratie religieuse?», *Maghreb-Mashrek*, No. 185.

Amghar, S. (2006) "Les Frères musulmans francophone: vers un islamisme de la minorité", in S. Amghar (dir.), Paris, Lignes de Reperes.

Amir-Moazami, S. (2007), *Politisierte Religion. Der Kopftuchstreit in Deutschland und Frankreich*, Bielefeld: Transcript.

Amir-Moazami, S. (2005), "Muslim Challenges to the Secular Consensus: A German Case Study", *Journal of Contemporary European Studies*, Vol. 13, No. 3, pp. 267-286.

Amiraux, V. (2002), "The Situation of Muslims in France", in *Monitoring the EU Accession Process: Minority Protection*, Open Society Institute, Budapest.

Amiraux, V. (2006), "Speaking as a Muslim: Avoiding Religion in French Public Space", in G. Jonker and V. Amiraux (eds), *Politics of Visibility. Young Muslims in European Public Spheres*, Bielefeld: Transcript.

Amiraux, V. and P. Simon (2006), "'There are no minorities here': Cultures of Scholarship and Public Debate on Immigrants and Integration in France", *International Journal of Comparative Sociology*, 47 (3-4), pp. 191-215.

Ansari, H. (2003), *'The Infidel Within' – Muslims in Britain since 1800*, London: Hurst.

Banque Européenne d'Investissement, "Etude sur les transferts de fonds des migrants méditerranéens d'Europe" (available at www.bei.org).

Barnard, C. (2001), "The Changing Scope of Equality Law?", *McGill Law Review*, 46.

Bamforth, N. (2004), "Conceptions of Anti-Discrimination Law" *Oxford Journal of Legal Studies* 24(4).

Barnard, C., (1996), "The Economic Objectives of Article 119", in T. Hervey and O'Keeffe (eds.) *Sex Equality Law in the European Union*, Chichester: Wiley Chancery.

Barry, B. (2001), *Culture and Equality: An Egalitarian Critique of Multiculturalism*, Cambridge, MA: Harvard University Press.

Bell, M. (2004), "Equality and the European Constitution", 33 *Industrial Law Journal*, 242.

Bell, M., "The Right to Equality and Non-Discrimination" in T. Hervey and J. Kenner (eds) (2003), *Economic and Social Rights under the EC Charter of Fundamental Rights: A Legal Perspective*, Oxford: Hart Publishing.

Bell, M. (2002), "Beyond European Labour Law? Reflections on the EU Racial Equality Directive", *European Law Journal*.

Besson, E. (1998), "For an emergency plan to support the creation of small entreprises", Information Report No. 1804, Observatory of European SME's, European Commission, DG Enterprise, Brussels.

Bin Ahmad, M. (2003), "Islam and Economic Growth in Malaysia", Naval Postgraduate School, Malaysia, December.

Blair, A. and W. Aps (2005), "What not to wear and other stories: Addressing religious diversity in schools", *Education and the Law*, Vol. 17, No. 1-2, March/June, pp. 1-22.

Blaschke, J. (2004), "Tolerated but Marginalised – Muslims in Germany" in *State Policies towards Muslim Minorities. Sweden, Great Britain and Germany*, Edition Parabolis Verlagsabteilung im Europäischen Migrationszentrum (EMZ), Kempten.

Blick, A., T. Choudhury, and S. Weir (2006), *The Rules of the Game: Terrorism, Community and Human Rights*, Joseph Rowntree Reform Trust, York.

Blion, R., C. Frachon, A.G. Hargreaves, C. Humblot, I. Rigoni, M. Georgiou and S. Dilli (2006), *La représentation des immigrés au sein des media, Bilan des connaissances*, FASILD, Paris.

Blommesteijn, M. and H. Entzinger, (1999) "Appendix: Report of the Field Studies carried out in France, Italy, the Netherlands, Norway, Portugal and the United Kingdom, 1999", in C. Butterwerge, G. Hentges, F. Sarigös (eds) (1999), *Medien und multikulturelle Gesellschaft*, Opladen, Leske und Budrich Verlag.

Body-Gendrot, S., E. Ma Mung and C. Hodeir (1992), "Entrepreneurs entre deux mondes. Les créations d'entreprises par les étrangers: France, Europe, Amérique du Nord", *Revue Européenne des Migrations Internationales*, Vol. 8, No. 1.

Bonnefoy, L. (2003), "Public institutions and Islam: A new stigmatization?", ISIM Newsletter, International Institute for the Study of Islam in the Modern World, 13, ISIM Newsletter, December.

Boubekeur, A. (2005), "Cool and Competitive: Muslim Culture in the West", *ISIM Review*, No. 16, International Institute for the Study of Islam in the Modern World, autumn.

Boubekeur, A. (2006), «L'islamisme comme tradition. Fatigue militante et désengagement islamiste en Occident», in Samir Amghar (ed.), *Islamismes d'Occident. État des lieux et perspectives*, Paris: Lignes de repères.

Boubekeur, A. and S. Amghar (2006), "Islamist Parties in the Maghreb and their Connections with Europe: Growing Influences and the Dynamics of Democratization", Euromesco report, November.

Boubekeur, A. and S. Amghar (2006), "The role of Islam in Europe: Multiple Crises?", in *Islam and Tolerance in Wider Europe*, Open Society Institute, June.

Boussetta, H. (2003), «L'Islam et les musulmans en Belgique, enjeux locaux et cadres de réflexion globaux», Synthesis note, Fondation Roi Baudouin, Bruxelles, September.

Bouvenkerk, F., M.J.I. Gras, D. Ramsoedh, M. Dankoor and A. Havelaar (1995), *Discrimination against migrant workers and ethnic minorities in access to employment in the Netherlands*, International Labour Office, Geneva.

Bowen, J. (2006), *Why the French do not like headscarves: Islam, the State, and Public Space*, Princeton, NJ: Princeton University Press.

Bréchon, P. and J-P Willaime (eds) (2000), *Media et religions en miroir*, Paris: PUF, coll. Politique d'aujourd'hui.

Brems, E. (2006), "Above Children's Heads. The Headscarf Controversy in European Schools from the Perspective of Children's Rights", *International Journal of Children's Rights*, 14, pp. 119-136.

Bribosia, E. and I. Rorive (2004), "Le voile à l'école: Une Europe divisée", *Revue trimestrielle des droits de l'homme*, 60, pp. 951-983.

Brown, M. (2000), "Religion and Economic Activity in the South Asian population", *Ethnic and Racial Studies*, 23(6).

Buijs F. and J. Rath (2002), "Muslims in Europe, the State of Research", Russell Sage Foundation, NYC, USA, October.

Bunglawala, W. (2005), 'Muslims in the UK and the Labour Market', in The Open Society Institute, *Muslims in the UK: Policies for Engaged Citizens*, Budapest: Open Society Institute, pp.193-251.

Burgat, F. (2005), *L'Islamisme à l'heure d'Al-Qaida*, Paris, La Découverte, pp. 32-39, 117.

Burgat, F. (2002), *L'Islamisme en face*, Paris, La découverte, p. 113.

Bying, M. (1998), "Mediating Discrimination: Resisting Oppression among African-American Muslim Women", *Social Problems*, 45(4).

Caeiro, A. (2005), "Religious Authorities or Political Actors? The Muslim Leaders of the French Representative Body of Islam", in J. Cesari and S. Mcloughlin (eds), *European Muslims and the Secular State*, Aldershot: Ashgate, pp. 71-84.

Calla, C. (2005), "L'intégration réussie des immigrés à Francfort", *Le Figaro*, December.

Carens, J. (2004), "The weight of context: Headscarfs in Holland", *Journal of Ethical Theory and Moral Practice*, Volume 7, No. 2, April.

Carré, O. and G. Michaud (Michel Seurat) (1983), *Les Frères musulmans*, Paris: Gallimard-Julliard, collection Archives.

Catarino, C. and M. Morokvasic (2005), "Femmes, Genre, Migration et Mobilités", *Revue Européenne des Migrations Internationales*, Vol. 21, No. 5.

Geissler, R. and H. Pöttker (Hrsg.) (2005), *Massenmedien und die Integration ethnischer Minderheiten in Deutschland*, Bielefeld: Transcript.

CEREI (Cercle d'Etudes et de Recherches en Economie Islamique) (2003), "Quantification of the Muslim Financial Needs", December, (see www.cerei.net).

Cesari, J. (1998), *Musulmans et Républicains, les Jeunes, L'islam et la France*, Bruxelles : Complexe.

Cesari, J. (2002), "Islam in France: The Shaping of a Religious Minority" in Yvonne Haddad-Yazbek (ed.), *Muslims in the West, from Sojourners to Citizens*, Oxford: Oxford University Press, pp.36-51.

Cesari, J., S. Bargach and D. Moore (2002), «L'islamismation de l'espace public français: vers la fin des conflits», *Les Cahiers du Cemoti*, No. 33.

Cesari, J. (2006), *Securitization and religious divides in Europe: Muslims in Western Europe after 9/11 – Why the term Islamophobia is more a predicament than an explanation*, Paris: Challenge, (http://www.libertysecurity.org).

Chan, K.B. and S.N.C. Chiang (1994), "Cultural Values and Immigrant Entrepreneurship: The Chinese in Singapore", *Revue Européenne des Migrations Internationales*, Vol. 10, No. 2.

Chonm, M. and D. Artz (2005), "Walking While Muslim", *Law and Contemporary Problems*, 68.

CEREQ (Centre d'études et de recherches sur les qualifications) (1998), Survey on "Generation 98", Paris.

Chopin, I. (1999), "The Starting Line Group: A Harmonised Approach to Fight Racism and to Promote Equal Treatment", *European Journal of Migration and the Law* No. 40, 1.

Choudhury, T., M. Aziz, D. Izzidien, I. Khireeji and D. Hussain (2006), *Perceptions of Discrimination and Islamophobia: voices from members of Muslim communities in the European Union*, European Union Monitoring Centre of Racism and Xenophobia, Vienna.

Clayton, D., "Data comparability, definitions and the challenges for data collection on the phenomenon of racism, xenophobia, anti-Semitism and Islamophobia in the European Union", paper presented at European Monitoring Centre on Racism and Xenophobia (EUMC) Colloque, Vienna, 25 June 2002.

Collins, H. (2003), "Discrimination, Equality and Social Inclusion", Volume 66, Issue 1 *Modern Law Review*, Blackwell Synergy.

Dahlab v. Switzerland, App. 42393/98, 15 February 2001 (http://www.echr.coe.int).

Dassetto, F., (1988), "L'organisation du Tabligh en Belgique" in T. Gersholm and Y.G. Lithman (eds), *The New Islamic Presence in Western Europe*, London, New York.

Dasseto, F. (1998), *Le Tabligh en Belgique. Diffuser l'islam sur les traces du prophète*, Louvain-la-Neuve: Academia Bruylant, Sybidi Papers.

Davie, G. (2000), *Religion in Modern Europe*, Oxford: Oxford University Press.

Dayan, J-L, A. Echardour and M. Glaude (1996), "Le Parcours professionnel des immigrés en France: Une analyse longitudinale", *Revue Economie et Statistique*, No. 299.

Deltombe, T. (2005), *L'islam imaginaire. La construction médiatique de l'islamophobie en France, 1975-2005*, Paris: La Découverte.

Demant et al. (2007), *Muslims in the EU City Reports – The Netherlands: Preliminary Research Report and Literature Review*, Budapest, Open Society Institute, forthcoming), pp. 16 and 24.

Demant et al. (2007), *Muslims in the EU City Reports – The Netherlands: Preliminary Research Report and Literature Review*, Open Society Institute, Budapest.

De Schutter, O., *Three Models of Equality and European Anti-Discrimination Law* (forthcoming).

Diop, M.A. (1994), "Structuration d'un réseau: la Jamaat Tabligh (Société pour la Propagation de la Foi)", *Revue européenne des migrations internationales*, Vol. 10, No. 1.

di Torella, E.C. (2005), "The Goods and Services Directive: Limitations and Opportunities", *Feminist Legal Studies*, 13.

Dreher, R. (2002), "Murder in Holland", *National Review*, 7, May.

Duits, L. and L. van Zoonen (2006), "Headscarves and Porno-Chic: Disciplining Girls' Bodies in the European Multicultural Society", *European Journal of Women's* Studies, 13, pp. 103-117.

Dwyer, C. (2000), "Negotiating diasporic identities: young British South Asian Muslim women", *Women's studies international forum*, 23(4).

Dwyer, C. (1999), "Veiled meanings: young British Muslim women and the negotiation of differences", *Gender, place and culture*, 6(1).

El Hamel, C. (2002), "Muslim Diaspora in Western Europe: the Islamic Headscarf (Hijab), the Media and Muslims' Integration in France", *Citizenship Studies*, 6(3).

El Guindi, F. (1999), *Veil: Modesty, privacy and resistance*, London: Berg.

Ellis, E., (2002) "The Principle of non-discrimination in the Post-Nice Era" in Arnull and Wincott (eds), *Accountability and Legitimacy in the European Union*, Oxford: OUP.

Enneli, P., T. Modood and H. Bradley (2005), *Young Kurds and Turks: A set of 'invisible' disadvantaged groups*, Joseph Rowntree Foundation, York.

Esposito, J. (1983), *Voices of Resurgent Islam*, Oxford: Oxford University Press.

EUMC (European Monitoring Centre on Racism and Xenophobia) (2006), "Antisemitism - Summary overview of the situation in the European Union 2001-05", EUMC, Vienna.

EUMC (European Union Monitoring Centre on Racism and Xenophobia) (2006), "Muslims in the European Union: Discrimination and Islamophobia", EUMC, Vienna.

EUMC (European Union Monitoring Centre on Racism and Xenophobia) (2005), "The Impact of 7 July 2005 London Bomb Attacks on Muslim Communities in the EU", EUMC, Vienna.

Fekete, L. (2004), "Anti-Muslim racism and the European security state", Race and Class, 46(1).

Foley, M.W. and B. Edwards (1996), "The paradox of civil society", Journal of Democracy, 7(3), pp. 38-52.

Ferrari, S. (ed.) (1996), L'Islam in Europa. Lo statuto giuridico delle comunità musulmane, Bologna: il Mulino.

Ferrari, S. (2005) "The Secularity of the State and the Shaping of Muslim Representative Organisations in Western Europe", in J. Cesari and S. McLoughlin (ed.) European Muslims and the Secular State, Aldershot: Ashgate.

Fredman, S. (2002), Discrimination Law, Oxford: Oxford University Press.

Fredman, S. (2005), "Changing the Norm: Positive Duties in Equal Treatment Legislation", Maastricht Journal of European and Comparative Law 369, 12(4).

Frégosi, F. (2005), «Les musulmans laïques en France: une mouvance plurielle et contradictoire», Maghreb-Maschrek, No. 185, printemps.

Gale, R., "The Multicultural City and the Politics of Religious Architecture: Urban Planning, Mosques and Meaning-making in Birmingham, UK" Built Environment, 30(1).

Gallala, I. (2006), "The Islamic Headscarf: An Example of Surmountable Conflict between Shari'a and the Fundamental Principles of Europe", European Law Journal, 12(5).

Gaspard, F. and F. Khosrokhavar (1995), Le foulard et la République, Paris: La Découverte, "Essais et Documents".

Geisser, V. (2003), La nouvelle islamophobie, Paris, La Découverte.

Geissler, R., H. Pöttker (Hrsg.) (2005), Massenmedien und die Integration ethnischer Minderheiten in Deutschland, Bielefeld: Transcript.

Girardet, R. (1990), *Mythes et Mythologies Politiques*, Paris: Le Seuil.

Goldberg, A., D. Mourhino and U. Kulke (1997), *Labour market discrimination against foreign workers in Germany*, International Migration Papers 7, International Labour Organisation, Geneva.

Goldstone, J. (2006), *Ethnic Profiling and Counter-Terrorism: Trends, Dangers and Alternatives*, New York, Open Justice Initiative.

Gökariksel B. and K. Mitchell (2005), "Veiling, secularism, and the neoliberal subject: National narratives and supranational desires in Turkey and France", *Global Networks*, 5(2).

Göle, N. (1996), *The Forbidden Modern: Civilization and Veiling*, Ann Arbor, MI: University of Michigan Press.

Gresh, A. (1997), "L'Islam dans les media", Centre socio-culturel de la rue de Tanger, Paris.

Gritti, R. (2003), *Torri crollanti. Comunicazioni, media e nuovi terrorismi dopo l'11 settembre*, Rome: Fillenzi, pp. 278-279.

Guénif-Souilamas, N. (2006), "The Other French exception. Virtuous Racism and the War of the Sexes in Postcolonial France", *French Politics, Culture and Society*, Vol. 24, 3, pp. 23-41.

Guenif-Souilmas, N. and E. Macé (2004), *Les féministes et le garçon arabe*, Paris: De l'Aube.

Guiso, L., P. Sapienza and L. Zingales (2002), People's Opium? Religion and Economic Activities, NBER Working Paper 9237, National Bureau of Economic Research, Cambridge.

Habermas, J. (1997), *Droit et Démocratie: entre faits et normes*, Paris: Gallimard.

HCI (2005), *La diversité culturelle et la culture commune dans l'audiovisuel*, Avis du Haut Conseil à l'Intégration au Premier ministre, Paris, 17 mars.

Hafez, Kai (Hrsg.) (2001), *Media and Migration. Ethnicity and Transculturality in the Media Age*, Schwerpunktheft der Zeitschrift NORD-SÜD aktuell 4.

Halliday, F. (1999), *Islam and the myth of confrontation: religion and politics in the Middle East*, chapters 4, 6, London: IB Tauris.

Halman, L. and O. Riise (eds) (2003), *Religion in a Secularizing Society: The Europeans' Religion at the End of the 20th Century (European Values Study, 5)*, The Hague: Brill.

Hamid, A.W. (2002), *The quest for sanity: reflections on September 11 and its aftermath*, London: MCB.

Hamzeh, N.A. and R. Hrair Dekmejian (1996), "A sufi response to political Islamism: Al-ahbash of Lebanon", *International Journal of Middle East Studies*, No. 28.

Hervey, T.K. (2005), "Thirty Years of EU Sex Equality Law: Looking Backwards, Looking Forwards", *Maastricht Journal of European and Comparative Law*, 12(4).

Holmes, E. (2005), "Anti-Discrimination Rights Without Equality", *Modern Law Review*, 68(2).

Hourani, A. (1962), *Arabic thought in the Liberal Age*, Oxford: Oxford University Press.

Housez, C. (2006), "L'obsession identitaire des médias français", 9 March (http>//www.voltairenet.org).

Housez, C. (2005), "*Charlie Hebdo* et *Prochoix*. Vendre le «choc des civilisations» à la gauche", 30 August, (http>//www.voltairenet.org).

Husband, C., L. Beattie and L. Markelin (2000), *The key role of minority ethnic media in multiethnic societies: case study, UK*, The International Media Working Group Against Racism and Xenophobia (IMRAX) and the International Federation of Journalists (IFJ), Bruxelles.

Hussain, S. (2003), *An Introduction to Muslims in the 2001 National Census*.

IHF (2005), *Intolerance and Discrimination against Muslims in the EU: Developments since September 11*, March, p. 78.

INSEE (2005), *Les immigrés en France* (Immigrants in France), Edition 2005, p. 130, cited in Tebbakh, S., *Muslims in the EU Cities Report – France: Preliminary Research Report and Literature Survey*, Open Society Institute, Budapest.

Jahangir, A. (2006), *Droits civils et politiques, notamment la question de l'intolérance religieuse (Additif mission en France)*, Rapport, Commission des droits de l'Homme, ONU, March.

Joppe, C. (2007), "Beyond Nationals Models: Civic Integration Policies for Immigrants in Western Europe", *Western European Politics*, 30(1).

Kabha, M. and E. Haggai (2006), "Al-Ahbash and Wahhabiyya interpretations of Islam", *International Journal of Middle East Studies*, 38(4).

Karakasoglu, Y. et al. (2006), "German report", in Cesari, pp. 148-149.

Keddie, N. (1968), *An Islamic Response to Imperialism, Political and Religious Writings of Sayyid Jamal al-Din `Al-Afghani*, University of California Press.

Kepel, G. (2003), *Jihad, Expansion et déclin de l'islamisme*, Paris, Gallimard/Folio, (Original Edition: Paris, Gallimard, 2000).

Kepel, G. (2004), *Fitna. Guerre au cœur de l'Islam*, Paris: Le seuil.

Kepel, G. (dir.) (2005), *Al-Qaïda dans le texte*, Paris, PUT, 2005.

Kerr, M.H. (1966), *Islamic Reform: The Political and Legal Theories of Muhammad `Abduh and Rashid Rida*, University of California Press.

Khosrokhavar, F. (2003), *Les Nouveaux Martyrs d'Allah*, Paris: Flammarion.

Khosrokavar, F. (1997), *L'islam des jeunes*, Paris: Flammarion.

Khachani, M. (1999), "La Femme Maghrébine Immigrée dans l'Espace Economique des pays d'accueil: Quelques repères", actes du colloque international "Femmes et Migrations". Numéro spécial de la Revue Juridique *Politique et Economique du Maroc* éditée par la Faculté des Sciences Juridiques Economiques et Sociales de Rabat.

Kira, K. (2000), "Building Bridges: Media for Migrants and the Public-Service Mission in Germany", *European Journal of Cultural Studies*, No. 3, pp. 319-342.

Kodmani-Darwish, B. and M. Chartouni-Dubarry (eds) (1997), *Les Etats arabes face à la contestation islamiste*, Armand Colin.

Kuran, T. (2005), *Islam and Mammon: The Economic Predicaments of Islamism*, Princeton, NJ: Princeton University Press.

Lane, R. J. (2001), *Jean Baudrillard*, London: Routledge.

Lavau, G. (1981), *A quoi sert le Parti communiste?*, Paris: Fayard.

Laurens, H. (1993), *L'Orient arabe: arabisme et islamisme de 1798 à 1945*, Paris: A. Colin.

Leiken, R. (2006), "The Quantitative Analysis of Terrorism and Immigration: An Initial Exploration", *Terrorism and Political Violence*, Nixon Institute, December.

Le Monde (2005), "De plus en plus de jeunes musulmans sont attirés par la consommation halal", 13 juin.

Leyens, J-P. et al. (1994), *Stereotypes and social cognition*, London: Sage.

Liguori, M. (2006), "Report on Islamophobia", in Cesari.

Lindley, J. (2002), "Race or Religion? The impact of religion on the employment and earnings of Britain's ethnic communities", *Journal of Ethnic and Migration Studies*, 28(3).

Lohlker, R. (2004), *Islam im Internet. Formen muslimischer Religiosität im Cyberspace*, Hamburg, Deutsches Orient Institut.

Lopez, A. and G. Thomas (2006), "L'insertion des jeunes sur le marché du travail: le poids des origines socioculturelles", Données sociales, INSEE, pp. 293–305, cited in Tabbak, *Muslims in the EU City Reports – France: Preliminary Research Report and Literature Review*, Open Society Institute, Budapest, 2007, forthcoming.

Lorcerie, F. (ed.) (2005), *La politisation du voile: L'affaire en France, en Europe et dans le monde arabe*, Paris: L'Harmattan.

Ludin (2003), 2 BvR 1436/02, 24 September.

Lyon, D., and D. Spini (2004), "Unveiling the headscarf debate", *Feminist Legal Studies*, 12, pp. 333-345.

Magnette, P. (2003), "European Governance and Civic Participation: Beyond Elitist Citizenship?", *Political Studies*, 51/1.

Mahlmann, M. (2003), "Religious Tolerance, Pluralistic Society and the Neutrality of the State: The Federal Constitutional Court's Decision in the *Headscarf* Case", *German Law Journal*, 4 (11).

Mahmood, S. (2005), *Politics of Piety: The Islamic Revival and the Feminist Subject*, Princeton, NJ: Princeton University Press.

Malik, M. (2005), "Muslims in the UK: Discrimination, Equality, and Community Cohesion", in *Muslims in the UK: Policies for Engaged Citizens*, Budapest, Open Society Institute, pp. 69-73.

Malik, M. (2007), "Muslim Women, the Headscarf and 'Law in Society': A British Perspective on l'Affaire du foulard", *Droit et Société*, forthcoming.

Malonga, M-F. (2007), «La représentation des minorités dans les séries télévisées françaises: entre construction et maintien des frontières ethniques», in Isabelle Rigoni (éd.), *Penser l'altérité dans les médias*, La Courneuve, Aux Lieux d'Être, forthcoming.

Malonga, M-F. (coord.) (2000), *Présence et représentation des minorités visibles à la télévision française*, Paris, CSA, mai.

Manço, U. (1997), "Les organisations islamiques dans l'immigration turque en Europe et en Belgique", in Felice Dassetto (ed.), *Facettes de l'islam belge*, Bruylant-Academia.

Manço, A. (2005), "L'Entreprenariat immigré en Belgique: Contextes, exemples et perspectives", IRFAM, Brussels.

Marcou, J. (2004), "Islamisme et post-islamisme en Turquie", *Revue Internationale de Politique comparée*, Vol. 11, No. 4.

Mawdudi, A. A. (1965), *The Political Theory of Islam*, Lahore.

Maussen, M. (2006), "Anti-Muslim sentiments and mobilization in the Netherlands: discourse, policies and violence", in Cesari, p. 122.

McGoldrick, D. (2006), *Human Rights and Religion: The Islamic Headscarf Debate in Europe*, Oxford: Hart Publishing.

Mervin, S. (2000), *Histoire de l'Islam, Doctrines et fondements*, Paris: Flammarion.

Mitchell, R. (1993), *The Society of the Muslim Brothers*, Oxford: Oxford University Press.

More, G. (1999), "The Principle of Equality Treatment: From Market Unifier to Fundamental Right?", in P. Craig and G. De Búrca (eds.), *The Evolution of EU Law*, pp. 517-543.

Moors, A. (2007), "'Burka' in Parliament and on the Catwalk", *ISIM Newsletter*, International Institute for the Study of Islam in the Modern World, Spring, 5.

Moussaoui, S. and F. Bouquillat (2002), *Zacarias Moussaoui, Mon frère*, Denoël – Impacts.

Muhe, N. (2007), *Muslims in the EU Cities Reports – Germany: Preliminary Research Report and Literature Survey*, Open Society Institute, Budapest.

Muller, L. and S. Tapia (2005), "Un dynamisme venu d'ailleurs: La création d'entreprises par les immigrés", Paris: L'Harmattan.

Nazroo, J. (2001), *Ethnicity, Class and Health*, Policy Studies Institute, London.

Nielsen, J. (2005), *Muslims in Western Europe*, Edinburgh: Edinburgh University Press.

Norris, P. and R. Inglehart (2004),"Sacred and Secular, Religion and politics worldwide", Harvard University, Cambridge, MA.

O'Cinneide, C. (2006), "Positive Action and the Limits of Existing Law", *Maastricht Journal of European and Comparative Law*, 13(3).

OECD (2004), *Learning for Tomorrow's World: First Results from PISA 2003*, OECD, Paris.

O'Fahey, S. and B. Radtke (1993), "Neo-Sufism Reconsidered", *Der Islam*, IXX.

Okkerse, L. and A. Termote (2004), Singularité des étrangers sur la marché de l'emploi, Etudes statistiques No. 111, Institut National de la Statistique, Bruxelles.

Open Society Institute (2005), "Muslims in the UK: Policies for engaged citizens", Open Society Institute, Budapest and EU Monitoring and Advocacy Program.

Open Society Institute (2002), *Monitoring de la protection des minorités dans l'Union européenne: La situation des musulmans en France*, OSI, Budapest.

Ortuno Aix, J.M. (2006), "Report on Islamophobia in Spain", in Cesari.

Palidda, S. (1992), "Le développement des activités indépendantes des immigrés en Europe et en France", *Revue Européenne des Migrations Internationales*, Vol. 8, No. 1.

Peach, C. (2006), "Islam, ethnicity and South Asian Religions in the London 2001 Census", *Transactions of the Institute of British Geographers*, NS 31(3), pp. 353-370.

Pecoud, A. (2005), "The cultural dimension of entrepreneurship in Berlin's Turkish economy", *Revue Européenne des Migrations Internationales*, Vol. 17, No. 2, pp. 153-168.

Perchal, S. (2004), "Equality of Treatment, Non-Discrimination and Social Policy: Achievements in Three Themes", *Common Market Law Review*, 41.

Perrin, N. and B. Van Robaeys (2006), "La Pauvreté chez les personnes d'origine étrangère chiffrée", in *Pauvreté chez les personnes d'origine étrangère*, Fondation Roi Baudouin and GERME, ULB, Bruxelles.

Pew Center (2006), "Muslims in Europe: Economic Worries Top Concerns About Religious and Cultural Identity Few Signs of Backlash from Western Europeans", Pew Global Project, Boston, June.

Poliakov, L. (1980), *La causalité diabolique, essai sur l'origine des persecutions*, Paris: Calmann-Lévy.

Poole, E. (2002), *Reporting Islam. Media Representations of British Muslims*, London: I.B. Tauris.

Poole, E., J. E. Richardson(2006), *Muslims and the News Media*, London: I.B. Tauris.

Popper, K.R. (1985), *Conjecture et réfutations. La croissance du savoir scientifique*, Pris, Payot (original edition: London 1963).

Robbers, G. (ed.) (2005), *State and Church in the European Union*, Baden Baden: Nomos.

Rath, J., R. Penninx, K. Groenendijk and A. Meyer (1999), "The Politics of Recognising Religious Diversity in Europe: Social Reactions to the Institutionalization of Islam in the Netherlands, Belgium and Great Britain", *Netherlands' Journal of Social Sciences,* 35(1).

Rath, J. and F. Buijs (2002), "Muslims in Europe: The State of Research", essay prepared for the Russel Sage Foundation, New York, NY, October.

Richard, J-L and A. Moysan-Louazel (2002), "De l'immigration étrangère parentale à la mobilité sociale des jeunes adultes: Lignée familiale et dynamiques professionnelles individuelles au début des années 1990", *Journées d'Etudes* CEREQ, Rennes, May.

Rigoni, I. (2004), "Médias musulmans britanniques. Les voix de la jeune generation", in Claire Cossée, Emmanuelle Lada et Isabelle Rigoni (dir.), *Faire figure d'étranger : regards croisés sur la production de l'altérité*, Paris: Armand Colin, coll. "Sociétales", pp. 281-300.

Rigoni, I. (2005), "Challenging Notions and Practices: The Muslim Media in Britain and France", *Journal of Ethnic and Migration Studies*, "Media and Minorities in Multicultural Europe", guest-edited by Myria Georgiou & Roger Silverstone, 31(3), pp. 563-580, May.

Rigoni, I. (2005), "De hoofddoek ter discussie. Een nieuwe islamitische identiteit voor de vrouw in seculier-burgerlijk Frankrijk" [The Veil in Debates. A New Feminine Islamic Identity in Secular France], in Gily Coene and Chia Longman (eds), *Eigen Emancipatie Eerst? Over de rechten en representatie van vrouwen in een multiculturele samenleving* [On Rights and Representation of Women in a Multicultural Society], Gent: Academia Press, pp. 95-111.

Rigoni, I. (2006), "Women Journalists and Women's Press: Western Europe", in Alice Horner and Seteney Shami (eds), *Encyclopedia of Women and Islamic Cultures*, Leiden: Brill.

Rigoni, I. (2006), "Islamic Features in French and British Community Media", in Elizabeth Poole and John E. Richardson (eds), *Muslims and the News Media*, London: I. B. Tauris, pp.74-86.

Rigoni, I. (dir.) (2007), *Penser l'altérité dans les médias*, La Courneuve, Aux Lieux d'Être, forthcoming.

Rigouste, M. (2002), *Les cadres médiatiques, sociaux et mythologiques de l'imaginaire colonial. La représentation de «l'immigration maghrébine» dans la presse française de 1995 à 2002*, Nanterre, Université Paris 10, Mémoire de maîtrise.

Ringelheim, J. (2006), *Strategic Litigation to Combat Discrimination against Muslims in Europe: "State of Law" Legal Memorandum*, New York, Open Justice Initiative, p. v.

Rougier, B. (2004), «L'Islam face au retour de l'islam», *Vingtième siècle*, No. 82, avril-juin.

Roy, O. (1992), *L'échec de l'Islam politique,* Paris: Le Seuil.

Roy, O. (2002), *L'islam mondialisé*, Paris: Le Seuil.

Roy, O. (2004), *Globalised Islam*, London: Hurst.

Runnymede Trust (1994), *A very light sleeper: the persistence and dangers of anti-Semitism*, Report of the Runnymede Commission on Anti-Semitism, London.

Runnymede Trust (1997), *Islamophobia. A Challenge for Us All*, report of the Runnymede Trust, Commission on British Muslims and Islamophobia, London.

Saddek, R, (1998), *L'islam dans le discours médiatique*, Beyrouth : Al-Bouraq.

Safran, W. (2004), "Ethno-religious Politics in France", *West European Politics*, 27/3, May, pp. 423-251.

Sageman, M. (2004), "Understanding Terrorist Networks", Pennsylvania University Press.

Saharso, S. and O. Verhaar (2006), "Headscarves in the Police Force and the Court: Does Context Matter?", *Acta Politica*, 41, pp. 68-86.

Sahin v. Turkey, App. No. 44774/98 (Eur. Ct. H.R. November 10, 2005) Grand Chamber, (All decisions related to religious freedom and article 9 can be found at http://www.echr.coe.int).

Schatz, H., Ch. Holtz-Bacha and J-U. Nieland (Hrsg.) (2000), *Migranten und Medien*, Wiesbaden: Westdeutscher Verlag.

Schiek, D., 'Broadening the Scope of the Norms of EU Gender Equality Law: Towards a Multidimentional Conception of Equality Law', *Maastricht Journal of European and Comparative Law,* 12(4).

Schiffauer, W. (2006), "Enemies within the gates. The debate about the citizenship of Muslims in Germany", in T. Modood, A. Triandafyllidou and R. Zapata-Barrero (eds), *Multiculturalism, Muslims and Citizenship,* London: Routledge, pp. 94-116.

Schlesinger, P. and F. Foret (2006), "Political Roof and Sacred Canopy? Religion and the EU Constitution", *European Journal of Social Theory,* 9.

Scott, J. (2005), "Symptomatic Politics. The Banning of Islamic Headscarves in French Public Schools", *French Politics, Culture & Society,* Vol. 23, 3, pp. 106-127.

SCP (2005), Jaarrapport Integratie [Integration Annual Report]. The Hague: Sociaal en Cultureel Planbureau, cited in Demant *et al. Muslims in the EU City Reports – The Netherlands: Preliminary Research Report and Literature Review,* Open Society Institute, Budapest, 2007, forthcoming).

Selignan, M. (2006), "L'example britannique", *Le Figaro,* 24 November.

Shadid, W. and Van Koningsveld (2005), "Muslim Dress in Europe: Debates on the Headscarf", *Journal of Islamic Studies,* 16(1).

Silberman, R. and I. Fournier (2006), "Jeunes issus de l'immigration: une pénalité à l'embauche qui perdure…" (Young people descended from the immigrant population: penalisation in the recruitment process that lasts…), *Bref,* No. 226, January, p. 3.

Silberman, R. and I. Fournier (1999), "Immigrants' Children and the Labour Market. The Mechanisms of Selective Discrimination. From one generation to another. How do the immigrants and their children see their position on the labour market?", paper prepared for Fourth International MigCities Conference, Lisbon, November.

Silvestri, S. (2005), "The Situation of Muslim Immigrants in Europe in the Twenty-first Century: The creation of National Muslim Councils", in H. Henke (ed.), *Crossing Over: Comparing Recent Migration in Europe and the United States,* Lanham, MD: Lexington, pp. 101-129.

Silvestri, S. (2005), "EU relations with Islam in the context of the EMP's cultural dialogue", *Mediterranean Politics,* 10/3, November.

Silvestri, S. (2005), "Institutionalising British and Italian Islam: Attitudes and Policies", forthcoming as a chapter in H. Yilmaz and C. Aykac (eds), *Rethinking Europe through Rethinking Islam,* proceedings of conference held at Bogazici University, Istanbul, December.

Silvestri, S. (2006), *Muslim Political Mobilisation in Europe and the EU Response,* PhD thesis, Cambridge University, Cambridge.

Silvestri, S., (2007), "Regards croisés sur l'institutionnalisation de l'islam au niveau national et européen", in F. Foret (ed.), *L'Europe à l.épreuve du religieux,* Bruxelles: Etudes européennes series, Editions de l'Université Libre de Bruxelles.

Silvestri, S. (2007), "Europe and Political Islam: Encounters of the 20th and 21st century", in T. Abbas (ed.), *Islamic Political Radicalism: A European Comparative Perspective,* Edinburgh: Edinburgh University Press, pp. 57-70.

Skach, C. (2006), "Leyla Sahin v. Turkey and 'Teacher Headscarf Case' BverfG Case No. 2BvR 1436/02", *American Journal of International Law,* Vol. 100, No. 1, pp. 186-196.

Skidmore, P. (2001), "EC Framework Directive on Equal Treatment in Employment: Towards a Comprehensive Community Anti-Discrimination Policy?", *Industrial Law Journal,* 30.

Spidla, V. (2006), "Relever le défi de l'immigration et de l'intégration", speech, European Commission, February.

Soper, C. and J. Fetzer (2005), "Explaining the Accommodation of Muslim Religious Practices in France, Britain, and Germany", paper prepared for Stream 3 on Public Recognition and Secular Democracy, IMSCOE Cluster B6 workshop on Ethnic, Cultural and Religious Diversity, Amsterdam, 26-28 May.

Socialist Worker (2006), London, 21 October (retrieved from http://www.socialistworker.co.uk/article.php?article_id=9977).

Stasi, B., (2003) Working group (Commission de réflexion) on the application of the principle of laicity. Report to the President of the Republic, La Documentation Française, Paris.

Statham, P., R. Koopmans, M. Giugni and F. Passy (2005), "Resilient or Adaptable Islam? Multiculturalism, Religion and Migrants' Claims-making for Group Demands in Britain, the Netherlands and France", *Ethnicities,* 5/4, pp. 427-459.

Taguieff, P-A (2005), *La Foire aux Illuminés: ésotérisme, théorie du complot et extrémisme,* Paris: Mille et une nuits.

Tebbakh, S. (2007), *Muslims in the EU City Reports – France: Preliminary Research and Literature Review,* Open Society Institute, Budapest, forthcoming.

Terray, E. (2004), "L'hystérie politique", in C. Nordmann (dir.), *Le foulard islamique en questions,* Paris, ed. Amsterdam.

Tévanian, P., "La loi sur le voile, un an après, un bilan désastreux", (www.mrap.fr).

Tévanian, P. (2005), *Le voile médiatique. Un faux débat: "l'affaire du foulard",* Paris, raisons d'agir.

Thomas, N.M. (2005), "On Headscarves and Heterogeneity: Reflections on the French Foulard Affair", *Dialectical Anthropology,* 29, pp. 373-386.

Torrekens, C. (2006), "La gestion locale de l'Islam dans l'espace public bruxellois", *Les cahiers de la sécurité,* No. 62, 3rd trimester, pp. 139-160 (available at http://www.inhes.interieur.gouv.fr/fichiers/RECH_ 62CSIinternet.pdf).

Verhaar, O. and S. Saharso (2004), "The weight of contexts: The wear of headscarf in Holland", *Ethical Theory and Moral Practice,* 7(2), 179-195.

Weber, M. (1967), "L'éthique protestante et l'esprit du capitalisme", 1905, Plon.

Weibel, N. (2000), *Par-delà le voile, femmes d'islam en Europe,* Bruxelles: Complexe.

Weil, N. (2006), "What's in a Scarf? The Debate on *Laïcité* in France", *French Politics, Culture & Society,* Vol. 24, No. 1, pp. 59-73.

Winock, M. (2004), *Nationalisme, antisémitisme, et fascisme en France,* Paris: Le Seuil.

Wohlrab-Sahr, M. (1999), *Konversion zum Islam in Deutschland und den USA,* Frankfurt/M, Campus.

Young, I.M. (1990), *Justice and the Politics of Difference,* Princeton, NJ: Princeton University Press.

Zine, J. (2006), "Unveiled sentiments: Gendered Islamophobia and Experiences of Veiling among Muslim Girls in a Canadian Islamic School", *Equity & Excellence in Education,* 39, pp. 239-252.

Official Documents and Special Reports

Beckford J. et al (2006), *Review of the Evidence Base on Faith Communities*, London: Office of the Deputy Prime Minister, p. 39.

Case C-144/04 Mangold v Helm, 22/11/05.

Case 409/95 Marschall v Land Nordrhein-Westfalen [1997] ECR I-6363. See also Case 158/97 Badeck v Hessischer Ministerpresident [2000] ECR I-1875 and Case 407/98, Abrahamsson and Andersson v Fogelqvist [2000] ECR I-5539.

Conseil d'Etat (2004), *Rapport public 2004: Jurisprudence et avis de 2003, Un siècle de laïcité, Etudes et documents No. 55, Paris, La Documentation française*.

Conseil de l'Europe, Recommandation relative aux migrants, aux minorités ethniques et aux médias, No. 1277, Strasbourg, Conseil de l'Europe, Assemblée parlemantaire, juin 1995. Conseil de l'Europe, Recommandation du Comité de ministres aux Etats membres sur les médias et la promotion d'une culture de tolérance, No. R(97)21, Strasbourg, Conseil de l'Europe, 30 octobre 1997.

COM(2001) 644 final, OJ C 75/E/269 of 26 March 2002.

Commission nationale consultative des droits de l'homme (2004), La lutte contra le racisme et al xénophobie.

European Commission, Council Directive 2004/113 of 13 December 2004 implementing the principle of equal treatment between men and women in the access to and supply of goods and services [2004] O.J.L. 373/37.

European Commission, Council Directive 2000/43 of 29 June 2000 implementing the principle of equal treatment between persons irrespective of racial or ethnic origin, [2000] O.J.L 180/22.

European Commission, Council Directive 2000/78 of 27 November 2000 establishing a general framework for equal treatment in employment and occupation, [2000] O.J.L 303/16.

European Commission, Council Directive 75/117 of 10 February 1975 on the approximation of the laws of the Member States relating to the application of the principle of equal pay for men and women, [1975] O.J.L. 45/19).

European Commission, Council Directive 76/207 of 9 February 1976 on the implementation of the principle of equal treatment of men and women as regards access to employment, vocational training and promotion, and working conditions, [1976] O.J.L 39/40.

European Commission, Council Directive 79/7 of 19 December 1978 on the progressive implementation of the principle of equal treatment for men and women in matters of social security, [1979] O.J.L. 6/24; EC, Council Directive 86/378 of 24 July 1986 on the implementation of the principle of equal treatment for men and women in occupational social security schemes, [1986] O.J.L 225/40 and EC, Council Directive 86/613 of 11 December 1986 on the application of the principle of equal treatment between men and women engaged in an activity, including agriculture, in self-employed capacity, and on the protection of self-employed women during pregnancy and motherhood, [1986] O.J.L. 359/56.

European Commission (2003), Rapport au Conseil européen de printemps du 21 mars 2003 sur la stratégie de Lisbonne pour le renouveau économique, social et environnemental, (COM(2003) 5 du 14 janvier 2003).

European Commission (2002), "Successful Integration on the Labour Market", report of a European Commission Conference, Copenhaguen, 4-5 July.

Framework Directive Article 4(2).

UK Cabinet Office, Ethnic Minorities and the Labour Market: Interim Analytical Report, London: Cabinet Office, 2001, p. 82.

UK Department for Work and Pensions. Households Below Average Income 1994/5 - 2000/01, London.

UK Department for Education and Skills (2006), *National Curriculum Assessment, GCSE and Equivalent Attainment and Post-16 Attainment by Pupil Characteristics in England 2005/06* (Provisional) London, Office of National Statistics.

UK Office of National Statistics (2004), *Focus on Religion*, ONS, London.

ABOUT THE AUTHORS

Chris Allen completed his PhD in Theology (Islamic Studies) at the University of Birmingham and in recent years he has taught Multiculturalism, Media, Culture & Society and Research Skills & Methods in the University's Sociology department. Author of "From race to religion: the new face of discrimination" in *Muslim Britain: communities under pressure*, London: Zed Books (2005) and co-editor of: *Summary report on Islamophobia in the European Union after September 11, 2001*, Vienna, European Union Monitoring Centre on Racism and Xenophobia (2002), among other works. He is a visiting lecturer at the University of Wolverhampton where he teaches a module on 'Islam'. He regularly undertakes work for the media (Channel 4, BBC, Central ITV, Islam Channel and Sky News) whilst also facilitating cultural awareness training.

Samir Amghar is a BA graduate in law and has an MA in political science at the Sorbonne University, Paris. He is completing his PhD in sociology at Ehess (Ecole des Hautes Etudes en Sciences Sociales, Paris) under the supervision of Olivier Roy. His thesis focuses on transformations in Islamism and the dynamics of re-islamisation in Europe. He is head of Islam in Europe's programme at the Institut d'études de l'islam et du monde musulman (Paris). He has also edited a book on Western Islam: *Islamismes d'Occident* (Lignes de repères, 2006) and conducted a special review on Moderate Islamists (Maghreb-Machrek, winter 2007).

Valérie Amiraux is Professor at the department of sociology of the University of Montréal where she holds a Canada Research Chair for the study of religious pluralism and ethnicity. Her research interests include religious minorities in the European Union, the politics of recognition, multiculturalism and religious pluralism. She recently co-edited *Politics of Visibility* with Gerdien Jonker and *Young Muslims in European Public Spaces* (Transcript, 2006).

Amel Boubekeur is a research fellow at CEPS and the leader of the CEPS Islam and Europe programme. She is completing her PhD at the

Ecole des Hautes Etudes en Sciences Sociales in Paris on the Contemporary Transformations of Islamism. Active in various international projects and research activities dealing with Muslim communities in Europe and the US, Islamist movements, terrorism and radicalisation processes, European foreign policy and the Arab world, Islam and gender development.

She is the author of "Le voile de la Mariée. Jeunes musulmanes, voile et projet matrimonial", L'Harmattan, Paris, 2004, and of "Beyond Islamism? What have Islamists become" (with Olivier Roy), To be published.

Tufyal Choudhury is a lecturer in law at Durham University. He is a senior research advisor to the Open Society Institute's project 'Muslims in the EU - City Reports' and a consultant to the Oxford Centre for Migration Policy and Society research project looking at Muslims and Community Cohesion. His research and writing focuses on religious and racial discrimination law and policy.

Michael Emerson is an Associate Senior Research Fellow at the Centre for European Policy Studies (CEPS), Brussels. A graduate in philosophy, politics and economics at Balliol College, Oxford, he joined the European Commission in 1973. From 1991 to 1996, he was the first ambassador of the European Commission to the USSR and then to Russia. From 1996 to 1998, he was a Senior Research Fellow at the London School of Economics. In 1998, he joined CEPS, where he leads the European Neighbourhood Programme. He holds a doctoral honoris causa from the Universities of Kent and Keele.

Bernard Godard has been an Advisor at the Central Office of Religions in the Ministry of Interior – France, since 2002 (expert on Islam). He was also an Advisor on Islam to the former Ministers of the Interior Jean-Pierre Chevènement (1997-2000) and Daniel Vaillant (2002-2004) and was in charge of questions concerning terrorism and Islamism in security services before 1997. He is author of several articles on Islam in France under the pseudonym Hervé Terrel and author of a book recently published (February 2007) entitled Les Musulmans en France, by Bernard Godard and Sylvie Taussig.

Imane Karich is the General Secretary of the CEREI (Cercle d'Etudes et de Recherches en Economie Islamique), a non-profit organisation dedicated to promoting and developing Islamic Finance in Belgium. She is also collaborating on two other projects: a French-speaking magazine respecting Islamic values and Belgian Muslim Professionals Organisation (ABPM: Association Belge des Professionnels Musulmans). She has also published two books on Islamic Finance – Le Système Financier Islamique, de la Religion à la Banque, Editions Larcier, 2002, Finances & Islam, Editions Le Savoir, 2004.

Isabelle Rigoni holds a PhD from the University Paris 8, France. She completed her post-doctoral research on ethnic media as an EU Marie Curie Research Fellow at the Centre for Research in Ethnic Relations (University of Warwick, 2001-03), and at the Centre Marc Bloch (Berlin, 2004-05). She has taught sociology and political science for several years in the universities of Paris 8 and Evry-Val d'Essonne. Among her books: *Faire figure d'étranger: regards croisés sur la production de l'altérité* (ed. with C. Cossée, E. Lada), Paris, Armand Colin, 2004; *Mobilisations et enjeux des migrations turques en Europe de l'Ouest,* Paris, L'Harmattan, 2001; *Turquie, les mille visages. Politique, religion, femmes, immigration* (ed.), Paris, Syllepse, 2000.

Olivier Roy (1949) is a Senior Researcher at the French National Center for Scientific Research (since 1985) and a Consultant for the French Ministry of Foreign Affairs (since 1984). He is a Professor at the Ecole des Hautes Etudes en Sciences Sociales (since 2003). He headed the OSCE's Mission for Tajikistan (1993-94) and was a Consultant for the UN Office of the Coordinator for Afghanistan (1988). His field works include Political Islam, Islam in the West, Middle East and Central Asia. Mr. Roy received an Agrégation de Philosophie and a Ph.D. in Political Sciences. He is the author of *Globalized Islam* (Columbia University Press), 2004, and *Secularism confronts Islam* (Columbia University Press), 2007.

Sara Silvestri is a political scientist based in the Centre for International Politics, at City University (London) and is an associate of Chatham House (former Royal Institute of International Affairs) and of the Centre for the Study of Faith in Society at Cambridge University. Her publications and current research are concerned with Muslim identity politics, the institutionalisation of Islam and public policies towards Muslim communities in Europe. At City University she teaches courses on Religion and International Relations, The Middle East, Political Islam and the EU. She also regularly advises international organisations and policy centres on the issue of radicalisation and the integration of Islam in Europe.